WORST CASES

WORST CASES

TERROR AND CATASTROPHE IN
THE POPULAR IMAGINATION

LEE CLARKE

The University of Chicago Press   CHICAGO AND LONDON

The University of Chicago Press, Chicago 60637
The University of Chicago Press, Ltd., London
© 2006 by The University of Chicago
Published 2006
Paperback edition 2021
Printed in the United States of America

30 29 28 27 26 25 24 23 22 21   1 2 3 4 5

ISBN-13: 978-0-226-10859-9 (cloth)
ISBN-13: 978-0-226-79010-7 (paper)
ISBN-13: 978-0-226-10860-5 (e-book)
DOI: https://doi.org/10.7208/chicago/9780226108605.001.0001

Library of Congress Cataloging-in-Publication Data

Clarke, Lee Ben.
    Worst cases : terror and catastrophe in the popular imagination / Lee Clarke.
        p.   cm.
    Includes bibliographical references and index.
    ISBN 0-226-10859-7(cloth : alk. paper)
        1. Emergency management. 2. Disasters—Psychological aspects. 3. Terror-
ism—Psychological aspects. 4. Risk assessment. 5. Catastrophical, The. 1. Title.
HV551.2.c533 2006
303.48'5—dc22

                                                                    2005008994

♾ This paper meets the requirements of ANSI/NISO Z39.48-1992 (Permanence of Paper).

FOR ALEX, MY BEST CASE

CONTENTS

PREFACE

People are worried, now, about terror and catastrophe in ways that a short time ago would have seemed merely fantastic. Not to say that horror and fear suffuse the culture, but they are in the ascendant. And for good reason. There are possibilities for accident and attack, disease and disaster that would make September 11 seem like a mosquito bite. I think we have all become more alert to some of those possibilities, and it is wise to face them down. The idea of worst cases isn't foreign to us. We have not, however, been given enough useful insight or guidance, either from academics or political leaders, regarding how to do that.

In this book I look the worst full in the face. What I see is frightening but enlightening. I believe that knowing a thing permits more comfort with that thing. Sometimes the comfort comes from greater control. Sometimes it comes from knowing the enemy, or the scary thing, which proffers a way forward, toward greater safety. There is horror in disaster. But there is much more, for we can use calamity to glean wisdom, to find hope.

Tragedy is with us now as never before. But that does not mean we need be consumed with fear and loathing. We can learn a lot about how society works, and fails to work, by looking at the worst. We can learn about the imagination, about politics, and about the wielding of power. We can learn about people's capacities for despair and callousness, and for optimism and altruism. As we learn, our possibilities for improvement increase. *Worst Cases* is about the human condition in the modern world.

Some say that September 11 changed everything. That's not true. But it did imprint upon our imaginations scenes of horror that until then had been the province of novels and movies. We now imagine ourselves in those images, and our wide-awake nightmares are worse than they used to be. We must name, analyze, and talk about the beast. That's our best hope, as a society, to come to terms with the evil, the human failings, the aspects of nature, and just plain chance that put us in harm's way.

Of course, talking about the worst can be a way to scare people into accepting programs that have other ends, and that they might not otherwise accept. The image of a nuclear mushroom cloud, for example, can be used to justify war because the possibility is so frightening that we would do almost anything to prevent it. The dark side of worst case thinking is apparent even at the level of personal relationships. Unleavened by evidence or careful thought it can lead to astonishingly poor policy and dumb decisions. No organizational culture can prevent or guard against it. The only response that will effectively mute such abuses is one that is organized and possessed of courage and vision. So warnings that the worst is at hand should be inspected closely, particularly if they call for actions that would serve ends the speaker cannot or does not freely acknowledge. I acknowledge my ends in this book. For better or worse, I always have.

Worst Cases is a book full of stories about disasters. But it is not a disaster book. It is a book about the imagination. We look back and say that 9/11 was the worst terrorist attack ever in the United States, that the Spanish Flu of 1918, the Black Death, or AIDS was the worst epidemic ever, or that the 1906 San Francisco earthquake was the Great Earthquake. Nothing inherent to the events requires that we adorn them with superlatives. People's imaginations make that happen. Similarly, we construct possible futures of terror and calamity: what happens if the nation's power grid goes down for six months? what if smallpox sweeps the world? what if nuclear power has a particularly bad day? what if a monster tsunami slams southern California? These too are feats of imagination.

There are those who say we shouldn't worry about things that are unlikely to happen. That's what your pilot means in saying, after a turbulent cross-country flight, "You've just completed the safest part of your trip." We hear the same thing when officials tell us that the probability of a nuclear power plant melting down is vanishingly small. Or that the likelihood of an asteroid striking the earth is one in a million, billion, or trillion. There is similar advice from academics who complain that people are unreasonable because their fears don't jibe with statistics. Chance, they reckon, is in our favor.

But chance is often against us. My view is that disasters and failures are normal, that, as a colleague of mine puts it, things that have never happened before happen all the time. A fair number of those things end up being events we call worst cases. When they happen we're given opportunities to learn things about society and human nature that are usually obscured.

Worst case thinking hasn't been given its due, either in academic writings or in social policy. We're not paying enough attention to the ways we organize society that make us vulnerable to worst cases. We're not demanding enough responsibility and transparency from leaders and policy makers. I am not an alarmist, but I am alarmed. That's why I wrote *Worst Cases*. It is also why my tone and language are not technical. I am a sociologist, but I wrote *Worst Cases* so that nonsociologists can read it.

This is the right place to acknowledge others' help in producing *Worst Cases*. Thanks to Ann Martin for being a generous technological enabler. Thanks to Douglas Mitchell and Timothy McGovern for being interested and interesting. Personal disasters have been softened, or intellectual stimulation charitably given, by Caron Chess, Kai Erikson, William Freudenburg, John Gagnon, James Jasper, John Lang, Charles Perrow, Patricia Roos, Michael Schwartz, Joel Score, Judith Tanur, Kathleen Tierney, and Diane Vaughan. I owe a special debt to John Gagnon, who is directly responsible for putting wheels under the project.

1

WORST CASES: BE AFRAID, BE VERY AFRAID

It was superlative, the most magnificent, most celebrated, most luxurious flying machine ever built. Never mind the Nazi swastika on the tail fin. The *Hindenburg* was a technological marvel, the best of the best, a testament to humanity's determination and skill in conquering nature. Radio announcer Herb Morrison was rightly in awe as he described the vessel's arrival in Lakehurst, New Jersey. It was May 6, 1937:

Well, here it comes, ladies and gentlemen. We're out now, outside of the hangar, and what a great sight it is. . . . It's coming down out of the sky pointed directly towards us and toward the mooring mast. The mighty diesel motors just roared, the propellers biting into the air and throwing it back into a galelike whirlpool. No wonder this great floating palace can travel through the air at such a speed, with these powerful motors behind it. . . .

The ship is riding majestically toward us, like some great feather. . . . It's practically standing still now. They've dropped ropes out of the nose of the ship and they've been taken ahold of down on the field by a number of men. It's starting to rain again. The rain had slacked up a little bit. The back motors of the ship are just holding it, uh, just enough to keep it from . . .

Then it happens.

It burst into flames. It's burst into flames and it's falling, it's crashing. . . . Get out of the way, get out of the way. Get this Charlie, get this Charlie.

It's fire and it's crashing. It's crashing terrible. Oh my, get out of the way, please. It's burning, bursting into flames. And it's falling on the mooring mast and all the folks. This is terrible, this is one of the *worst catastrophes in the world*. . . . Oh, the humanity, and all the passengers screaming around here. . . . I can't talk, ladies and gentlemen. Honest, it's just laying there, a mass of smoking wreckage, and everybody can't hardly breathe. . . . I'm going to step inside where I *cannot* see it.

Morrison's horror is palpable. His voice is smooth and admiring as the Nazi dirigible—a behemoth almost as long as the *Titanic*—floats down. But then in a flash the airship catches fire. Morrison is shocked, and his voice starts to crack, giving us some glimpse into the terror that must have touched the souls of the hundreds of spectators. "This is one of the worst catastrophes in the world," says Morrison, and it really does look and sound like one. It must have felt, and smelled, like doomsday.

*

The succession of plagues that started with what we call the Black Death emerged in Europe in 1347 and within four years had wiped out two-thirds of the populations of many cities. People were healthy one day and dead the next. The Italian author Boccaccio wrote in the *Decameron* that people would have "breakfast in the morning with their relatives, companions, or friends, and . . . dinner that evening in another world with their ancestors!" The plagues continued for three hundred years, claiming nearly *one-third* of the European population. The effects were catastrophic. Economies collapsed. Millenarian and penitential doctrines, such as that of the flagellants, arose amid the death and disease, as people sought meaning in a world that suddenly had none. Anti-Semitism predictably increased. Family members were set against one another. Said Agnolo di Tura del Grassi, a fourteenth-century chronicler, "Father abandoned child, wife husband, one brother another, for the plague seemed to strike through breath and sight. And so they died. And no one could be found to bury the dead, for money or friendship." Death and misery became so commonplace as to be normal. People lost hope. It may well have been that the living envied the dead.

*

On June 30, 1908, at about 7:00 in the morning a meteorite (most likely—scientists still aren't sure) exploded some three to five miles over Siberia, near the Tunguska River. The object was probably 150 to 250 feet in diameter. Trees within a nine-mile radius were incinerated; those within twenty-five miles were flattened. The Tunguska Event, as astronomers call it, was fifteen times as powerful as the nuclear weapon that destroyed Hiroshima. Shock waves from Tunguska circled the globe twice. If an object of similar size exploded five miles over Manhattan millions of people would be incinerated. Survivors would say it was the worst disaster that ever happened. They would call it a worst case.

*

It can be comforting to regard events like these as things of the past and people who talk about such things as ongoing threats as alarmist, extremist, or even crazy. Nowadays, we have science to protect us, technology to serve us, and experts to predict the paths that calamity might take. We understand better than ever how probability works; thinking in terms of probabilities is a hallmark of the modern scientific mind. In some ways science and technology do make us safer. We live longer, and far more comfortable, lives than people did a hundred years ago. This is especially true of people in rich countries. Certainly the rise of probabilism as a way of thinking about the future—and especially any dangers the future may behold—benefits us in countless ways.

But neither the passage of time nor accumulated riches nor fancier technology nor greater expertise protect us from worst cases. Not even the magic of probabilistic thinking can save us. In fact, we humans are making some kinds of worst cases *more* likely and potentially *more* devastating. Huge airliners, rather than hydrogen-filled dirigibles, now fall out of the sky, killing hundreds in a flash. The frightening thing about the 2003 outbreak of SARS—severe acute respiratory syndrome—was less its lethality (fewer than 10 percent of those infected died) than the speed of its global transmission. Other viruses, as deadly as Ebola and as fast moving as the common cold, likewise have the potential to circle the globe, on the planes that don't crash, in twenty-four hours. One might kill millions of people before doctors even knew what was happening. NASA is tracking hundreds of NEOs—near earth objects—including an asteroid called XF11. In 1997 some highly reputable scientists started to worry that XF11 might come dangerously close to earth sometime in the next thirty years. With a diameter of about a mile, XF11 could, if it hit us, be a planet killer, releasing as much as a million megatons of energy. We now know that we're safe from XF11. But that's no reason to think we're safe from NEOs. It's only a matter of time, so a reasonable person might conclude that we should be afraid.

Thinking about worst cases may seem neurotic, but it should be seen as normal. It starts early. A child wants to learn to ride a bicycle but is afraid. "What's the worst that can happen?" her parent intones, failing to understand that the child imagines not just the physical danger of failure but also the social risk of embarrassment. Later, as a teenager, she drives with abandon, operating on the unarticulated presumption that the worst "can't happen to me." And it doesn't. Worst cases are rare, she believes. She survives to become CEO of a major industrial concern, for which she must consider "worst case scenarios" and then decide whether to cover them up. When an accident causes half of her plant to explode, killing two hundred workers and contaminating two neighboring towns, the carnage exceeds everyone's worst nightmares. The lead paragraph in the paper begins, "No one could have planned for it. It was the worst industrial accident in 60 years."

Worst cases happen frequently. For that simple reason thinking about worst cases is normal at all societal levels—individual, group, organizational, national. Private industry and government increasingly use worst case analyses in making decisions. For example, the Environmental Protection Agency, following a mandate from the Clean Air Act, started a process in 1996 that requires industrial facilities that hold or produce toxic chemicals to create "worst case scenarios." These scenarios, in one form or another, will be made available to local citizens. This is unprecedented. At the very least, the program itself is a crude indicator of how important such scenarios are becoming in our lives.

As a society we tend to adopt a reactive posture toward worst cases. The government has, for example, tried to create some policies that work as prophylactics against the worst fiscal year, the spread of AIDS, the deadliest terrorist attack, and the like. While corporations *do* sometimes paralyze themselves worrying about worst case lawsuits and individuals *do* buy life insurance policies, mostly we worry about worst cases when they're upon us. Especially regarding disasters. David King is the director of the Centre for Disaster Studies at James Cook University in Australia. His research shows that after cyclones and floods there are always wonderful stories of heroism and neighbors helping each other in situations of great danger. King points out, however, that such acts wouldn't be necessary in the first place if people paid more attention to worst case possibilities. We should all take his advice. In spite of all the ways our lives are better than those of our ancestors, we're also more vulnerable to large-scale disasters.

Studying worst cases, and ideas about worst cases, can teach us about a lot more than just disasters. It can teach us, generally, about how society works. It can afford a glimpse into human nature. For to reflect upon worst cases is to reflect upon the imagination. It's natural to think of "the imagination" as something outside of the influences of society. The death penalty or fashion are obviously open to social and political influences. But the imagination? It seems different somehow. In fact it isn't. What we imagine and how we imagine it are very much open to society's influences, some of which I explore in this book.

Most people seem to have spent at least some time imagining the worst thing that could happen to them. Those who dwell on those imaginings are called paranoid. But having the thoughts, and controlling them or perhaps even working them into a plan, is considered intelligent and wise. American intelligence agencies, to take a counterexample, have been criticized for being caught off-guard by the terrorist attacks of September 11, 2001. They failed to consider and prepare for a devastating worst case.

Conceptions of the worst also vary by culture and subculture; each group provides a different set of images for its members to use in imagining the superlatively bad. Those are the things that this book is about. We will weave into and out of people's ideas about horror, and we will delve into some truly horrifying events.

I have several messages.

1. Worst case thinking is very different from the modern approach to risk. The modern approach is based on probabilistic thinking—what's the likelihood that the nuclear plant will melt down?—and is often used to justify dangerous systems. Worst case thinking is *possibilistic* thinking—what happens if the nuclear plant has a really bad day?—and can be more progressive.

2. Big disasters are something we're more prone to as a society, and therefore they are something we ought to spend more resources preparing for. However, such preparations can actually put us at *greater* risk if they are implemented incorrectly.

3. Disasters aren't special. They are as normal as love, joy, triumph, and misery. Looking at disasters as normal is both interesting and practical.

DIMENSIONS OF WORST CASES

Doom is everywhere. Worst cases, and worst case thinking, cross-cut society. This is not entirely a bad thing. Individuals do worst case analysis whenever they buy health or life insurance. People who buy life insurance, showing generosity toward their heirs, are betting that they will die. If people weren't worst case thinkers the insurance industry would be in a lot of trouble, as would a great many heirs. At the community level, city governments pass laws that limit the times and speeds that toxic trains can pass through town. In doing so, they are acting on their assessments of the worst consequences should a train car fall over in a populated area, releasing dangerous gases or chemicals. Organizations, especially in the United States, are increasingly consumed with worst case analysis. One reason for corporate hysteria over lawsuits in the United States is fear of a worst case financial judgment against them. Even entire countries have worst case worries. After 9/11 politicians fostered in Americans the idea that terrorist threats were lurking behind every corner.

Before getting to any of that, though, we really ought to see if we can figure out what a worst case is.

That worst case thinking happens over such a broad swath of society raises the question of the dimensions of worst cases. Are there characteristics that worst cases have in common? In one sense this question doesn't make much sense. That's because trying to divine common dimensions of something assumes that there are enough particular instances of it to constitute a category, a *type* of event. But we usually think of failures and catastrophes as rare, if not unique, and as striking randomly and without warning. If so, then it makes little sense to speak of patterns and common dimensions.

No one would have predicted that a tree would fall on top of a moving car, killing a minister, his wife, and two children in Indiana. The sheriff who investigated the crash said that the "chances of that tree falling at the time they were directly underneath it are astronomical." I'm sure he meant extremely tiny. Perhaps equally unlikely is that a third child survived the crash. That case was a lot like the one of a

Pennsylvania woman accidentally killed by a hunter's bullet. That in itself is not so surprising—people are killed in hunting accidents all the time. But this woman was in her house. The bullet traveled through a window, a door, and a wall and hit her in the neck as she was standing in her bedroom. A game commissioner was probably underestimating when he said that the "odds of [a bullet] coming through the woods, not hitting a tree, going through all that material in the house and hitting a person is . . . million-to-one odds." Then there was the case of the woman who tripped while trying to unlock the door to her house with a key that was strung around her neck on a strap. She fell, the strap caught on the door handle, and she strangled to death. That was like the poor Long Island chap who bled to death after falling on the shards of his broken coffee cup. I mean here just to give some examples of the bizarre character of individual-level worst cases.[1] These people likely never anticipated the scenarios in which they died, but, alas, there are many others who live with worst case thinking all the time—people with phobias, inmates on death row, and those who find themselves in the grip of suicidal depression.

At other levels of society, too, worst cases can be sudden or chronic. Toms River, New Jersey, is a community that's permeated by a mood of gloom and doom, and with good reason. Toms River has *two* Superfund sites, places that the Environmental Protection Agency has deemed among the worst polluted places in the country. There are about twelve hundred such sites throughout the United States. A lot of children in Toms River suffer from brain cancer, spinal melanoma, neural blastoma, or leukemia, afflictions that we don't normally think children will get. In Toms River, homes and communities are now places of pain and despair rather than the safe havens they should be. How else would people respond when, as one mother put it, you "have a child with leukemia living two houses down from a child with a tumor, drinking the same water and breathing the same air"?[2]

Compare that to what happened when a train carrying skiers caught fire in a tunnel inside an Austrian mountain. There was, apparently, a faulty radiator in the driver's cab. That wouldn't have been enough to cause a fire, but a leaky hydraulic cable dripped combustible fluid onto the radiator. The resulting fire led to the failure of the hydraulic system; as the hydraulic pressure dropped the brakes engaged, stopping the train in its tracks. The passengers could still have survived, but the train had no emergency exits and only the driver could control the doors. The skiers were trapped inside the train, which was trapped inside the tunnel. Emergency personnel couldn't even get to the wreckage for twenty-four hours. It's hard to imagine worse conditions for survival. One hundred and fifty-five people died; a mere dozen survived. Reflecting sentiments of the local community, a reporter called it "a catastrophe of unprecedented proportions." A political official said, "It is one of the darkest and hardest days for Salzburg that we have ever seen." An official from the train company said, "The idea that a fire could break out in the tunnel was considered to be something unimaginable." Worst cases are like that.[3]

Reading these kinds of stories one might conclude that worst cases are so bizarre that trying to find patterns in and among them is fruitless. I see things differently. I think that catastrophes are common and that failures are a normal part of life. Courts of law become corrupt. Schools do not educate. Doctors make people sick. More people die in U.S. hospitals from medical errors every year than in industrial facilities, in car crashes, or from AIDS.[4] There are repeated and serious security breaches at nuclear plants. Even where officials and systems have strong built-in incentives to operate reliably, they don't. Doom, failure, and catastrophe are part of ordinary life. They are normal.

In fact, disasters strike often enough for us to make some important predictions about them, although not with a high degree of precision. For example, the American midwest is at greater risk of tornadoes than the northeast, the southeastern coast is at greater risk of hurricanes than the midwest, and the western states are at greater risk of earthquakes than the southeast. Of course we can't predict with much confidence that a hurricane will destroy the east coast of Florida several years from now, as we can predict with great confidence that the sun will rise at a precise time several years from now. And I doubt we'll ever be able to predict, say, when the next earthquake will happen. Still, these are important predictions.

Any phenomena that are so widespread ought to have some fundamental attributes in common. Figuring out those kinds of characteristics is one of the things that scientists do all the time. Take divorce. People who do research on the topic count up divorce rates, the effects of divorce on the people breaking up, the effects on children, and so on. Summing it up, scholars say, "Here's what we know about divorce," and then run off the numbers. Sometimes they can even tell a story in which the characteristics are connected to each other—"crime and drug abuse are rampant in a culture of poverty that leaves people without self-respect or hopes for the future." Such stories give people the sense that the issue is well understood. Similarly, in 2000 and 2001 the National Science Foundation held a series of invited conferences on the issue of "extreme events." The NSF was trying to establish if there was enough interest by scholars, and coherence in the empirical events, to fund a research agenda on the topic. The idea of "extreme events" was given a lot of currency after September 11. One of the main issues that the NSF, and the conference attendees, were concerned with was the definition of an extreme event: how do you know one when you see it? The NSF meetings didn't resolve the question of whether there are patterns of worst cases, but that they tried indicates the importance of the issue.

Let us explore, then, the issue of the dimensions of worst cases.

Body Counts

It seems obvious that one distinguishing property of worst cases is body count. After terrorists destroyed the World Trade Center in New York a lot of people compared the event to Pearl Harbor. It was a natural comparison: both were massive surprise attacks on American people and property. It was also natural because we were scrambling to get a grip on the magnitude of the devastation. Counting the number of dead seemed like a good way to do that. For example, I was on television the evening of the attacks, discussing various aspects of the day's events. In talking about the possible number of casualties I said something like, "If even half of the people who could have been working and visiting the World Trade Center were there when the buildings fell, it would mean there were 10,000 people in each tower. That would mean roughly *ten times* the number of people who were killed at Pearl Harbor." It was a dramatic moment. I was, we now know, wrong by a factor of seven (2,749 people died in New York).[5] Nonetheless, it was a useful comparison; at the time we had few other ways to gauge the magnitude of the day's horror. The point is that body counts are a common way to measure whether something is a worst case or not.

Comparing body counts is common with train accidents. In February 2002 an overloaded train caught fire in Egypt. The conductor didn't realize an inferno was raging behind him and so didn't immediately stop the train. He made the situation worse by racing on, feeding oxygen to the fire. In the end almost four hundred people died, many of whom jumped from the moving train. To get a sense of how bad that disaster was, think about Amtrak's super-fast Acela train, which can carry about three hundred people between Boston and Washington, D.C. Just imagine how terrible it would be if one of those trains caught fire and everyone on board perished. It would be one of the worst train catastrophes in American history.

But neither the Egyptian fire nor our American hypothetical would be the worst in terms of body count. In December 1917, a thousand French soldiers on leave from the war packed into a train heading home from northeast Italy. The war had made everything scarce, even locomotives, so the train had only one when it should had have two, which made the train difficult to control. It needed more than one locomotive because it was really *two* trains' worth of cars strung together. There were also not enough cars with brakes. In Modane, France, the train careened down an embankment, killing eight hundred. People still call it the worst railway accident ever. But, I should note, the Modane wreck holds only the *official* worst case record. There are suspicions that a train accident in India in the early 1980s may have killed as many as three thousand! The victims there couldn't be counted reliably, however, and so, as often happens with poor people, were ignored.

If we look at plane crashes, we again find that body count is a key dimension of a worst case. In 1977 two Boeing 747s crashed at an airport in Spain's Canary Islands. The jumbo jets—one from Pan Am, the other from KLM—had been diverted to Tenerife because of a reported terrorist attack at their intended destination. The KLM captain was taxiing to takeoff position and once there started down the runway. But he throttled-up too soon, before he had been given clearance by the control tower. He careened down the runway, smack into the Pan Am 747. Five hundred and eighty-three people died in what to date is still called the worst accident in aviation history. Airbus, the French aircraft manufacturer, has built the A380, a four-engine, four-aisle, two-story behemoth that will carry 555 potential casualties. Imagine the first time an A380 slams into a mountain or falls into the sea or has its tail snapped off in turbulence. The headline will read: "Worst airline crash in history."

It is certainly a cause for great concern when large numbers of people are harmed or killed. It is proper and significant to underline the horror of some catastrophe by pointing to the amount of human carnage it causes. Ultimately, though, the usefulness of body count as a measure of "worstness" is limited to a certain kind of disaster: ones we have a lot of experience with. A lot of events widely considered worst cases do not have the highest body counts. Think of the *Challenger* space shuttle accident, which killed only seven people, or the *Hindenburg* crash, with a death toll of a few dozen. Or even, I daresay, the World Trade Center attack. While that horror killed more people than any other terrorist attack on U.S. soil, the worst disaster in U.S. history, at least in terms of numbers killed, was a 1900 hurricane that hit Texas, killing perhaps eight thousand people.

So body count does matter, but only sometimes. What vaults body count into prominence as a measure of the worst in some cases is that there is a string of similar cases to serve as a framing device. Our experience with other similar events allows us to create templates for stories about train wrecks, plane crashes, surprise attacks, and so on. These stories help us make sense of horror and tragedy, rendering them more psychologically manageable. The story that is used for plane crashes is pretty much the same for all plane crashes: There is "human error," usually on the part of the pilot, and, newspapers and television announcers tell us, "panic" among the victims. Innocent victims are obliterated, their clothes and other possessions scattered. Anyway, it's accurate to say that when there are similar cases the body count, or kill number, will be used to establish whether the event is a worst case.

The *worst case* label, though, is flexible. The Modane crash or the Egyptian train fire may have had the highest kill number, but people still refer to other train disasters as worst cases. When in 1998 a passenger train derailed in Germany and about a hundred people were killed, it was called the worst train wreck in Germany's postwar history. And recall the Austrian train fire, which a reporter termed "a catastrophe of unprecedented proportions." I don't want to sound unfeeling, but what exactly would warrant such judgments? The death tolls weren't all that high; neither came close to those in Modane or Egypt. In the moment, though, the sentiments were reasonable.

What made people think of the Austrian train wreck as a worst case were other characteristics: Most of the victims were teenagers. Children are icons of innocence and purity, and the idea of young people suffering so terribly tugs at our heartstrings. The accident happened in a tunnel, which quickly filled with dense, black, choking smoke, making any rescue attempt impossible. There were a few survivors, who broke out windows in the back of the train and ran for their lives, but their escape made the story all the more poignant—if a few could get out perhaps more should have. Then there was the completeness with which the train was destroyed. Train workers who inspected the wreckage found that only its metal base remained. All of these characteristics add poignance to the story. So the Austrian train disaster *was* a worst train disaster. There are many worst train disasters, because people use different points of comparison in making their judgments. Similarly, the destruction of the World Trade Center was a worst case, not because of the number of people who died but because it overpowered people's imaginations and made doom and disaster seem a normal part of daily life, at least for a while.

When events are novel, body count doesn't matter as much. *Challenger* can be a worst case even though only seven perished, but a commuter airplane crash that kills twice as many is not one. (*Challenger*, and later *Columbia*, were certainly worst cases for NASA because they threatened the space program in general.) About one hundred Americans die in lightning strikes every year, none of which are worst cases, except for those who die. But if next year's hundred are killed all at the same time while attending an open-air wedding in Maine it will be a worst case. People will say it's the kind of thing that never happens. If a calamity is in a recognizable genre then the kill number will probably be used to measure its worstness.

What besides Body Count?

Untoward events are likely to be judged worst cases to the extent that the people doing the judging feel out of control. We really hate to be out of control. In the language of social scientists, the *less controllable* the risk is felt to be the more likely it will be called a worst case. Forty thousand people die on American highways every year, an average of more than one hundred a day, and people don't think of this as a chronic, never-ending catastrophe. But imagine if every year a thousand soccer moms driving with their children—fewer than three a day on average—were accosted by carjackers, who stole their cars but otherwise didn't harm them. It would be regarded as disaster of great proportions, a worst case, a sign of the decline of civility as we know it. People feel in control of their automobiles, even with the prevalence of fatal crashes, but much less in control if marauders are endangering mommies and their babies.

When planes take off it's not unusual to see people grasping the arms of their seats in pure terror, even if the takeoff is perfectly smooth. After a particularly turbulent flight people often applaud when the plane lands. For whom are they applauding? Some of it may be for the pilot, but I think most of it is a collective expression of relief. They're saying, "We're alive and darned glad of it, and we want to share our joy publicly." They're glad to be in control again.

The fire at the Triangle Shirtwaist factory has been called "one of the worst disasters since the beginning of the Industrial Revolution." Near closing time on March 25, 1911, a fire broke out on the top floor of the Asch Building (which now houses classrooms and offices for New York University) and quickly spread to other parts of the structure. The ten-story building was a death trap, lacking sprinklers or adequate fire escapes. It was a garment factory, a sweatshop, and the cloth provided an excellent fuel for the fire. Although the first fire engines arrived in about ten minutes, that was not soon enough for many victims. And the firefighters' ladders reached only to the sixth floor. Many of the five hundred workers got out of the building—worst cases can always be worse—but 146 did not. The vast majority of the dead were females, many in their teens. Some of the survivors reported that exits were locked, which would not have been surprising given the grinding oppression that working class immigrants were forced to endure in that era.

People in the street yelled at the girls and women not to jump. But the prospect of burning to death was apparently too horrible for many of them. I estimate, from reading witness accounts, that half of the casualties were jumpers. A journalist at the scene described it this way: "Thud—dead, thud—dead, thud—dead, thud—dead. Sixty-two thud—deads. I call them that, because the sound and the thought of death came to me each time, at the same instant." One police officer said it was "the worst thing I ever saw."[6]

Imagine that you're standing outside the factory, looking up at the inferno. Smoke and flame are billowing out of the building. The firefighters can't quite get to the trapped women. You see some of them at windows, backlit by flames, hug each other, clasp hands, and leap to their deaths. It's hard to imagine a situation in which you would feel more *out of control.* And that, I think, is why some disasters come to be seen as worst cases. It is important in this particular case, too, that so many of the dead were females. That fact carries its own meaning, because women, especially young ones, were and are seen as more innocent and in need of protection than men. Even immigrant girls warranted that sentiment. Here again, the characteristics of the victims add emotional value.

Social similarity matters for judging whether or not something is a worst case. A ferry goes belly-up in the Philippines, drowning two thousand, and occasions barely a paragraph at the end of the first section of the *New York Times*. But when a twenty-car pileup outside Atlanta kills fifty, we say it's one of the worst transportation disasters in fifteen years. Thousands die in a big earthquake in Turkey or Peru and Hollywood doesn't even make a movie out of it, but when sixty people died in the Loma Prieta earthquake in California, a mini-industry was mobilized around engineers' "worst case scenarios." The capsized ferry and the third world earthquake may be worst cases for the victims, but they don't matter much to people far removed. I don't mean to say that the ferry accident is not a worst case, only that people far from the Philippines aren't likely to consider it one. Nearly three hundred people burned or drowned when a ship cracked up off the coast of China in November 1999. The tragedy was barely noticed in the rest of the world. Had three hundred perished off the coast of North Carolina, the event would probably have been dubbed a worst case, in the United States at least, perhaps even if the fatalities were Chinese.[7]

One of the things that people do when judging how well off they are is to look up, down, and sideways. They look up to people who are richer, smarter, or luckier. They look down on people who are poor, sick, or enfeebled. They glance sideways at people they consider peers, usually on the basis of age, sex, and education. When people make these comparisons they are imagining the networks of meaning in which their lives are, or could be, embedded. They are building mental maps that locate people they come into contact with, or might come into contact with if their station in life were different.

Two months after the World Trade Center attack American Airlines Flight 587, an Airbus A300 bound for the Dominican Republic, broke apart soon after takeoff and crashed into Queens, New York. Five people on the ground were killed, as were all 260 in the plane. A man who had a loved one on Flight 587 illustrated the significance of social similarity to perception of worst cases when he said, "Today is worse than [September] 11th. On the 11th, there were people crying, but it was for everybody. Today it is for Dominicans."[8] In 1974,

179 people died in what was then the worst high-rise disaster ever, at least in terms of body count. But the fire was in São Paulo, Brazil, and while the disaster is commemorated there, probably few people outside of Brazil even know about it. On July 17, 1998, a tsunami killed more than twenty-two hundred people in Papua New Guinea. The U.S. Geological Service said, prior to the much deadlier December 2004 tsunami, that it "may have been the most devastating tsunami in this century."[9] Over the following week the disaster garnered six stories in the *New York Times,* only one of which was on page 1. Imagine the coverage if a tsunami had killed two thousand people in New Jersey. The more like us the victims are, the more likely we are to judge their suffering relevant to our own experience.

Finally, worst cases are almost always described as beyond imagination. They are *unthinkable.* When there are multiple failures that no one in their right mind would have thought possible—not one but two jumbo jets smashing into the World Trade Center *and* both towers completely disintegrating—the imagination is overwhelmed. Consider the case of United Airline Flight 232, which cartwheeled into the Sioux City, Iowa, airport in 1991. One hundred twelve souls were lost. Of course airplanes will crash from time to time, but could anyone have imagined that a defect in an engine rotor, the size of a grain of sand, would cause the rotor to fail? Perhaps. When the rotor failed it sent broken engine parts flying. That too may have been imaginable. But the flying parts sliced through *three* hydraulic lines, and if any of them had remained intact the plane would have been flyable. Worst cases overwhelm the imagination.

Before October 1991 nobody had ever imagined that a cold front from Canada would meet up with a hurricane from the Caribbean *and* a large storm from the Great Lakes. The hurricane would eventually become embedded inside a much larger cyclone, feeding the latter's destructive energy so that it too would become a hurricane. The National Weather Service called it "the perfect storm." Sebastian Junger, whose best-selling book *The Perfect Storm* was made into a hit movie, wrote that it created "among the very highest waves measured anywhere in the world, ever." Waves themselves are extreme forces. To again quote Junger, "The seas generated by a forty-knot wind aren't twice as violent as those from a twenty-knot wind, they're seventeen times as violent." The storm was so strong that "the ocean gets piled up against the continent and starts blocking rivers. The Hudson backs up one hundred miles to Albany. . . . Storm surge and huge seas extinguish Isle of Shoals and Boone's Island lighthouses off the coast of Maine."[10] The perfect storm was perfectly overwhelming.

CULTURE AND WORST CASES

These three attributes—inconceivability, uncontrollability, and social identification—seem to be common to unfamiliar events that people label worst cases. Even so, we don't want to get too hung up on definitions. What really makes something worst is not the event itself but what people *think about* the event. That involves culture, which concerns what people think and believe. People's conceptions of the kinds of things that they will fear and loath are often quite broad. Newspaper editors, for instance, decide whether they'll cover some catastrophe, and how prominently and extensively, partly on the basis of whether they can imagine themselves or their readers in the situation. What an editor deems a worst case may or may not correlate with how many people died. Let's look at some examples.

On May 7, 1915, three years after the *Titanic* sank, the passenger liner *Lusitania* was torpedoed by a German submarine. There were 1,962 people aboard, and 1,198—61 percent—were lost. The *Titanic* lost 1,490 of 2,201, or 68 percent. In terms of either total numbers or percentages of lives lost the events weren't drastically different. But the *Titanic* is the disaster that looms larger in the popular mind, and not just because of the Hollywood movie. I think the comparable body count mattered less because there were other things going on that drew attention *away* from the *Lusitania*. The *Titanic* had already sunk, setting a precedent for a large number of people being lost at sea. More importantly, World War I had started, so attention was naturally focused there.

Were someone to ask you what was the worst marine accident in American history, you probably would not think of the *Sultana*. The *Sultana*, a Civil War steamboat, was on a routine trip in April 1865, carrying Union soldiers north from New Orleans to Cairo, at the southern tip of Illinois. The vessel was terribly overcrowded and started experiencing troubles with its boilers. When the boilers finally exploded, just north of Memphis, the boat split in half, sending flames into the sky and bodies into the cold water. Men not injured in the explosion threw themselves from the burning ship, apparently preferring the risk of drowning to that of burning alive. Between seventeen hundred and two thousand perished.

As with the *Lusitania,* the main reason the *Sultana* disaster isn't part of popular lore is because of the larger context in which it occurred. The Civil War was nearing its end. Johnston had surrendered on April 8, Lee the next day at Appomattox. On April 14 Abraham Lincoln had been shot, and the dramatic search for his killer, John Wilkes Booth, dominated the headlines. People on both sides of the Mason-Dixon Line were weary of death and destruction. It was fairly easy to turn away from the *Sultana*. Whether a problem or event is deemed worthy of significant attention depends on the configuration of things competing for attention at the time. There wasn't much news coverage of the disaster, and there hasn't been commemoration of it. *Sultana* does not resonate in the nation's collective disaster memory. That's why it's not a worst case.

Imagine a ruler used for measuring damage (fig. 1).[11] The "zero" end corresponds to no harm; the other end, let's give it the value 12, indicates the most extreme damage one can imagine. At point 0 on someone's ruler, they read a book, watch a sitcom, prune the rose bushes, walk the dog; at point 12, the person may imagine being diagnosed with a brain tumor or losing his or her family in a house fire or plane crash.

WORST CASE RULERS

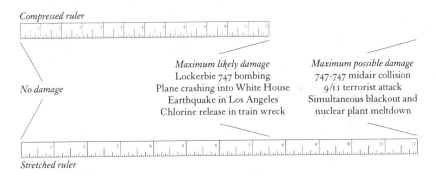

Compressed ruler

No damage

Maximum likely damage
Lockerbie 747 bombing
Plane crashing into White House
Earthquake in Los Angeles
Chlorine release in train wreck

Maximum possible damage
747-747 midair collision
9/11 terrorist attack
Simultaneous blackout and
nuclear plant meltdown

Stretched ruler

Imagine now that the ruler is made of rubber and can be stretched or compressed. The more you stretch the ruler, the more things are included as plausible dangers. The Federal Aviation Administration, for example, may consider some particularly devastating crashes but is unlikely to stretch its ruler so far as to include, say, the possibility of four jetliners crashing in the middle of New York City. Elites and institutions will tend to be bound by probabilistic thinking and to neglect more extreme possibilities. Such improbable events will simply be off their scale.

Official rulers won't cover the following scenario, which actually happened in Holland in 1992. As an El Al 747 was taking off, one of its engines fell off and took a second engine with it, which led the four-hundred-ton plane to shear the top five floors off two buildings and then explode in a fireball. Then, because that wouldn't be a worst case, they would have to further imagine that the plane was carrying most of the chemicals needed to make sarin gas *plus* not-so-depleted uranium in the tail (which is used as a counterweight in hundreds of older 747s). For realism, they might want to add a mitigating factor, and so could posit that eighty-three tons of what officials call "oil industry explosives" had been offloaded just before the crash. Had those explosives blown up when the plane crashed the disaster would have been much worse, of course, but the point is that even without them elites are unlikely to create such a scenario. The rubber ruler used by airline officials and regulators is consistently short. But it would be long for others, such as victims' families or environmentalists.

Above I said that designating something a worst case depends on someone's point of view. Perhaps, though, there is an "ultimate worst case"—the total annihilation of humanity. Imagine a comet a mile wide striking the earth somewhere. It doesn't matter where, because if anything that size hit the earth we would all, sooner or later, be plunged into a deep, dark climatic catastrophe. Millions of tons of dust and dirt would be blown into the stratosphere where winds would distribute them around the globe. The ambient temperature would drop and much of the sun's light would be prevented from reaching the earth, probably for years. There would be massive crop failure. In the end, as it were, in spite of all our modern technology, we are utterly dependent on crops. If the crops die, we become the dinosaurs. Would that not qualify as an essential, inherent worst case?

It would for humans, but from the point of view of the universe it would be fairly normal and would probably not disrupt even our solar system. There would even be winners in the event of the total annihilation of humanity, but they would be nonhuman organisms. Among the eventual beneficiaries of the total annihilation of the dinosaurs, after all, were humans, who simply could not have coexisted with building-size reptiles. But the larger point about the actual end of people as we know them is that while the issue is clearly important (!), it is not interesting. For if all the people were gone then there would be no witnesses to judge it a worst case. So, even the death of everyone, the highest possible body count, isn't enough to qualify as an objective worst case. And yet sometimes a single death can be considered a worst case—many regard the loss of Martin Luther King Jr. or John F. Kennedy as overwhelmingly devastating.

The malleability in the definition of "worst case" is not a bad thing; it doesn't mean there's no there there. What it does mean is that we have to be careful to understand how it is that some things rather than others come to be considered worst. We have to figure out those aspects of a situation that influence peoples' points of view, which is ultimately what makes something a worst case.

IT DEPENDS . . .

There is a larger principle at work here. Basically, whether something is a worst case depends on the context that people use to make sense of the event. Think of the word *society*. It some situations it means an entire nation that shares a culture. In other situations it means a secret club of hate-mongering bigots. In still other situations *society* can refer to a collection of highbrows who hang out together and exclude nonrich people from their parties. The meaning depends on the context in which it is used. Imagine the following scenario. You're walking down the street and you look up to see someone throwing a three-year-old child out of a second-story window. What do you make of this situation? Based on just the facts given so far you'd probably conclude that an evil person, or a deranged one, was committing an act of unspeakable cruelty. But if you then see smoke pouring from the roof of the building and fire trucks on the street, you might revise your judgment and designate this particular baby thrower a hero.

We can say the same things about the ideas "danger," "disaster," and "worst case." An earthquake that happens in the middle of nowhere isn't a disaster because no one is affected. A tsunami can wash over an entire island in the Pacific but if no one is on the island there's no sense in calling it a catastrophe. Is it dangerous to fly in airplanes? The answer can depend on the kind of airplane you fly in, the prevailing weather, and the alternative methods of travel available to you. In some ways cars are much more dangerous than airplanes. If we count up the *number of people who die* every year in each mode of transportation, cars are more dangerous. In 2000, 36,249 people died in car crashes on American roads. But there were only 92 fatalities on U.S. air carriers that year. If we count the *number of crashes* for the same year, then cars, again, are more dangerous than airplanes. In 2000 there were 50 airplane crashes but 6,394,000 car crashes.[12] If you think about the risk in taking a long trip, for instance across the country, then, yet again, cars are more dangerous because on the road you're at greater risk from drunk drivers, drowsy drivers, bad road conditions, poorly built cars, and so on. These are the kinds of statistics that airline officials always use to ease people's fear of flying. It is another example of how elite risk rulers are shorter than those of the people who take risks for their benefit.

But that's not the only way to tell the story. There are other ways of looking at how dangerous flying is. Airplanes are not a substitute for getting to work every day, or going to the store, or taking the kids to school. In those contexts, it makes no sense to say that planes are safer than cars. In fact, it's irrational. Airplanes are also not safer in cars *in any given crash*. Think about how likely someone is to die once they get into an airplane crash or a car crash. Car crashes are more numerous but regularly have survivors; some walk away uninjured, and no one is too surprised. Plane crashes serious enough to kill one person often kill everyone on board; survival is reported as somewhat miraculous. Considering *that* context, it's much more dangerous to fly than to drive.

Worst cases require this kind of thinking. Let's take the following statement: Forty thousand people died last year. That statement is senseless without more information: Who were the people? Where were they? What were they doing? How many *could* have died? If they were all in a town that was wiped out by a tornado, we'd probably call it a worst case. If forty thousand people at a college football game were obliterated by a terrorists' bomb, it'd be a worst case. If forty thousand American children died from second-hand smoke or radiation poisoning, that too would be a worst case. But if forty thousand poor Africans died from AIDS then it wouldn't be, at least not in the United States. Words and numbers have to be placed in a larger context before they mean anything.

I'll have more to say about the issue of context dependency, and especially how creating some contexts as opposed to others works to normalize or control the uncontrollable aspect of worst cases. For now I'll just make the point that something can be "worst" only from a certain point of view, and compared to something else. The reason that matters is that it reminds us that the actual location of "worst cases" is *in the imagination*. When we delve into horrible catastrophes we are, at bottom, delving into the social organization of thoughts and minds. Think about the three dimensions that we usually find in worst cases: they are uncontrollable, they are overwhelming, and they happen among socially similar people. Each of these dimensions inherently involves people's considerations of the value of other people, their sense of mastery, or their feelings of power. As soon as we realize that the worst is not the same for everyone it becomes apparent that looking at ideas about worst cases is an opportunity to look at *social imaginations*.

TIME AND THE WORST CASE IMAGINATION

The idea of the worst case draws our attention to the past and pushes it into the future. For thinking about worst cases involves both thinking about negative futures and evaluating past events as superlatively bad. "What's the worst than can happen?" we ask children. Most people can look back and say, "That was the worst day of my life." Such thinking and evaluating is fundamentally about the expansion and contraction of imagination.

Labeling something "the worst" involves both prospective and retrospective orientations to disaster. Let me say a few more words about that. Sometimes we imagine futures that are particularly awful or construct scenarios that are overwhelmingly bad or sad, then attach the worst case moniker to them. Since the 9/11 terrorist attacks many people and organizations have created projections of that sort. Government leaders have made solemn announcements regarding when another attack might be coming—especially after it was discovered that officials actually had pretty good indications that something big was coming *before* September 11. Everyone has been urged to go on "high alert." Reporters and others have set off to assess preparedness levels at nuclear plants, water treatment facilities, and key points on the electric power grid.

Some of the 9/11 terrorists were reported to have asked questions of airport personnel in the small south Florida town of Belle Glade. Belle Glade is a farming community and crop dusters are a common sight there. Those reports were probably false, but at the time they prompted worst case projections about the use of crop dusters to distribute chemical or biological weapons. Similar speculation followed reports of a March 2001 visit by Mohammed Atta, a key player in the September 11 attacks, to a small town in Tennessee. Tanks at a nearby plant hold 250 tons of sulfur dioxide, and the plant's worst case scenario said that perhaps sixty thousand people could be killed or hurt if it were sabotaged. Recall the EPA-required scenarios I mentioned earlier. Journalists looked through some of those scenarios after 9/11 and discovered that many of America's most populated areas are next to facilities with large amounts of toxic chemicals. For example, in Kearny, New Jersey—which is very close to Manhattan—there's a facility that has 180,000 pounds of sulfur dioxide which, if released in a toxic cloud, could kill or injure *twelve million* people. Similar scenarios exist for Los Angeles, Detroit, and Philadelphia. Officials of the companies responsible for these dangerous chemicals say they're taking precautions that make such a catastrophe "unlikely"—there's that short risk ruler again. That's not very reassuring, though, because terrorists aim precisely to create *unlikely* horrors, which is to say they aim to make worst cases.

To construct *prospective worst cases,* like the ones I just mentioned, we must somehow imagine the unimaginable. That isn't easy to do. Before they built the Tacoma Narrows Bridge, engineers calculated that it would perform well under its own weight and the weight of the traffic it was to carry. That sort of projection often gets us into trouble, because once people convince themselves that they *have* imagined the worst then they stop imagining more possibilities. The engineers didn't consider the possibility that wind could set up a wave in the deck of the suspension bridge that would, if sustained, shake the thing apart, but that's exactly what happened on November 7, 1940, only four months after it opened to traffic. Their thinking was trapped in experience, depending on past successes and failures for models of what could go wrong. I'll explore later how worst case thinking expands and contracts the imagination. For now, I just want to make the point that prospective worst case thinking is doomed to failure, in an absolute sense, because the mere act of imagining a worst case renders it something less of one. An emergency planner captured the idea well when he said, "People who are terrorists and sociopaths don't have the normal thinking we have, so they would imagine things that would never occur to most of us. I would never say, 'Oh, yeah, we're as prepared as we can be.' "[13]

Forward-looking worst case creation isn't just about terrorists. Millennialists, millenarians, and other religiously inspired apocalyptics do it when they look forward to the end of the world. Organizations do it too, when they make plans and scenarios for chemical facilities, such as those noted above or the contingency plans the U.S. Army has developed in case of a major mishap at its facilities for destroying our chemical weapons stockpile. To look at prospective worst cases is to look at how people think about and judge the future and their place in it.

In constructing *retrospective worst cases,* people instead look back on events and fit them into a story, the ending of which is something like "that's the worst thing that's ever happened to me" or "that was the worst airplane accident ever." The construction of retrospective worst cases helps people make sense of society and nature, providing a way to shoehorn the calamitous and the threatening back into their sense of normalcy.

The meanings of retrospective and prospective orientations toward the worst are different. Retrospective worst cases are events that would probably not have been imagined before they came to pass. They are occurrences about which we say, "Nobody in their right mind would say that can happen." Listen to Stewart Carroll, a resident of Rockaway, New York, after American Airlines Flight 587 broke up over his neighborhood:

You think of Rockaway as being away from it all. And yet it's Rockaway that had so many people in the World Trade Center, so many Fire Department people, so many police. And now this. No one would have thought this would be ground zero.[14]

We go back and look forward at a failed imagination. That is what's involved with retrospective worst cases.

In contrast, prospective worst cases are less likely to encompass the inconceivable, especially when experts and high-level decision makers are doing the prospecting. Indeed, these cases are often constructed as "reasonable" possibilities. The problem is that worst cases are never reasonable. The U.S. Department of Energy plans to bury high-level nuclear waste in Nevada for many thousands of years. In its "preliminary evaluation" DOE models "external events": tornadoes, earthquakes, and the like. DOE says its plans guarantee "no loss of isolation" of the radiological materials. "This strategy," says the document, "ensures that there are *no credible* radioactive release scenarios associated with external design basis events and natural phenomena, even though the initiating events are deemed credible."[15] The Department of Energy is projecting future competence and control, based on its present capabilities and expertise. *Could* the DOE consider the possibility of terrorists detonating a small nuclear weapon at the site, which would kill all the good guys so the bad guys could invade and create a "loss of isolation?" *Could* it consider an 9.5 magnitude earthquake? That's the estimated size of the largest recorded earthquake, which happened off the coast of Chile in 1960; earthquakes of similar force have repeatedly struck the Pacific Northwest. Sure it could. But the *chances* of those things happening are, as risk experts say, vanishingly small. DOE's environmental impact statement says the department considered a 6.3 magnitude quake within three miles of Yucca Mountain. "DOE regards this annual frequency as appropriate and conservative because it reflects the annual probabilities of design ground motions for nuclear powerplants in the western U.S."[16]

We look forward, but pressing circumstances hem in the imagination. That is what's involved with prospective worst cases.

This book asks how extreme events happen, how they come to be thought of as worst cases, how projections of the worst are built, and what worst cases do. Failure and catastrophe are all around us. They happen all the time, and for that reason they are not special. People's lives are punctuated with terror just as they are punctuated with joy. Worst cases are normal. My central argument is that disasters are normal parts of life—spectacular, but prosaic in their cognitive and institutional patterns. All that is special about them is the searchlight they throw upon power, politics, and imagination. I will turn on that bright light.

2

THE SKY *COULD* BE FALLING: GLOBALLY RELEVANT DISASTERS AND THE PERILS OF PROBABILISM

Who would ever predict that a jetliner would crash into a bridge in a major city just when thousands of people are going home from work early because of a massive snow storm *and* just about the same time that a subway train, in the same city, crashes and causes a fire, putting extra stress on the city's emergency response system? Wouldn't it be ridiculous to expect, even in fancy, that someone could aimlessly fire a .22 caliber rifle—the bullets are smaller in diameter than a pencil—into the air and hit a sunbather a mile away? Might not someone question your mental acuity were you to suggest that an asteroid half a mile wide would come perilously close to the earth?

All those things happened. In 1937 an asteroid named Hermes came to within twice the distance from Earth to the moon; in 1989 another asteroid came even closer. The problem isn't going away either. In March 2002 an asteroid estimated to be between fifty and a hundred kilometers across—big enough to blow up a large city—zipped past us at a distance of about one and a half times the distance to the moon. In June 2002 an asteroid the size of a football field missed Earth by a mere seventy-five thousand miles, less than a third of the distance to the moon. Something that size could release the energy equivalent of a large nuclear explosion.

In August 1998 Andres Perez was testing his new .22 rifle on Long Island. He pointed the gun into the sky and fired. A minute or so later Christina Dellaratta, who was sunbathing in her backyard, felt a sting. She initially thought it was a mosquito bite. Ms. Dellaratta lived, though she became "afraid to go outside and sunbathe." Mr. Perez was charged with reckless endangerment and assault.[1]

On January 13, 1982, an Air Florida jetliner with too much ice on its wings tried to take off from National Airport in Washington, D.C. The plane failed to get enough lift and slammed into the Fourteenth Street Bridge, which connects Washington and Virginia. As if that weren't bad enough, at just about the same time a Metro subway train crashed and caused a fire. Such coincident accidents created what many considered a worst case for the D.C. area.

In November 2001, two months after the World Trade Center and Pentagon disasters an American Airlines jetliner broke apart soon after takeoff from New York's Kennedy Airport, crashing into Queens and killing 265. The plane's tail broke off in midflight. Nuclear power plant accidents, chemical contaminations that slowly obliterate communities, terrific explosions at petrochemical plants, nuclear waste that will last thousands of years, people dying from contaminated mouthwash, and all manner of transportation disasters that kill hundreds or even thousands at a time. I haven't even mentioned the massacres we can expect once terrorists get their hands on weapons of mass destruction. How much worse can a worst case get?

There's a good deal of advice, from various quarters, *not* to think in terms of the worst. "Don't panic," goes one oft-repeated admonition. "Chances are that the cruise ship won't be torpedoed." "Don't overreact," says the public relations specialist. "The probability that the wings will fall off the airplane is too small to calculate." It's as if anyone who worries about worst cases were akin to the deeply religious who try to predict the end of the world as we know it—TEOTWAWKI, as they call it.

But worst cases are not chimerical. Machines do sometimes go haywire and kill when they're supposed to save. Killer bees do sting people to death, hundred-foot waves do inundate populations, and people's immune systems do turn on them as if *they* were the disease. Airplanes do smash into each other in midair. Houses do explode. Sometimes the sky falls.

GLOBALLY RELEVANT DISASTERS

It must have seemed like the sky was falling to the good people of Pompeii in AD 472. Others, across the continent, must also have felt dread. A sixth-century writer describes the scale and intensity of the event:

Vesuvius, a burning mountain of Campania, seething with internal fires, vomited up its completely consumed inner parts and turned day into night, covering the whole surface of Europe with a fine dust.

Mount Vesuvius has that habit. It had also blown its stack in AD 79 and buried Pompeii, Herculaneum, and other cities. It did much the same thing in 217 BC.

In fact the sky has fallen for a lot of people. What they experienced were *globally relevant disasters*—globally relevant because their impacts were felt well outside their immediate environs. Following are a few examples.

For eighteen months, sometime around 848, in Mesopotamia and probably throughout the northern hemisphere, the sun shone for only four hours a day, and even then the "light was only a feeble shadow . . . the fruits did not ripen and the wine tasted like sour grapes." A similar "dry fog" had appeared around the Mediterranean in 536 and lasted some twelve to fifteen months. Dry fogs happen when volcanoes push vast quantities of ash and sulfur gases into the troposphere and stratosphere. Very dense and widespread dry fogs happen every few centuries. Richard Stothers, a scientist at NASA's Goddard Institute for Space Studies, has spent a good deal of time worrying about worst cases, especially worst cases that involve monster volcanic eruptions. In 1983 Stothers and Michael Rampino, also of Goddard, published the definitive catalog of huge volcanic eruptions in the Mediterranean before A.D. 630. Their catalog reveals some very disturbing facts. Very large volcanic eruptions can bring about the total destruction of cities and even civilizations. Stothers and Rampino note that an eruption in the fifteenth century BC ruined the Minoan civilization on Crete.

The 1883 eruption of Krakatau in Indonesia killed perhaps thirty-five thousand people, mostly through tsunamis, one of which reached the Arabian Peninsula, some forty-three hundred miles away. The Tambora eruption in 1815 was even worse, with more global consequences. It was 150 times larger than Mount Saint Helens, and shot a volcanic column twenty-eight miles into the air. It darkened the skies entirely, over a distance of 370 miles. Estimates are that ninety-two thousand people died because of Tambora, eighty-two thousand of them from starvation caused by cooler temperatures across the northern hemisphere—1816 is known as the "year without a summer." In 1783 over ten thousand people died in Iceland, in a famine caused by "dry fog." A fissure had opened and let loose the largest "terrestrial lava flow of the present millennium."

This is the stuff of disaster movies. It is not common, even after September 11, to think that entire cities, or countries, could disappear. But it should be.

Some respectable people are pondering these issues. For example, S. Pete Worden, a brigadier general in the U.S. Air Force and deputy director for Command and Control Headquarters at the Pentagon, says we should pay more attention to "Tunguska-class" objects—near earth objects with average diameters of a hundred meters or so that can strike up to several times per century with the destructiveness of a nuclear weapon. I mentioned Tunguska in chapter 1. It's possible, even probable, that the next time an object that size crashes to Earth it will do no damage. Most of Earth's surface, after all, is uninhabited, so any random fifteen-megaton explosion would most likely devastate nothing. But if it exploded over Seattle it would be a worst case catastrophe.

It would be comforting to think that monstrous disasters were a thing of the past. In many ways, as I've said and will say again, modern, rich, open societies are safer than their opposites. But we're still very much at risk for a globally relevant disaster. Massive volcanic eruptions, to take but one genre, produced real worst cases for the ancients. They can visit us too. In fact, the way we live and consume makes us increasingly vulnerable to globally relevant disasters. More people are at risk from a supervolcanic eruption today than were two hundred or three hundred years ago. Modernity doesn't protect us from everything.

Even influenza. Most people think of the flu as a nuisance that visits every winter. But tens of thousands of Americans die every year from flu. And it could be much worse, although modern vaccines help prevent pandemics. The so-called Spanish flu of 1918 was a plague of biblical proportions—and it was often interpreted in just that way. (There was nothing "Spanish" about this particular strain of the virus; Spain just reported its incidence more accurately than other places.) It started in September of 1918, reached nearly every corner of the earth, and was gone in a matter of months. But during that time *conservative* estimates are that it killed twenty to forty *million* people worldwide, more than any other disease in the history of the world. Some believe it may have killed a hundred million.

In the US, theaters and shops closed around the country as 25 percent of the population fell ill. Streets were deserted. At a New York minor league baseball game everybody in attendance, including the players, wore a gauze mask. Tucson passed a law requiring that anyone out in public wear a mask that covered nose and mouth. It even affected the conduct of World War I: a draft of more than 140,000 men was canceled because of the high infection rate at military training camps and bases. The Spanish flu was particularly bad in Philadelphia, and that poor city was particularly unprepared to deal with it. Public officials there didn't appreciate that gravity of the situation. Within a month eleven thousand people in the city had died.

Globally relevant disasters are events whose effects reach far beyond their initial locales. They may not kill more people than other disasters, at least directly. A massive earthquake that shook Los Angeles to the ground might kill half the population—about five million people. A supervolcanic eruption might not kill nearly that many, though its consequences could traverse, say, the southern hemisphere. It's tempting to think of such things as relics of a long lost past. Maybe the dinosaurs or Minoans in the fifteenth century BC saw such eruptions, but not us. That's wishful thinking. We should not be surprised if we wake up tomorrow morning and learn that Yokohama, Auckland, Honolulu, or San Diego has been wiped out by a tsunami caused by such an eruption.

The tsunami of December 26, 2004, is the kind of thing I'm talking about. A huge earthquake broke around eight in the morning near the Indonesian island of Sumatra. The quake produced a tsunami that crossed the Indian Ocean; it traveled seven hours to kill in eastern Africa, though the greatest damage was done within three hours. It even passed into the Pacific and was recorded as far away as the west coast of North America. Hundreds of thousands of people were killed. Entire communities were wiped from the earth; it threw into doubt the continued existence of the Maldives as a country. We need to look closely at that disaster for several reasons. The obvious reason is that it shows just how horrible globally relevant disasters can be.

There are other reasons. Should such an event—twenty- to forty-foot waves moving at five hundred miles per hour—befall the American west coast it could be a catastrophe of almost unimaginable proportions. Many thousands of people could be at risk. A huge part of the physical infrastructure could be wiped out: the Port of Los Angeles, Los Angeles International Airport, San Francisco International Airport, San Onofre nuclear power plant (with two live reactors and one dead one and the waste that's sitting in its cooling pools), Diablo Canyon nuclear station (there's a big fault five thousand meters off shore), and naval and air force bases. It's not just that California could be shut down for a significant period of time. The Port of Los Angeles is the largest international gateway for moving goods. The U.S. economy could be crippled, at least for a while, and the world economy depends on the U.S. economy being in good shape. And that's just the American west coast, where earthquakes are *expected*. A tsunami, though probably not one caused by an earthquake, could also hit the American east coast. Imagine the outer quarter mile of the U.S. eastern seaboard destroyed. It would be worse than all our worst case scenarios.

HOW WE CREATE CONDITIONS FOR DISASTERS: CONCENTRATION AND INTERDEPENDENCE

In 1968 biologist Paul Ehrlich published a book called *The Population Bomb*. His argument borrowed from that original worst case thinker, Thomas Malthus. He said that if population growth continued at its present rate, at some point in the not too distant future we'd run up against resource limits. Ehrlich's book was followed a few years later by the first commissioned report from the Club of Rome, called *Limits to Growth*. The books' long-term value lies not in their specific models or predictions, but in the attention they brought to the issues of population and interdependence and in the debates they generated—both were hugely controversial. They very effectively brought to the forefront of political debate the fundamental connections between population, energy, resources, and industrialization. That specific dire predictions have not come true does not gainsay the vital importance of emphasizing, as both books did, that if we ignore pollution, resource depletion, and patterns of population growth, then the quality of life for everyone, sometime in the future, will be significantly diminished. Today, in 2005, the earth's population is about 6.5 billion. In 1970 it was about 3.5 billion. Most of that growth, and almost all of the projected growth over the next forty-five years, is in the so-called developing world.

There are many good reasons to worry about population growth, including massive urban expansion, abandoned children, starvation, poverty; I'll only say softly that China and India, each projected to have populations of 1.5 billion in 2050, could have *huge* armies. The key concern, for my purposes, is that population growth—especially growth among poor, illiterate populations, people without much purpose in the world economy—intensifies pressures on the world's resources.

Human connections to disaster are broad and deep. First of all, people have to be hurt before we can even say a disaster has happened. If a hurricane with two-hundred-mile-per-hour winds slams into a string of islands but people don't live there, there is no catastrophe. If there are no people on the planet it doesn't matter if an asteroid throws the place into a deep, dark permanent winter.

We can go further. We can even say that humans cause ourselves to be victims. We put ourselves in harm's way by the ways we organize, and fail to organize, our lives. There are two particular ways in which we create the conditions for large-scale worst cases. One is that we concentrate ourselves. The seemingly trivial fact of having a lot of people live close to each other—the United Nations says population density nearly doubled between 1970 and 2005—creates unprecedented opportunities for mass destruction. It doesn't help when people concentrate in dangerous places. The other way that societies organize for catastrophe has to do with interdependence. This is a more complicated topic than concentration, but certainly as important. I'll explain each in turn.

When people concentrate in dangerous areas they become worst cases waiting to happen. In 1935 a huge storm killed over four hundred people in the Florida Keys. The Labor Day hurricane's fifteen-foot storm surges were so strong that they knocked a train over, tossing some of its cars a hundred feet. Of course, it was and is perfectly normal for hurricanes to blow over south Florida. What made the Labor Day storm worthy of superlatives were not only the high winds and other physical attributes but the high body count. Especially significant was that several hundred out-of-work veterans—it was the depths of the Great Depression—had relocated to the Keys to help build U.S. Highway 1. Most of those men were living in tents and similarly flimsy structures. At the time, the Keys were relatively unpopulated. Today about eighty thousand people live there, and although they evacuate when hurricanes come barreling through, there could easily be complications. There are two nuclear plants about twenty-five miles south of Miami, which is just north of the Keys. If one of them melted down just when a category 5 hurricane came to town, the evacuation routes could be blocked. The people in the Keys would be sitting ducks. Putting people in harm's way increases the risk of death and destruction when the sky starts to fall.

The Pacific Ocean is surrounded by mountain chains that make up what is often called, because of the volcanoes that live among the mountains, the "ring of fire." The ring of fire is capable of producing monstrous earthquakes and huge tsunamis. Millions of people are at risk, because people congregate near coastlines. Concentration of population is also facilitated by our new technologies. Creating larger jumbo jets creates a bigger body count when one crashes. Building nuclear power plants close to urban centers does the same. Holding sports events with twenty or fifty thousand spectators creates the opportunity for a high-order terrorist attack. And that's just in the United States. There are soccer stadia in Mexico, South America, and Europe that can hold a hundred thousand or more.

When people congregate in one place they makes themselves into a target. They may also change the character of the place in ways that can make run-of-the-mill calamities become worst cases. That's true of the people who insist on living in the San Gabriel Mountains at the edge of Los Angeles. It is part of the natural order of things for the vegetation in the canyons there to catch fire periodically. When the chaparral burns off and large rains follow, the mountains can't hold the water and huge floods result. The floods carry with them sediment, rocks, and boulders. In fact, with some regularity huge mud flows careen down the San Gabriels and wipe out communities. There's a lot of denial of worst case possibilities going on there. Noted author John McPhee quotes a geologist, who describes the situation like this:

Developers will buy a piece of property without thinking, for example, that it's at the mouth of a drainage. The engineers should be cognizant of it, but they're not. There are ordinances now, but in the past there were not. Every bad year, the agencies stiffen their rules. All this assumes that we know what the maximum situation is. Maybe we have not yet seen the hundred-year flood, or even the fifty-year flood. There are a lot of disasters up there waiting to happen. The people want to live in these areas. When they buy houses, they don't know what they are getting into. . . . Damn few know the story. They're newcomers. Ninety per cent of them never know that the water can go down there like the milltails of Hell. They have no perspective on the possibilities.[2]

As if living there at all weren't dangerous enough, people then do things to make matters worse. Local, state, and federal agencies, as well as private developers, build roads in the mountains, which provide efficient conduits through which fires can travel. They take measures to keep the chaparral from burning, ignoring the fact that prolonging its life means there's more combustible material available when the inevitable fires come. They build structures in the mountains—blockades and catchment basins—to prevent sediment and debris from cascading toward the streets below. But when the big rains come, the milltails can come out of the mountains with greater force than would be the case had people not built these safety devices. The city of Los Angeles is a major builder of barriers against boulders and mudflows and also tries to prevent or ameliorate fires. And the federal government provides flood insurance and other disaster protection. All of these factors facilitate catastrophe.

Concentration of population puts more people at risk from a devastating local event. But time and the processes of globalization have also created new "disaster vectors," ways of bringing catastrophe to people far removed from the initial threat that are unique to the modern day. Modern people create wonders beyond the imaginations of those in earlier generations. But we also create horrors, worst cases, increased risks of globally relevant disasters.

Interdependence is a disaster vector. Social networks are mechanisms for the transmission of harm. Faster and cheaper modes of transportation, for example, can spread diseases exponentially. AIDS wouldn't have taken as large a toll a hundred years ago. A large part of Richard Preston's novel *The Hot Zone* is about a guy who becomes sick deep in an African jungle, then takes a plane to Nairobi where he spreads Marburg virus to others. Marburg is similar to Ebola, and both are highly contagious and have high fatality rates. Preston was severely criticized for sensationalism in *The Hot Zone*, but the 2003 SARS outbreak showed that his descriptions of how disease can travel make sense:

A hot virus from the rain forest lives within a twenty-four-hour plane flight from every city on earth. All of the earth's cities are connected by a web of airline routes. The web is a network. Once a virus hits the net, it can shoot anywhere in a day—Paris, Tokyo, New York, Los Angeles, wherever planes fly.[3]

Modern forms of interdependence also make it harder to recover when worst cases happen. Very large volcanic eruptions have in the past led to famines and pestilence. Would they do so today? We might postulate that people a thousand years ago lived closer to the edges of starvation and disease than at least those in rich countries do today. Perhaps it didn't take much to push them over the edge. The tropospheric cooling caused by a large volcanic eruption usually led to crop failures and disease fairly quickly. But, while it is difficult to know for sure, it may be that we moderns would suffer more. Our massive urbanization has led the world's population to be more interdependent. If there were a widespread failure of crops in America's heartland large parts of the world would suffer—starting with the rich peoples of the world who can best afford to buy American products. People in the cities would have no chance to rely on husbandry. It's not as if the twenty million people in the New York City metropolitan area could feed themselves by fishing in the Hudson or the East Rivers (which wouldn't be very safe anyway). Most of those people probably don't even having fishing rods. And the guns that city people have are not helpful in killing food.

Modern social organization and technologies bring other new opportunities to harm faraway people. Nuclear explosions, nuclear accidents, and global warming are examples. We are increasingly "at risk" of global disasters, most if not all of which would qualify as worst cases. This situation presents us with unprecedented challenges in terms of both anticipating worst cases and responding to them.

After one of the Soviet-built nuclear reactors at the Chernobyl power station blew itself to pieces in 1986, radioactive materials were spread as far away as California. Imagine how bad it could be if terrorists destroyed five or ten reactors in a single strike. I noted above that when Tambora erupted in 1815 ninety-two thousand people perished, mostly from famine. Imagine the horror if three or four large volcanoes in the ring of fire erupted in the space of a few years. Between 1811 and 1812 a series of earthquakes emanated from the New Madrid fault, which is actually a 150-mile-long series of faults stretching from Arkansas to southern Illinois—a sparsely populated area at the time. Three of those quakes are estimated to have had magnitudes of greater than 8.0 on the Richter scale, and at least two aftershocks were nearly as large. The great San Francisco earthquake of 1906 registered between 7.7 and 7.9 and killed perhaps three thousand people. Imagine the loss of life should a temblor that size break near Manhattan. Sometimes you have to wonder how have we lasted so long.

I think we haven't paid enough attention to how vulnerable we are to worst case events. I think we ought to prepare more for possible untoward events that are out of control and overwhelming. I think it's perfectly sensible to plan for the consequences of global warming (even if we can't agree on what causes it), colossal airplane disasters, nuclear waste releases, volcanic eruptions, and asteroid strikes. I'm not alone. Increasing amounts of resources are going toward worst case thinking and planning. Those resources include money, expert knowledge, organizational efforts, governmental regulations, and defensive moves by corporations. Yet in some ways we are like Cassandra, the mythical Trojan whose prophesies were never believed; we do have our detractors.

THE ANTI-CASSANDRAS

The way modern society is organized creates the potential for more, and more serious, worst cases. Interdependence and population concentration work against us. Interdependence works against us by providing disaster vectors that can channel damage to expanding networks of people. Interdependence also makes recovery from some kinds of catastrophe more difficult. Concentration works against us by providing bigger targets for myriad threats.

Modern technologies also help to make worst cases. This is especially so for toxic substances, which some scholars argue persuasively are a "new species of trouble."[4] One reason toxics are special is that when they escape their containers they can threaten many people far away from the point of the leak. This is true in spatial terms; Chernobyl made that clear. It is also true in temporal terms—the U.S. Department of Energy's contamination of huge tracts of land will touch generations far into the future. But it isn't just the extensive damage that toxics can cause that makes them contribute to worst cases. Nuclear and chemical production require large-scale enterprises that are very complex. Such complex systems are known to be susceptible to rapid and extreme failure, often with catastrophic consequences. In other words, very complex systems are given to the kind of compounding factors that lead to worst case failures.

But that's not the whole story. The great paradox is that despite this greater risk of worst cases we've never been safer or healthier. Even the poorest denizens of the rich, modern world are vastly better off than their counterparts in the third world, or their counterparts two hundred or four hundred years ago. Our lives are much improved by having modern technologies at our disposal. It is unquestionably better—not just more comfortable but safer and cheaper—to fly between New York and California than to bump across the continent in a horse and buggy. As unfortunate and unsafe as it is to have nuclear weapons, it is hard to argue that the United States would have been safer had it unilaterally disarmed. The weapons were needed as a deterrent against China and the Soviet Union, although their usefulness as a deterrent is more ambiguous these days.

As the vociferous political scientist Aaron Wildavsky used to say, "richer is safer." Problems of water and air pollution are worse in the third world than in the first. People live longer in rich countries. The "healthy life expectancy," as the World Health Organization calls it, of someone born in the United States, where 12 percent of the population lives in poverty and the gross domestic product, per capita, is $36,000, is sixty-seven years. In Rwanda, where 70 percent are below the poverty line and per capita GDP is $900, the healthy life expectancy is thirty-two.[5] Some of the quality of life in rich countries, I hasten to add, comes at the *expense* of poor countries. The world's economic systems work in ways that drain capital, brainpower, and natural resources away from the poor and toward the rich. Still, people simply live longer and better when they have fewer children, eat better, drink cleaner water, and stop animals from defecating in the streets. We benefit from modern medicine too, although less from high-tech (and high-revenue producing) specialties than from the low-tech provision of vaccines and control of infectious diseases.

Poor countries are also at greater risk from other disasters. A 7.4 magnitude earthquake broke near Izmit, Turkey, on August 17, 1999, and killed seventeen thousand; a 6.8 magnitude quake hit the Seattle area on February 28, 2001, and one guy died from a heart attack, although seventeen thousand *were* left without electricity for a time. There are a lot of reasons that Seattle was safer than Turkey, but the most important one is that buildings in Seattle are built better and with earthquake protection in mind. Poor people the world over tend to live in structures that collapse when shaken.

As time marches forward and societies develop surplus resources they become better positioned to protect people against the vagaries of nature, including the vagaries of human nature. We are, by many measures, safer than people ever have been. So why, in the midst of all this health and safety, should anybody worry about disasters and worst cases? The question hasn't been completely neglected.

One position holds that people worry because they are overly emotional and irrational. Their fears and risk perceptions, the argument goes, are molded by sensationalistic media, which distribute propaganda that scares people unnecessarily. Mary Douglas, the famous anthropologist, and the aforementioned Aaron Wildavsky, for example, wrote a widely read political screed called *Risk and Culture,* which equated public concern over environmental hazards with worry about Satan and "the evil world." Since worrying about Satan is not something educated, modern people do, the implication was clear: people are stupid. Another respected scholar has compared worrying about the risks of nuclear power to worrying about the evil eye. Still others have suggested that our ability to measure substances in smaller and smaller quantities has led to conflict and argument over correspondingly trivial issues. Why worry about parts per million or billion of 2,3,7,8-tetrachlorodibenzo-*p*-dioxin? Most people don't even know how to say those words, let alone know what they mean. From this perspective the great advantages of expertise and science, which have given us much of what we enjoy, are lost to the hysterical demands of an uneducated public.[6]

Such judgments have typically come from the right of the political spectrum. Denunciations of the general public's cognitive abilities imply that experts and high-level decision makers should be left alone to make choices about important risks as they see fit. This kind of argument is blatantly elitist in that it advises ignoring the concerns and interests of the bulk of the population. It says that experts and decision makers are in the know and nonexperts aren't; thus choices about risk ought to be made by elites. It treats the general public as parents often treat children. Also, and not coincidentally, it is exactly the argument you would expect from professors, who live and die for expert knowledge, and the powerful, who live and die for their positions.

Of course, there are a lot of decisions that we happily give over to experts and the powerful. No one would say that airline passengers ought to have any direct influence over how the pilot flies the plane. No one would argue that Joe and Josephine Doe should have any say over how to work the valves in a nuclear power plant. No one thinks that the operating theater in a hospital is any place for participatory democracy.

There are many situations where we all gladly relinquish control over our lives, trusting them to the greater knowledge of others, assuming and hoping that their knowledge is current and that their skills and qualifications have been adequately evaluated and monitored.

Yet having a significant degree of popular input and oversight concerning projects that pose significant risks promotes both health and safety. When airlines and transportation authorities set the routes that airplanes will follow, it is perfectly appropriate for the general public to have some influence over the deliberations and even the final disposition. Mr. and Mrs. Doe should certainly be able to weigh in on the question of whether a nuclear plant will be built outside their town. Vigilant citizen oversight groups, for instance, help prevent the oil industry from repeating its oil spills in Alaska. When such groups take on the role of watchdog over private or government agencies and make their views widely known, they may prompt those agencies to second-guess their choices, which have often been arrived at too hastily in the first place. Democracy may be less efficient but is often safer.

It is a tired, clichéd complaint that the political right voices. Their position dismisses as irrational the interests of social movements, community organizations, and protest groups that try to influence decisions about risk issues, as if democracy were supposed to exist only in the voting booth. (Of course, such restrictions apply only to liberals. Antichoice, anti–gun control, and pro–death penalty protests are seen as exemplifying the American spirit.)

In any case, criticism directed at nonexperts for involving themselves in technical disputes is misguided. It makes little sense to say that conflict and unrest arise simply because average citizens don't understand things measured in ever minuscule units. There's nothing about the hazards themselves, or the measures of the hazards, that necessarily leads to conflict. But people often care about different things than experts and officials. They care about threats to their communities and families, not just abstract probabilities. They worry about the *consequences* of an explosion at the chemical plant down the road. Such fears are dismissed by elitists as an irrational, not-in-my-backyard attitude, or NIMBYism. But they're just using a different metric to gauge safety. They're using a stretched ruler and worry about worst cases.

As I've noted, these complaints about people's risk perceptions have usually come from political conservatives. Recently, though, the public-irrationality position has become popular on the left too. Sociologist

Barry Glassner argues, relentlessly, that people "worry about the wrong things." "Why," he asks, "are so many fears in the air, and so many of them unfounded?"[7] He means, as did Wildavsky, that people's worries don't match the probabilities of actual harm. After the Columbine massacre, and others like it, people began to worry about high school shootings. That's unreasonable, according to Glassner, because school shootings really aren't on the rise statistically. Similarly, people overestimate the likelihood of women dying from breast cancer, which shows they're panicky and emotional, given to easy manipulation by the media and fearmongers. People overworry about plane accidents, drug addicts, and violent crime. What they *should* worry about are maldistribution of income, concentrations of political power, and social policies designed to line the pockets of the rich at the expense of everyone else.

The meaningful difference between critics on the left and on the right is that the former point to ways in which elites and the media benefit from fearmongering, while the latter are content to emphasize public irrationality. But they share more than separates them. What they have in common is the conclusion that because we live longer and better, and because natural catastrophes don't do as much harm in rich, modern societies as in poorer ones, people who think about catastrophe are irrational. Both are correct in the sense that people's estimates of risk are often at odds with probability distributions of threats to life and property. But both are also wrong. Their focus is too narrow: people are often far more sensible than the right allows, and worrying about children being shot in school does not necessarily preclude worrying about larger political issues. The left and the right alike are worrying about the wrong things.

There's also a raft of popular works that admonish us not to think in terms of worst cases. We have, for example, *Beating Murphy's Law: The Amazing Science of Risk* by Bob Berger and, from Larry Laudan, a noted philosopher of science, *Danger Ahead: The Risks You Really Face on Life's Highway* and *The Book of Risks: Fascinating Facts about the Chances We Take Every Day*. These treatments try to bring to the general reading population what our academic anti-Cassandras bring to scholarly debate. They interpret risk assessment approaches for the nonexpert. In *Beating Murphy's Law* Berger teaches us that the use of "risk theory" is widespread in business and government, by which he seems to mean those institutions are more rational than individuals. It's only the everyperson who doesn't use it to make choices, and we're much the poorer for it. What about worst cases? They're pretty much dismissed, just as they are in more academic treatments. Berger considers the risks, for example, of introducing himself to someone at a bus stop. The worst case here is that she "might be a pistol-carrying serial killer and blow me away. She might reject me in a manner that emotionally scars me for life. These risks seem tiny."[8] And off he goes. These books are great fun, as long as you maintain a critical attitude. Some of what the authors say is useful and interesting. But inevitably we return to the central role of perception, and how people's flawed risk perceptions make them fear peanut butter and flying, how they overfear being murdered and underfear smoking and drinking.

Of course it's a good idea to be informed, and being informed about the risks of surgery, working on Wall Street, and the like can't be bad. But in these books we "learn" that flying really isn't risky, that driving cars is, even that "being a full-time cigarette smoker is tantamount to a death wish." Berger counts up all the people who get sick and die from cigarettes and then compares that to numbers associated with other activities. It's an aggregate number and not meaningless, obviously, but neither is it the whole story. Then finally we come to it: the announcement that nuclear power and natural gas are our "least risky" means of energy generation. Control is the grail. "Worry," he says, "is the poison secreted by unassessed risk. Worry is the paralysis suffered when the future is a dark, mysterious cloud. Worry is the disorder afflicting us when we're not in control."

Laudan's books are laundry lists of the "chances we face every day." We learn that "Oklahomans are 3 times more likely to have serious accidents at home than people in Maine," that Saturday is "the most likely day of the week to die," and that Alaska is the riskiest state to live in vis-à-vis accidents but the safest in terms of cancer risks. He warns that the "idea of curtailing everything risky" is a problem and that "risks are almost always a matter of *probabilities* rather than certainties." "Too often," he tells us, "we end up preparing ourselves for the improbable risk while failing to take precautions against more likely ones." And of course this leads to prescriptions for how society ought to be organized. "Our collective risk dollars should be used to tackle the most serious risks first and . . . relatively minor risks (such as asbestos insulation in public buildings) should receive treatment and attention only after the largest risks have been tackled." Airbags in cars aren't worth the added risk they pose, he says, unconvincingly. In *Danger Ahead* Laudan tells us that "everything is getting better on the risk front" and that the reason we worry is that we can measure risks in ever-finer detail. There are the obligatory swipes at environmentalists and government agencies, who have "vested interests" in scaring us (there's a vague acknowledgment that corporations have interests too). Erring on the side of caution is often the "worst" thing to do, he writes. "High profile risks don't matter much." And so on and on and on.

THE PERILS OF PROBABILISM

Probabilism Is "Normal"

The arguments of the anti-Cassandras, whatever their political predilections, rest on the idea of probabilism. More than that, they actually *equate* probabilistic thinking with reason and rationality: people who don't think the way they do are labeled irrational, or worse. Don't get me wrong. We need probabilistic thinking. We need to think in terms of chances and odds and likelihoods. But we shouldn't concentrate so much on probabilities that we forget the *possibilities*. Failing to keep a proper balance skews our vision; as a result our ability to learn about danger, and safety, is stunted or at least hampered.

It must be acknowledged, though, that thinking in terms of worst cases is a peculiar way of thinking about the future. At least it's peculiar for modern people. We've grown so used to approaching the future probabilistically that it seems natural. But it's been only a few hundred years that we've known what probability is! A huge amount of early mathematical effort was spent on thinking through the throwing of dice. Mathematicians were most concerned to figure out how to conceptualize causes, as a repudiation of determinism, and to decrease uncertainty about the physical and social universe. Stephen Stigler, a noted statistician from the University of Chicago, says that one of seventeenth-century Swiss mathematician Jacob Bernoulli's great contributions was to puzzle out "the vague notion that the greater the accumulation of evidence about the unknown proportion of cases, the closer we are to certain knowledge about that proportion." That is, the bigger the sample size of some thing, the closer to knowing something true about that thing. Today, this idea is taken for granted.[9]

Adolphe Quetelet, a gifted mathematical thinker of the 1800s, created several fascinating ideas that we now take for granted. One of those was the notion of the "average man," which he thought could be used to establish what was normal for a particular group of people. Quetelet put forth the idea that "the greater the number of individuals observed, the more do individual peculiarities, whether physical or moral, become effaced, and allow the general facts to predominate, by which society exists and is preserved." These great thinkers were conceptualizing sampling, populations, and other, related ideas, all of which are indispensable in the modern world. More important, they, along with others, were gradually creating the modern conception of probability.

What they created was a collection of ideas about how things happen. These ideas are ones that even nonspecialists have heard of: the normal curve, the average man or event, regression to the mean. Taken together, these ideas comprise what we call probability. It is certainly an advance to think of causes and effects as matters of contingencies and likelihoods, rather than mystical actions of gods and magic. But, like other aspects of modernity, the consequences of probabilism are not all good.

One problem is that when it comes to worst cases there are no average events. There's no real equivalent to the "average man." How could we talk about a normal distribution of extreme events? Even though they happen a lot, I don't think trying to plot them on a curve would be very helpful. That's one reason we see them as odd or rare—it's hard to see common elements and to apply the usual broadly familiar concepts of statistics.

But the key problem is that equating probabilism with reason crowds out consequential thinking. If we imagine the future in terms of probabilities, then risks look safe. That's because almost any future big event is unlikely. You're probably not going to die tomorrow. Terrorists probably won't destroy the White House, the Sears Tower, and Harvard University all in the same day. Four tornadoes probably won't converge on Toledo at the same time. Thinking in terms of probabilities will usually lead to the conclusion that most actions are safe.

If we imagine the future in terms of possibilities, however, horrendous scenarios appear. Could there be an accidental detonation of a nuclear weapon? Yes, there could. Could a hurricane stall over Miami, slip back out to sea, then loop back into Miami again? Definitely. Could an asteroid obliterate Los Angeles? No doubt about it. Of course, the future we imagine doesn't *have* to be filled with doom and gloom. It could just as readily be one of hope and achievement. Could enlightenment and equality spread throughout the world? Could war be eliminated? Could we eliminate hunger? The answer is yes to all of these. The point is not, then, that thinking in terms of the possible is necessarily negative: worst cases are generically similar to best cases. Still, there is an affinity between worst case approaches and possibilism.

I don't think the 9/11 terrorist attacks made worst case thinking more prevalent *in general*. I do think they made worst case thinking more prevalent when it comes to terrorist attacks. The Hart Senate Office Building was closed for three months, in late 2001 and early 2002, because those responsible were worried about the *consequences* of anthrax exposure rather than the probabilities. Were their risk estimations too conservative? Not according to the safety metric. Since 9/11 there's certainly been a lot more attention directed toward the consequences of a nuclear attack by terrorists. A 2002 article in the *New York Times Magazine* reported that a very small "dirty bomb"—a twelve-inch, pencil-sized canister of cobalt, which terrorists might steal from a food irradiation plant, along with ten pounds of TNT—would be enough to irradiate everybody in Manhattan and contaminate the ground for miles around.[10] Does it make sense to talk about the probability that such an event could happen? Of course. But the consequences of such an event are not nothing.

Various pressures influence people's efforts to assess risk and solve or at least respond to big problems. The usual, "reasonable" answer is to take it slow, feel your way, inch carefully toward some unspecified resolution. But probabilism, as a way of thinking about choices that must be made or situations that must be faced, is only one of a number of tools that we can use to get through the day. Figuring the odds of something, especially something bad, happening, is but one input, however important, into someone's decision procedures. Sometimes it is best to think about the future in terms of chance and likelihood, the fractional values of probability. Sometimes, though, it's better to think in terms only of zeros and ones.

In the PBS documentary *Meltdown at Three Mile Island*, Harold Denton—then director of the Division of Nuclear Reactor Regulation at the Nuclear Regulatory Commission—says that "within the NRC no one really thought that you could have a core meltdown. It was more a *Titanic* sort of mentality. This plant was so well designed that you couldn't possibly have *serious* core damage." Denton was right; the probabilities of all the individual things that went wrong at Three Mile Island were quite small. Nuclear officials ignored the possibilities, to our peril.

On August 27, 1900, a hurricane passed over Cuba. Nine days later, on September 5, it moved through the Florida Keys and into the Gulf of Mexico. Cuban meteorologists, who had pioneered hurricane forecasting—they had a lot of experience with hurricanes—warned the U.S. Weather Bureau that the monster was on its way. But "experts" at the Weather Bureau had no faith in Cubans and, more to the point, thought it was highly unlikely that the hurricane would turn right and head toward Texas. But it did and by the afternoon of Saturday, September 8, it was over Galveston. The worst natural disaster in American history killed eight thousand people.

Most scientists with the relevant expertise think that human activity is leading to higher temperatures in Earth's atmosphere. They're worried about global warming and a "greenhouse effect." In my view their argument is important not because of overwhelmingly convincing scientific evidence. Even if their evidence turns out to be wrong, there's still a good argument for changing the way we consume fossil fuels, which are the chief sources of greenhouse gases. The scientists' argument is important because of the worst case possibilities.

These examples show that probabilistic thinking is not the only way to be reasonable. In fact it can be downright dangerous to neglect possibilities in favor of probabilities.

Let's consider the problem in another context. The American intelligence community has been roundly criticized for failing to pay adequate attention to the numerous signals prior to 9/11 that al Qaeda was planning a large attack. I don't believe any organization deliberately disregarded certain knowledge that something was going to happen. But they did fail to see. One reason is that probabilism blinkered their vision. Between 1998 and 2001 the FBI and CIA received information from several sources that terrorist organizations, including al Qaeda, were planning some sort of attack with hijacked aircraft. One plot was to fly an explosive-laden plane into New York's World Trade Center. Neither the FBI nor the Federal Aviation Administration acted on the information, however, because they "found the plot highly unlikely."[11] It probably was. But who now would say that concentrating on probabilities was wise?

You would have thought that managers and engineers at NASA would have learned to be smarter about possibilities. In the pre-*Challenger* days a lot of decisions at NASA were made on grounds of probability. We know from close research inside NASA, by sociologist Diane Vaughan, that many decision makers thought there was a fairly high risk of a catastrophic failure of the space shuttle that day in 1986. At least that's the way it looks in hindsight. In any case, NASA personnel were unwilling, before they sent the *Challenger* to its doom, to stretch their rubber rulers very much, and they used probabilities to justify their risk taking. They knew what a bad day for the space shuttle would look like—they weren't dumb. But they looked the other way.

Apparently, not enough changed after *Challenger*, although before *Columbia* broke up NASA officials claimed otherwise. In fact, they said that they were now emphasizing possibilities over probabilities, that they were thinking in terms of the worst. In some ways, they were. In January 2001 NASA people were inspecting a solid rocket booster than had helped push the shuttle *Endeavor* into orbit on one of its missions. They discovered that a wire had come loose, and that the connection was so important that had it failed the shuttle could have been lost. Because of its importance, the connection had a redundant backup, which functioned as it was supposed to. NASA then inspected the over *six thousand* similar connections and discovered that four were loose. That sounds like pretty good odds, but NASA wasn't taking the chance. Said the shuttle chief at the time, "Based on statistics alone, you might be comfortable proceeding with flight, and there was a number of folks that felt comfortable with just a statistical analysis." That chief was Ron Dittemore, who would represent NASA at daily press briefings after the *Columbia* tragedy. He decided the odds were "irrelevant." "In this case," he said, "just to do a mathematical exercise is not justification to proceed."[12] In that instance NASA was emphasizing safety—a zero or one proposition—rather than the likelihood of disaster. They were thinking consequentially. But when it came to *Columbia* they weren't. The Columbia Accident Investigation Board found that NASA personnel came to see foam debris problems not as signs of danger, as their own design called for, but as signs that the risk was acceptable. If consequential thinking were more pervasive at NASA perhaps the seven *Columbia* astronauts would still be alive.

Possibilism Is Also Normal

Consequential, possibilistic thinking has been commonplace among antinuclear activists and other environmentalists for years. They have a fairly long rubber ruler. They've always worried about the zeros and ones of a nuclear accident. Perhaps it is becoming more common for managers to think that way too. In September 1999 Japan suffered its worst-ever nuclear accident when production pressures and shoddy procedures at a fuel reprocessing plant, led to a "criticality accident," an uncontrolled nuclear reaction. Several people died and many more were unnecessarily exposed to radiation. A Japanese scientist voiced the sentiments of many when he said, "In nuclear power matters, there should always be fail-safes. Even if a mistake occurs, safety must be assured."[13] That's the safety metric talking, not the probabilistic one.

Boston's fire chief uses the safety metric. He worries about the 920-foot tankers, each carrying thirty-three million gallons of natural gas, that pass through Boston Harbor. Close to a million people are at risk if one of those tankers catches fire. The Federal Aviation Administration requires U.S. commercial pilots to train, in simulators, to fly upside down in a jumbo jet. It's called "unusual attitude training." Will pilots ever need that skill? Experts would call it a low-probability, high-consequence event. The consequences are severe enough that to not plan for the worst could mean the difference between recovery and severe loss in unusual conditions. It is, increasingly, wise to think in terms of zeros and ones.

It's not that people think statistics and probabilities are irrelevant. It's more that a lot of life's everyday activities are seen and felt to be under people's control. Lack of control, recall, is one of the key characteristics that we find in situations that are dubbed "worst cases." There is good reason to think of marriage and driving as within one's control. To a substantial degree we *are* in control of those things. There's no inexorable push of probability on an individual's life. We can, after all, take actions that strongly affect the chances of being hurt or killed while driving. It is a choice to wear seat belts, to slow down, or not to talk on the phone while driving. It is a choice to ignore all the pressures to not stay married.

The contrast with flying couldn't be more stark. If you're five miles in the sky and something goes badly wrong with the plane, you're stuck.

There's nothing you can do, and you are going to die. In July 2002 a Russian passenger airliner smashed into a cargo jet thirty-five thousand feet over Germany, taking seventy-one souls. It would make no sense to talk about their *chances* of survival. In automobile crashes a range of outcomes are possible: you might walk away, break an arm, cut your leg, be paralyzed, die. But airplanes—big and fragile and totally out of the control of passengers—are different. When people imagine airplane crashes, and what the Federal Aviation Administration euphemistically calls "hull loss," there is no *range* of injuries, no probability. There is only surviving or dying.

Alex is a businessperson in Los Angeles who needs to visit New York City. He books a flight. Standing at the doorway of the jumbo jet, he takes a moment to think through all the factors that are relevant to stepping into the plane. Of course, Alex has had training in statistics and probability, decision making, and forecasting. He's read the anti-Cassandras so he's predisposed to fly. He ponders the probabilities and crosses the threshold, because the data show that his chances of getting into a car crash while driving across the country are much higher than his chances of getting into a plane crash. Alex is a rational decision maker.

As the trip proceeds, though, the plane runs into turbulence. The pilot has kept the seat-belt sign on for most of the flight. She's warned people that getting out of their seats could lead to serious injury, or worse. The plane has had to travel around a huge thunderstorm, and it's being tossed about like a child on a trampoline. The passengers are nervous. The wings are bouncing up and down. Every bump has them looking around in fear. The religious among them are praying and fondling their talismans; the nonreligious have removed the pens from their pockets and are counting the number of rows to the exit. As for Alex, our rational frequent flier, he's gotten nervous along with the others. He's sweating a bit and has even turned on his cell phone, preparing to make one last call to his family should the need arise.

Has Alex lost his mind? What in the world is going on in the passengers' heads? Planes run into turbulence all the time. The wings of a Boeing 777 can easily flex above the top of the fuselage. These planes can even fly upside down. If you look at how airline executives and regulators act after a major plane crash you'd have to conclude that people are superstitious and prone to emotionalism. Elite responses are typically condescending and even insulting; they are premised on an image of regular people as closer to children than rational adults. "Flying is the safest part of a trip," they always say. "This is an isolated incident." In truth Alex has not lost his mind. He knows the probabilities are with him. He also worries about what happens if his chances run out. Both approaches are sensible.

Political Uses of Probabilism

Focusing on the minute probabilities of individual failures will usually make a system seem safe. What is the likelihood than an O-ring will fail in a huge rocket, which will then explode and drop seven people to their deaths? Low, most of us would have thought before *Challenger*. And what is the likelihood such a failure will occur the one time the space shuttle is carrying plutonium to refuel a satellite? The chances would have to be, to use a phrase we've heard before, "vanishingly small." Probabilistically speaking, how could one have argued against launching plutonium on the space shuttle *Challenger*?

Now turn the question around and ask what happens to the people of Florida if the shuttle explodes and plutonium rains down on them. Then the situation looks very different. If you actually *tell* the people of Florida of the risk you're exposing them to, it becomes likely that the situation will generate more than a little political controversy. Once that happens, engineers and NASA officials will complain about the public having the NIMBY—not in my backyard—syndrome, faulty risk perceptions, and irrational fears. They might employ some of the anti-Cassandras as consultants in "risk communication," a profitable endeavor whose main function is to convince the public to accept risks that other people create. In short, officials will tell Floridians that all's well—the probabilities of failure are too low to worry about.

So one of the perils of probabilism is that precise statements of probabilities aren't as scary as statements about possibilities. As soon as someone starts talking about worst case scenarios, issues of probability, likelihood, and chance fade in importance. In June 2002 India and Pakistan came perilously close to exchanging nuclear warheads. Pentagon officials ran a worst case scenario and announced that as many as twelve million people could die. It was a perfectly sane way to talk. Few were talking about the chances. It was all about possibilities.

Chance and probability do provide a useful vocabulary for thinking about dangers, so we should be clear that we're not just talking about wild fantasies. But it is common for those who disagree with people who think in terms of the worst to say that they are being unreasonable or even a little crazy. After all, isn't almost *anything* possible? If so, then isn't it much more reasonable to focus on the most likely futures? Otherwise, we might never make a move for fear that doing so would result in catastrophe.

The regularity with which epithets like "unreasonable" and "irrational" are lobbed toward political opponents is a tip-off that they are rhetorical devices, intended to divert attention from danger, or potential danger. For who, really, is against reason?

Both kinds of question—about chances and about consequences—are legitimate approaches to keeping self and family safe. But each yields a particular kind of answer. The probability metric has a range of values; the safety metric has only zeros and ones. The safety question is more conservative. The safety metric is one of extremes and more easily leads to thinking in terms of the worst.

Because of its range of values, the probability metric is more permissive, whatever the action one might be evaluating. Should people go parachuting today? At what point on the metric does risk become unacceptable? Different and reasonable people will accept different levels of risk, so there is no single, best answer. Should we have space flights with people on them? Probabilistically speaking, there is no right answer. If, on the other hand, risk is figured according to the safety metric, which focuses on consequences, then things start to look different. The chance might be low that the parachute won't open, so the odds are good that everything will be alright. But not going at all means you *definitely* will not die in a parachuting accident. Maybe it's better not to go parachuting today. Is it OK to manufacture toxic, explosive chemicals near population centers? The plant probably won't explode, but if it does and spreads its contents over a couple hundred thousand people, it will be a massive worst case.

There is another problem, too, with probabilistic thinking: it tends to favor those who benefit from dangerous systems. This is no mere mind game. High-level officials understand the issue quite well. Just think of the arguments of tobacco companies. For years tobacco executives held that it was impossible to say cigarettes caused diseases because smoking was but one of a number of factors that could make people sick. We now know that those executives were being cynical. They really did believe their products were dangerous. The point, however, is that tobacco executives understand the significance of probabilistic arguments. They aren't the only ones.

After World War II, the government rushed pell-mell to develop the nuclear industry, mainly because doing so facilitated the production of nuclear weapons. But in 1956 Westinghouse, a major reactor builder, told Congress that it would leave the industry if it had to accept responsibility for a big accident. So the Atomic Energy Commission did a study, called WASH-740, that attempted to assess the risks of a major accident at a nuclear power plant. The AEC was legally both the protector and the regulator of the nuclear industry, but in truth, it was more the industry's booster than its regulator. AEC officials believed that a safety study would prove that nuclear power was safe.

The AEC study assumed that *some* of a reactor's radiation would be released. Imagine everyone's surprise when the study found that a big accident would kill thirty-four hundred people, injure forty-three thousand more, and cause seven billion dollars' worth of property damage! Nuclear power didn't look so safe after all, so the government covered up the study. In the meantime Congress passed legislation, known as the Price-Anderson Act of 1957, that let the industry off the financial hook if there were a major radiation release. In the mid-1960s the AEC conducted a follow-up to WASH-740. It was still trying to prove that nuclear power was safe. But the new study came up with even worse numbers: forty-five thousand deaths from a big failure at one plant. The worst case didn't fit the interests of the AEC, and that study was also suppressed.

The *next* study, this one by the Nuclear Regulatory Commission, the AEC's successor, took an entirely different approach to proving the safety of nuclear power. The study, called WASH-1400, used a different method of estimating failures. That the method—probabilistic risk analysis—had fallen into disrepute among engineers didn't matter. It allowed the government to assure the public that "a person has about as much chance of dying from an atomic power accident as of being struck by a meteor."[14] That sounds pretty safe.

I don't mean to imply that high-level officials are incapable of thinking and talking in possibilistic ways. Of course they can. My claim is that probabilism *tends* to protect the powerful. More important, it often results in the nonpowerful being placed in danger.

The Wisdom of Possibilism

Why should people think *only* in probabilistic terms? Why is it irrational to think in terms of worst cases? I don't believe that it is, although people certainly can't live their lives as if a worst case was around every corner. A more nuanced view of life recognizes the complexity of how people think and the various forces that shape their behavior. Sometimes it is entirely appropriate to adopt the worst case perspective. If you're preparing to jump out of an airplane, thinking about your safety gear in probabilistic terms isn't helpful. It would even be irrational. We're urged to wear seatbelts along with our airbags not because of the chances of injury but because of the worst case possibilities. We shouldn't smoke for the same reason. Most smokers do not contract lung diseases—you might even say the odds are in their favor. Getting some dread disease is a worst case outcome. Sure, we say that someone's chances of getting lung cancer are higher if they smoke than if they don't. But it's the worst case consequences that provoke the fear, and the admonition.

There's no credible evidence that normal people run around like Chicken Little. Even those who live near potentially dangerous industrial facilities aren't consumed with worry. People just don't lead their lives as if they were a point on a distribution of probabilities. To say, as the CDC does, that 20 percent of all first marriages end in divorce within five years proffers no useful counsel for someone considering whether to marry. People marry for many reasons, but few, I'd wager, say to themselves, "There's a four-in-five chance that I'll still be married in five years. That's a pretty good bet so I'll try it." Similarly, drivers don't operate their vehicles according to abstract probabilities. If they did, they would *never* step foot inside an automobile, because the risk of harm is so high. A lot of people will divorce and a lot will get into car crashes—some will even die in car crashes on the way home from their divorce hearing. But people don't, can't, live probabilistically, and it's wrong to call them irrational because of it.

Think of how older people think about crime. Old people fear being victimized more than any other group and yet are statistically less likely to become victims. These "irrational" fears baffle criminologists. But when we look at the situation from the worst case point of view the fear seems quite reasonable: they're worried about the consequences, not the probabilities. Imagine you're on a fixed income and you get burgled or, worse, robbed of your money for the week or the month. A lot of older people are socially isolated, with few sources of support to rely on when times are tough. Too, older people often have more health-related vulnerabilities and might not easily recover from a violent attack. The point is clear: for seniors to worry about being victimized by criminals is quite sensible, because the consequences could easily be a worst case for them.

Our modern technologies promise high reliability, and most of the time they deliver. It really is true that Alex can more safely travel to New York and back in a large passenger jet than in even the safest car on the road. Planes carry us across oceans and nuclear plants generate lots of power without contributing to global warming. As for toxic chemicals, well, there's truth to the slogan Monsanto used in ads that aired a couple years after Love Canal made national headlines: "Without chemicals, life itself would be impossible." That our technologies are so generally reliable partly explains our high expectations; we come to take them for granted.

But the pivot point for a lot of choices isn't the probability of occurrence but the severity of the consequences if the probability is realized. It's a zero and one problem. What is often missed in denunciations of public fears about, say, flying, nuclear power, or toxic chemicals, is the high potential for disaster should they fail. What if chance goes against us? When people think in terms of consequences rather than the probability of occurrence they go against the scientific impulses of professors and the political impulses of elites. Potential victims confront the actuaries. People *do* ask what is the probability of an airplane crash? but they also ask will I or will I not be safe? They understand that it's unlikely that we'll have a full meltdown at a nuclear power station, but they also understand—especially after Chernobyl—the devastating consequences should a nuclear plant have a particularly bad day.

Obviously we can't lead our lives always thinking only in terms of zeros and ones. But just as obviously we often must.

One hot day in June 2003 in Tavares, Florida, twelve-year-old Brian Jeffery Griffin was swimming near a marina when a ten-foot alligator popped out of the water and swam away with him in its jaws. His friends had warned him not to go in the water, but he wouldn't listen. Florida's Fish and Game Commission says that the chance of a person dying from an alligator attack is less than that of drowning or being hit by lightning. Maybe so. But that doesn't mean it's wise to swim with alligators, especially in a thunderstorm. Probabilistic thinking advises that swimming in the vicinity of alligators increases the chances of an undesirable interaction with potentially unpleasant outcomes. Possibilistic thinking says simply, don't swim with gators.

RISING EXPECTATIONS AND EXPANDED DOMAINS OF DAMAGE

A lot of the time people are less worried about the risks of substances or technologies or events than they are about the people who claim to be in control of such things. Important sociological research on the issue of institutional trust, or confidence, shows that people think and worry about whether officials can be trusted to do their jobs properly. They worry, in other words, just as much about promises of safety as about probabilities of destruction. People fear the consequences of nuclear or chemical contamination. They also fear that experts, managers, and officials won't or can't live up to high standards of honesty and competence. This is relatively new in history.

Imagine the poor fellow in thirteenth-century Asia. He farms and occasionally enjoys a piece of meat for supper. But he's regularly subject to the vagaries of nature and marauders. Floods come and he runs for his life. Genghis Khan comes and everyone is subject to a death sentence. Nowadays these might be worst cases, but our hapless peasant probably did not judge them so. He did not expect the government to channel the flow of the Yellow River, and he didn't expect the police or the National Guard to protect him from the ruthless Khan. Destruction was just part of the natural order.

Things are different now. We have higher expectations for safety and security. It used to be routine that cargo ships would go down in rough seas with casualties that today would be unacceptable. For example, in September 1857 the SS *Central America,* bound for New York from San Francisco, sank in eight thousand feet of water off Cape Hatteras, killing more than four hundred people. It was tragic but not considered a worst case because safety at sea was not assumed to be the normal state of affairs. (Bankers, however, considered it a worst case, because the ship was carrying a huge amount of gold, the loss of which prevented banks from paying their bills and set off the "panic of 1857.") Were a vessel to sink off Hatteras today with four hundred people aboard it would be called one of the worst maritime tragedies ever. There would be investigations and calls for reform. There might even be calls for tougher regulation.

After 9/11 surviving victims expected that the government would make them whole. Of course, the government couldn't bring back the dead, but it could give survivors money. Congress obviously thought this was a reasonable expectation and passed one of the most stunning welfare programs ever proposed. The standard practice before that was to help people rebuild their houses or finance their businesses. But to expect the government to pay people because they lost loved ones, however tragically, crossed a new threshold in what people expect their government should do for them. Not only that, but rich people even expected that their lost loved ones were worth more than the less financially fortunate. In this, too, the government assented. I see no inherent or moral difference between a death in the 9/11 attacks and one caused by a drunk in a Saturday night bar fight. It is only political expediency that prevents expanding the 9/11 program into a governmental obligation to the survivors of anyone who dies a violent death. Imagine this proposition: the government should compensate people whose loved ones commit suicide. No one would support that idea. But is there really a difference between a run-of-the-mill suicide and the suicides of those poor people who jumped out of the World Trade Center towers?

As I said, it's only in recent historical times that we've come to expect protection from *any* sort of carnage. Tuberculosis, typhus, cholera, smallpox, and the like were simply part of the natural order of things. Gina Kolata, science writer for the *New York Times,* notes that mortality rates used to be so high in urban areas that it was not until "1900—the first time since cities came into existence five thousand years earlier— that large cities could maintain their populations without constant influxes of immigrants."[15]

Why do we have such expectations now? Partly because we've gotten used to living well. The standard of living in rich countries, especially in the United States, has increased by leaps and bounds over the past couple hundred years. Every decade, more Americans get high school and college degrees than did the decade before. We live longer, and fewer of us are homeless. Access to medical care is better than a hundred years ago, and many fewer people work outside or in dangerous occupations. A chemical plant may blow up in Texas and kill twenty people (something impossible in the not too distant past when there were no chemical plants), but a job in a large, modern chemical plant is much safer than being a cowboy or working on a cargo ship in the eighteenth century.

We're born safer and we work safer. We eat better and we practice public sanitation. We're richer and we're better educated. Almost all—not just most—children in modern societies survive childbirth (childhood is a little dicier, but only relatively). We're shocked if a woman dies in childbirth. So much more is in our control, concerning health and quality of life, even though wealth and power are highly centralized and concentrated. Our culture and the very facts of our existence lead us to take for granted these rising standards of living. It is the normal state of affairs to be well, to live well, and to live long.

William Freudenburg, the Dehlsen Professor of Environmental Studies at the University of California, Santa Barbara, says that rising expectations about safety go along with rising living standards. What makes societies "modern" has to do in part with the role of information, especially technical information. Over time, we come to know more and more things about how nature and society work. Actually, it's more accurate to say that *experts* know more and more things. Average folks can't even tune their own cars. Even people who could tune their cars twenty years ago can't now, because cars are computerized and complicated in ways that preclude anyone but experts working on them.

Society's greater reliance on information and technical experts provides benefits our forebears could not have imagined. Technical expertise permits expanded domains of control over social and natural life. But it also entails risks and potential disasters. Dams and levees extend our control over the often destructive nature of rivers and lakes. That people along the Mississippi continue to live on floodplains attests to their expectations that experts and organizations will control that mighty river. In controlling the splitting of atoms and making behemoths fly we demonstrate our abilities to harness nature for our own purposes. Our capacity to deflect the damaging forces of nature is evident in nearly earthquake-proof buildings, massive evacuations in front of hurricanes, and the obliteration of traditional scourges such as smallpox, polio, and malaria. Social control, too, has increased dramatically. Another Great Depression is unlikely thanks to expanded knowledge of how to regulate demand and the money supply. Along with these expanded domains of control comes an expanding worry about being out of control. Expectations for safety go up, but when those expectations are thwarted we fear the worst.

People are safer and healthier than ever before, but they also have higher expectations. We expect officials to do their jobs, and we expect experts to abide by the rules of their professions. Enron executives were so reviled because they used their corporate positions and knowledge to enrich themselves at the expense of the company and their customers. Of course, all corporate executives are trying to get rich. That's part of their job. What is not part of the job is to blatantly abuse the power that goes along with the position, in the interests of personal enrichment. When fealty is sacrificed, when officials use their organizations to feather their own nests or experts lie to cover up mistakes they've made, people's trust in the institutions that they represent declines. People feel they've been cheated, not by a person but by "the system," "the bureaucracy," or "the organization."

Two aspects to this problem of institutional trust are particularly relevant to understanding worst cases. One concerns hubris, the other domains of damage.

Large, complex organizations are a signal feature of our time. Such elaborate enterprises as the United States government, General Motors, and Microsoft make possible the creation and provision of goods and services unprecedented in history. Large organizations aren't new. It took perhaps twenty thousand people to build a pyramid four thousand years ago, and organizing that much labor must have required many rules and many bosses. The same has to be true of ancient armies and perhaps even governments. Still, large enterprises are much more common today than in ancient times and because of that their actions, and failures, affect many more people. Too, the large enterprises of today are far more complex than in the past. The reason they are more complex is that they do more things and manage more variation.

By "manage more variation" I mean two things. However large the collection of people who built the pyramids, they were a much more homogenous group than the denizens of, say, the Westinghouse corporation. Westinghouse is itself a component of a larger collection of organizations and has employees all over the world. Although all of its senior executives, as of 2005, were white men, Westinghouse must nonetheless create rules and procedures that span cultures and individuals in ways that the ancients couldn't have imagined. Modern large organizations are just a great deal more heterogeneous than in eras past. Managing that heterogeneity (the popular word is "diversity") requires high levels of complexity.

Modern enterprises also manage more variation with regard to their external environments. Let's stay with Westinghouse. Westinghouse makes components for nuclear power plants all over the world. As a result, it has to conform to safety regulations of various governments and local communities. It must recognize and respond to security issues. It must take into account laws and cultural expectations. It must manage its public face so that the inherent danger of its products doesn't arouse too much alarm. The political, social, and economic environments in which modern corporations operate are considerably more demanding and complex than was true for ancient organizations. This, too, contributes to high levels of complexity.

All of this means that the modern enterprise must increase its scale, scope, and complexity. As organizations get bigger, they affect more and more areas of our lives. In many ways, the expansion of organizational reach makes life better for us. We get more products that are better built and cheaper. We get greater tolerance of cultural diversity. Over time, organizations are smarter than individuals and have more resources to accomplish difficult tasks. There is much to admire about modern complex organizations, although never enough to love.

This expansion of domain extends to many areas, and its ill effects have not gone unnoticed. In his book *Organizing America,* Yale professor Charles Perrow laments the increasing density and concentration of large organizations in American society since the nineteenth century. One consequence has been that more and more of people's work lives are governed by the rules and regulations of organizations. This influences the community generally, he says, and not just their lives as employees. Large organizations have had considerable influence over what is considered normal family size, age of marriage, and other aspects of nonwork life. Perrow's point is that big bureaucratic organizations have expanded their domains of influence in everyday life.

Not only have modern systems expanded organizations' domains of control, they have also created more extensive *domains of damage.* Modern large-scale enterprises bring with them large-scale threats. It would have been hard for the Aztecs to ruin life for their grandchildren. They could have cut down the forests, which apparently they did with abandon. But population density was low, and there were a lot of forests. They had no ability to wreak long-term or far-reaching havoc in the way that modern enterprises have. If all the pyramids fell in an instant, crushing their builders, thousands might die, but the catastrophe wouldn't continue to rumble several decades into the future. The modern organization has expanded its domain of damage so that people far removed from a threat, both in distance and in time, can be put at risk of worst case harm.

Nuclear power plants are our pyramids, their waste a poisonous legacy to our great-great-great-grandchildren. When the nuclear industry was being created, little or no thought was given to the trash it would leave behind. This is no ordinary trash, of course, but trash that will be a threat to life and the environment for thousands of years. Nuclear-generated power has always provided society with awful dilemmas. Alvin Weinberg, a former director of the Oak Ridge National Laboratories, once said, "We nuclear people have made a Faustian bargain with society."[16] He was referring to the promise of unlimited energy as balanced against the demands for oversight of nuclear waste. It is a technology that *requires* an antidemocratic governance structure. Government oversight must be relatively less open than is the case, say, for the plumbing industry. The problem of insurance I've already mentioned; in the early years the U.S. government wanted so badly to develop nuclear power that officials indemnified utilities and contractors from responsibility in the event of a worst case. The industry still enjoys that perk. Not many industries get that kind of welfare.

The waste from nuclear plants presents similar dilemmas. For decades the spent nuclear fuel rods have been stored in "cooling pools" close to the plants that used them. As of 2003, there were about 108 million pounds of radioactive materials at these locations. The U.S. Department of Energy says that number will double in thirty years.[17] The chief dilemma is that it is not very safe to keep the waste on-site. Plus, there are physical limits to the amount of material that can be stored that way. Yet it's not clear that storing it underground in a central location is a great idea either. The DOE claims that it can keep the material safe for "thousands of years" by putting it under Yucca Mountain in Nevada. But there's so much uncertainty involved that such statements seem more like fantastic hopes than real plans. In July 2002 some scientists calculated that if any of the nearby volcanoes now presumed dead came back to life they could send molten rock toward the site at six hundred miles per hour, potentially reaching the buried waste. DOE risk assessments reassuringly tell us that the risk of volcanic activity around Yucca is between one in one thousand and one in ten thousand *over the next ten thousand years.*[18] Putting aside the questionable practice of projecting probabilities over ten millennia, we should stop to consider: Will Nevada even be there in thousands of years? Will the United States? Even if the geology does remain stable, how do we ensure that posted warnings will remain intelligible? Languages can disappear in a heartbeat, when the last speaker dies. It has happened before—why not again? The collection of marks and noises that we call English could well be gibberish to our successors. In truth, statements about keeping nuclear waste safely isolated from people for thousands of years reflect the desperate position nuclear officials find themselves in.

Expectations for increased safety are part of the more general phenomenon of expectations for better living. And our leaders—especially corporate and political leaders—promise greater safety, at least when times are good. The problem is that when our leaders and organizations don't live up to their promises, for whatever reason, it results in what I've elsewhere called "social liquefaction."[19] In geology, liquefaction happens when an earthquake shakes ground that is so saturated with water that it becomes unstable. When that happens buildings can fall down. Social liquefaction occurs when trust or confidence in institutions and leaders falls apart. It happens in areas other than the kinds of disasters I've spent the most words on. Business scholars make the point, for instance, that banks don't fail because of monetary losses. They fail because people have completely lost trust in them as stewards of their money. Once social liquefaction happens to a bank, its days are numbered, because people and organizations will withdraw their cash and other business.

We rich, modern people may live longer and better than our ancestors. But the world is in many ways a more dangerous place for us. We compare our lives to those who lived a hundred years ago and rejoice. It's fine to do that. It was less than 150 years ago that some Americans thought it was acceptable to own other human beings. But it's also legitimate to compare the present with the future—or with different futures. One such future might not have nuclear waste, for example. We're more likely to think of that future if we're in the worst case mood.

3

WHAT'S THE WORST THAT CAN HAPPEN?

On the night of June 20, 1967, President Richard Nixon spoke to the first humans to walk on the moon, Neil Armstrong and Buzz Aldrin. Five hundred million people were watching on television. Drearily, the president said, "Hello, Neil and Buzz, I'm talking to you by telephone from the Oval Room at the White House." But Nixon was ready to say:

Fate has ordained that the men who went to the moon to explore in peace will stay on the moon to rest in peace. These brave men, Neil Armstrong and Buzz Aldrin, know that there is no hope for their recovery. But they also know there is hope for mankind in their sacrifice. . . . For every human being who looks up at the moon in the nights to come will know that there is some corner of another world that is forever mankind.[1]

These haunting words, written by speechwriter William Safire, anticipated the worst case events for Apollo 11. As it happened, there was no catastrophe. But officials were prepared for it, and in preparing they had to engage their imaginations in horrible ways. To imagine Armstrong and Aldrin stuck on the moon they must have recognized that various failures could prevent their lunar module from lifting off. They must have imagined how the astronauts would die.

What if American cryptologists hadn't cracked the Japanese spy code during World War II? They wouldn't have learned that the Japanese planned to invade the Midway Islands. Had that happened, and given the amount of damage done to the U.S. fleet at Pearl Harbor, Japan would likely have wiped out American naval power in the Pacific, leaving the Hawaiian Islands and the entire west coast open to Japanese attack.

There is a moment in Nevil Shute's novel *On the Beach*, which is about the last days of a handful of people in Australia following a nuclear cataclysm, when a young Aussie naval officer is talking to a scientist, who has been busily explaining the mechanisms and progress of radiation poisoning. The officer finds it hard to believe that *everything* human is about to end, and the scientist woodenly accuses him of a lack of imagination. The officer replies—whether sardonically or with confused regret is hard to tell—"I suppose I haven't got any imagination. . . . It's, it's the end of the world. I've never had to imagine anything like that before."[2]

There's an asteroid named 1950 DA with an average diameter of about 1.1 kilometers, about two-thirds of a mile. It is the first asteroid forecast to possibly strike Earth that hasn't quickly been ruled out by scientists—there really is a credible chance that 1950 DA will collide with Earth on Saturday, March 16, 2880. What if it hits? Some scientists at the University of California, Santa Cruz, considered what would happen if the asteroid, zipping along at 38,000 miles per hour, struck the Atlantic Ocean about 375 miles from the U.S. coast. It would not be good. As the Santa Cruz experts put it, "Humanity lives with a calculus of infinite devastation times infinitesimal probability."[3]

At splashdown, 1950 DA creates a sixty-thousand-*megaton* explosion (the atomic bomb dropped on Hiroshima had a yield of about twenty *kilotons*). The asteroid easily reaches the sea floor, blowing a hole in the ocean about twelve miles across. Then the real trouble starts. Water rushes back in to fill the void, generating waves that spread out in all directions. Two hours after impact four-hundred-foot waves—almost one-third as tall as the Empire State Building—overtake beaches from Massachusetts to North Carolina, and within four hours the entire east coast has seen waves at least two hundred feet high. Europe will be better off because it will take eight hours for the waves to get there, by which time they will be only thirty to fifty feet high.

The American eastern seaboard will be devastated. "On a bright note," the scientists write, "the impact tsunami have limited run-in potential," which means the waves will come ashore two and a half miles at the most. Still, that's enough to make Boston, New York, Norfolk, Savannah, Miami, and possibly Baltimore and Washington, D.C., very wet. Tens of millions people live within a few miles of the American eastern coastline; surely more will by 2880.

Such examples raise the question of how worst cases are imagined. More generally, what are the mental and institutional mechanisms at work when people imagine things? The issue isn't as obvious as it might appear. Things can be less or more bad. To judge an event or phenomenon the worst requires a point of comparison. There is always the question "compared to what?" One framework for comparison, as I've said, is the set of instances with similar characteristics: airplane accidents, epidemics, forest fires. But we can also compare an event to hypothetical versions of *the same event* with some slightly different characteristic or characteristics. If less of the housing stock in San Francisco were wooden, the fires caused by the great earthquake of 1906 would have been less devastating and it wouldn't be called the worst earthquake disaster in American history. If only the Soviets had designed their nuclear reactors differently Chernobyl wouldn't have exploded.

In conducting such comparisons we pick apart and reassemble events, phenomena, and causal pathways so that a *different* sense is made of catastrophe. Whether looking forward in anticipation (what's the worst that terrorists can do?) or looking back to make sense of a situation (how did the American intelligence community fail to notice the blundering 9/11 terrorists?) the imagination is at work, holding some factors at bay while highlighting others, creating scenarios and then trying to convince ourselves and others of their reasonableness. There is much to learn from these kinds of exercises that can be put to practical use to decrease damage to people and property. But there are also pitfalls, because of how imaginations can be stifled. Too, we have to figure out what makes for truly useful scenarios and then think through what we might use them for. We can't just play around in our imaginations all day long.

WHAT IFS

Anticipating the worst entails trying to see the future. While fortune-tellers and soothsayers are generally scorned in modern cultures, the fact is that most people try to foresee the future. And most of the time they succeed! There is a big difference, however, between clairvoyants gazing into crystal balls and those whose visions of the future are grounded in experience. Planning for a major earthquake in Los

Angeles, for instance, demands that planners imagine the kinds of interactions that public agencies will likely have—what they'll talk about, whether they'll get along with each other, whether they'll trade resources, and so on.

We look into the future all the time and so take it for granted. Chances are you barely have to think to know how you'll start the day tomorrow. But consider less routine events and the complexity of foreseeing the future becomes apparent. Imagine that you live in Chicago and need to fly to Boston for a business meeting. If you go, you will miss a meeting at home, which may be equally important, or perhaps something will happen at your office that will create a disaster that would not have happened if you'd stayed. But not going could result in a career crash. And there's always "What if my plane crashes?" The possibilities seem endless.

Oddly, looking into the past is often just as hard. I say it's odd because looking *back* at events seems like it should be easy. Was Kennedy killed? Did the *Titanic* sink? How many people perished when the World Trade Center towers crumbled? These are simple matters of fact. But again some questions are more complex. What would have had to happen to prevent Saddam Hussein from using poison gas against his own people? How many American soldiers would have died if Harry Truman hadn't initiated nuclear attacks against Japan? In January 1968 an America B-52 bomber carrying four 1.1-megaton thermonuclear bombs crashed in Greenland near the North American Air Defense Command (NORAD) communications center. What if it had hit that center? What if one of the weapons had detonated? For events dubbed worst cases it can be especially hard to look back; they are usually very complex events. We look at them and wonder, Did that have to happen? What would have had to happen to have avoided that?

What if American Airlines Flight 93 hadn't been delayed by forty minutes on September 11? Flight 93, you may recall, crashed into a field in Pennsylvania after passengers fought the terrorists for control of the plane. Had Flight 93 taken off on time its brave souls would never have learned of the catastrophes at New York's World Trade Center and at the Pentagon. They wouldn't have realized that their hijackers were on a suicide mission and so would most likely have responded as the passengers did on the three other hijacked planes. That in turn would have made it much more likely that the plane would reach its intended target, which was probably the Capitol in Washington, D.C. Conversely, had Flight 93 been delayed a short time longer, it never would have left Newark airport, because all flights were grounded soon after its departure at 8:41 a.m.

The American Enterprise Institute and the Brookings Institution have a program called the Continuity of Government Commission, charged with the question of "how Congress could function if a large number of members were killed or incapacitated." So many in the government might be killed that, with no adequate way to fill the positions quickly, constitutional rules on how laws are to be made and enforced couldn't be followed. Had Flight 93 hit the Capitol, such a scenario might have played out. "What," the commission asks, "if the plane had hit the Capitol the week before, on September 6, 2001, when Mexican President Vicente Fox addressed a joint session of Congress with the vice president and the president's cabinet in attendance? What if the attack had been carried out during a major vote when almost all members were present?"[4]

What if conditions had been slightly different? What if the *Challenger* had been carrying plutonium when it exploded (the next mission was to launch a space probe powered by twenty-five pounds of plutonium)? What if Kennedy had not been assassinated?

What if questions look back and make us imagine alternative histories. In so doing, we imagine a panoply of causes and consequences; we imagine different ways of organizing society; we imagine nonworst cases. *If only* statements work in much the same way. The difference is that *if only* statements imply or express their own answers. If only there weren't so much production pressure on oil tanker captains, the *Exxon Valdez* wouldn't have run up on a large rock, creating the worst water-borne oil spill in American history. If only Union Carbide had provided masks to the workers who dug a tunnel in West Virginia in the mid-1930s, hundreds, possibly thousands, of poor southern blacks would not have died of silicosis.

If only statements and *what if* questions are what scholars call counterfactuals. Counterfactuals are fundamentally about the imagination. They can be used to reimagine history or to posit different futures, inquiring into ways that different conditions might produce different outcomes. Predicting the future is a form of forward counterfactual thinking in which complications are assumed away so that the future can be thought to be known. Of course no one can really know the future. Worst case counterfactuals are more useful in spurring creative thought than in actually predicting what will happen.

It's common for historians to use counterfactuals, although they disagree about their proper use.[5] Some think they're too fanciful to bother with while others think they're indispensable. There are endless arguments, for example, over how the world would be different had the South won the American Civil War.

We shall leave the historians to their squabbles. If we're going to wonder about worst cases, if we're going to ask What is the worst that can happen? we'll have no choice but to use counterfactuals.

Let's look in detail at a few cases to see how *what ifs* and *if onlys* work.

On May 29, 1914, about two years after the *Titanic* sank, a Canadian steamship named the *Empress of Ireland* left Quebec, headed north out of the Saint Lawrence River with almost fifteen hundred people on board. But a fog descended on the *Empress* and a Norwegian vessel, the *Storstad,* struck it amidships. The *Empress of Ireland* sank in fourteen minutes and nearly a thousand people lost their lives. The boat sank so fast that only a handful of lifeboats could be lowered into the water.

It's not entirely clear what happened that night. There were communication failures, to be sure; neither vessel's officers had accurate information about where the other ship was. The *Empress* seems to have suffered some mechanical trouble with the steering gear. The collision occurred at 2 a.m., which complicated the evacuation; as it happened, many passengers died in their beds. Moreover, the *Storstad* was the worst possible ship to have run into you. It was designed to break through ice, so when it struck the *Empress* in the side, it sliced into it like a surgeon's scalpel. Worse still, the *Storstad* was loaded with ten thousand tons of coal, which only added to its punch. And it hit the *Empress* between her two boilers, leading to a swift and complete loss of power.[6]

A lot of things had to come together in just the right way for the *Empress* disaster to happen. It may well be that without any one of the conditions listed in the last paragraph many fewer lives would have been lost. Perhaps the accident wouldn't have happened at all! In the *Empress of Ireland* case, as in many cases, we can't identify a single factor that's most important in explaining what happened. But that in itself is sometimes a lesson learned in thinking through counterfactuals.

This is the *small causes problem*. It's natural to look back to important events and extract the Key Issue or the Main Problem that caused the event: Ronald Reagan's massive military buildup caused the Soviet Union to collapse. Human error causes 80 percent of airline accidents. And so on. In fact there is rarely a single cause of anything, or at least anything important. The small causes problem is a simplifying technique in which the imagination winnows potential causes away. It's a way of thinking that fits well with courtrooms.

But it is often not the right way to characterize catastrophe. Recall the Tenerife catastrophe that I noted in chapter 1, where one 747 slammed into another 747 taking 583 souls. University of Michigan business professor Karl Weick analyzed the Tenerife disaster in great detail and discovered there were perhaps a dozen causes involved. If any one of them had operated differently, the accident never would have happened. Sensitivity to carefully built what ifs—a judgment wholly appropriate to Professor Weick's reconstruction—leads away from unfruitful oversimplifying.

On November 18, 1987, at about 7:30 p.m., a fire started under a wooden escalator in the Kings Cross subway station in London. Thirty-one people lost their lives in what is called one of "the worst transport disasters in British history."[7] Apparently, a passenger on the escalator lit a cigarette and dropped the match. The match ignited grease under the tracks, and about fifteen minutes later there was a "flashover," which is when everything in a space (a room, say, or a subway station) ignites suddenly and explosively. There was no escape passage between the two escalators. It just so happened that the slope and shape of the escalators were such that they provided an unusually efficient channel for the smoke and fire to rise to the ticket station. A train just happened to be coming into Kings Cross, which pushed oxygen into and up the flaming escalator.

What if the match hadn't been dropped? What if the grease hadn't been there? What if the escalators had been shaped differently? What if the fire had occurred at 5 p.m.?

Is there any point in asking what had to have been different to avoid these events? Is there anything to be learned from asking how these events could have been *worse*? The answer to both questions is yes. We can learn from counterfactuals, we can stretch our imaginations, and we can learn how imaginations are stifled. Most importantly, we can see how power and interest mold what is considered legitimate to worry about. This is one more way to use worst case thinking to see how society works.

VIRTUAL WORST CASES

In Tom Clancy's 1991 novel *The Sum of all Fears* we're treated to a virtual worst case. The U.S. president and national security advisor are both fairly incompetent. Tensions between the United States and a dying Soviet Union are escalating. The Israelis lose a nuclear weapon. Arab terrorists find it, smuggle it into the Super Bowl, and tens of thousands football fans are incinerated. Not too long ago Clancy's scenario would have been thought an impossible counterfactual, a virtual worst case appropriate for a novel but so complex and implausible that no one would think it a proper projection of reality. Too many things would have to come together in just the right way for such a thing to happen. That's the epitome of the worst case approach. Before 9/11 only those on the fringe would have thought Clancy's story plausible. Now it is not a question of if but of *when* terrorists will detonate a nuclear device in the United States. What once was a fancy now becomes the worst that can happen.

You can really get bogged down in imagining worst cases. I live in a flight path of Newark's airport, in New Jersey. Sometimes the 747s fly so close that it almost seems we can see people's faces in the windows. What if an engine falls off a plane onto my house? Engines do sometimes fall off planes. What if a jumbo jet crashes into my neighborhood? But danger doesn't have to fall from the sky. What if you go for a walk with your kids and a drunk driver turns the corner just as you're crossing the street? What if SARS, which is particularly deadly for the elderly, strikes in a dozen nursing homes at the same time? Thinking about all that puts me in mind of the sign at the gates of hell in Dante's *Inferno*: "Abandon all hope, ye who enter here." People who concentrate too much on what ifs are said to be obsessed, and may be prescribed medication.

Virtual worst cases, though, don't have to be so wild and crazy that thinking about them means we need psychiatric help. Indeed they can be incredibly interesting and useful in myriad ways. They come in two main varieties: there are virtual worst cases that *have happened* but could have been worse—we might say they *almost happened*—and others that *might happen*. Virtual worst cases that almost happened are actual incidents, accidents, and disasters that with a small change in how events unfolded could have turned out much worse. Virtual worst cases that might happen are usually unrealistic, but only because they live purely in the imagination. Among the latter we would include simulations, tabletop exercises, scenario building, red teaming, and nightmares.

Some of these virtual worst cases show us how dangerous our lives really are. They show the great catastrophic potential of systems we don't fear enough. But they also show the great utility of engaging in disciplined worst case thinking, because there are cases where doing so helps avoid disaster.

Let's look first at a few *almost happened* worst cases. All it would have taken for them to turn into real worst cases was a slightly different configuration of events. We owe more to lady luck than we realize.

Trains threaten us every day. They fall off their tracks, slam into each other, and smash into cars and trucks. They are an excellent terrorist target, as the March 2004 attack in Madrid demonstrated so well. But Madrid provides just a taste of the dangers that trains pose. The *worst* worst case scenarios involve trains that carry few people but dangerous cargoes. It is on trains, by and large, that America ships its hazardous materials. In 2001 there were 6,908 railcars in the United States that carried hazardous materials. Of that number 925 suffered damage in one way or another, and 57 released some or all of their contents. Following is the story of one such hazmat release, an almost happened virtual worst case that could have been much, much worse.

One summer morning in 1992, at about 2:15 a.m., a Burlington Northern Railroad freight train pulled out of Superior, Wisconsin. Five of its fifty-seven cars contained hazardous materials: one held aromatic hydrocarbons (including deadly benzene), one held liquefied petroleum gas, one held butadiene (which is also highly inflammable), and two held molten sulfur. Thirty-five minutes into its trip, the train's automatic emergency brakes kicked in, with part of the train on a river trestle. Fourteen cars derailed, including three containing toxic materials. The benzene car fell off the eighty-foot-high bridge, landed upside down on the river bank, and broke open. The hydrocarbons evaporated, creating a vapor cloud twenty miles long and five miles wide that swept across the narrow tip of Lake Superior toward Duluth, Minnesota. The LPG and the butadiene cars also derailed.

Eventually the benzene death cloud dissipated. But it wouldn't have taken much for this virtual worse case to become an actual one. The evacuation of thirty to forty thousand people could have become snarled, just at the time that the massive cloud descended on them. Instead of being *close* to Duluth, which has a population of about eighty-five thousand, the accident could have happened in the city. The gas cars could have exploded, blowing benzene over the people who survived the blast.

Duluth dodged a bullet. A retired railroad worker pointed out as much when he said, "Someday this is going to be butane or propane and it's going to happen at a switch in some city and lots of people are going to die. It's not a matter of if, it's a matter of when."[8]

It gets worse.

In Arkansas on September 19, 1980, during routine maintenance in a missile silo, a technician caused an accidental leak in a Titan II missile's pressurized fuel tank. The fuel vapors accumulated and nine hours later exploded inside the silo, blowing both 740-ton doors off and lobbing a nine-megaton nuclear warhead about six hundred feet.

The U.S. military assures us that such incidents, known as broken arrows, can't possibly result in a nuclear detonation. This is a comfortable and reassuring thing to believe, and the evidence seems to verify it. After all, no nuclear accident has resulted in a nuclear explosion in the sixty years since nuclear weapons were born. And there have been plenty of opportunities. There've been scores of broken arrow accidents, and roughly *fifty* nuclear warheads lie on the oceans' bottoms. Good design probably explains why one of them hasn't gone off. But luck may be involved too. The rather benign term, broken arrow, doesn't well convey the potential for disaster of the worst sort.

A vital link in the United States' early warning system is the Thule air base in Greenland. In the late 1950s the Strategic Air Command became concerned with the possibility that Thule might be destroyed before SAC knew what had happened.[9] If that happened we would lose a key aspect of early warning, giving the Soviets an advantage in a nuclear first strike. SAC's solution to this potential risk was a program called Operation Chrome Dome. The idea was to constantly fly a B-52 with advanced communication capabilities around Greenland and North America. The plane also carried nuclear warheads. The reasoning was that even if Thule were wiped out SAC would still have defenses and communications.

In January 1968 a fire on a Chrome Dome B-52, with four 1.1-megaton thermonuclear bombs, robbed the plane of electricity. The pilot ordered everyone to bail out, and the headless, burning nuclear hazard passed directly over the Thule air base and slammed into the ice seven miles away at five hundred miles per hour. The 225,000 pounds of jet fuel and the high-powered conventional explosives on the nukes exploded. Radioactive debris was spread over a wide area. Luckily none of the thermonuclear weapons detonated.

As in Duluth, the outcome could easily have been otherwise. What if the burning B-52 had crashed into the communications center at Thule? NORAD wouldn't be able to talk to the air base, and the bomb alarms in the United States would show the base had been destroyed. It would look as if Thule had been attacked with conventional weapons. The prevailing assumption was that the Soviet Union would be the aggressor in a conflict with the United States, so NORAD would probably assume the Evil Empire had begun its attempted takeover of the world.

Or what if, upon crashing, one of the nukes had accidentally exploded? Stanford political scientist Scott Sagan, who has worked with the Joint Chiefs of Staff, the Office of the Secretary of Defense, and the Los Alamos National Laboratory and who first detailed the frightening Thule story in his book *The Limits of Safety*, has shown that an accidental detonation was *not* impossible.[10] Again, in a scenario where the bomb alert system was working properly, SAC and NORAD would get the message that a *nuclear attack* on American forces was in progress.

None of the potentially confounding conditions were inconceivable, in Duluth or in Thule. Imagine that one of these situations had actually escalated out of the virtual category, graduating to a real worst case. We'd look back and ask incredulously, "How in the world did they not see that coming?"

It is tempting to see these almost happened virtual worst cases as evidence of safety and resiliency. We should resist the temptation.

One reason to resist it is that we can't trust high-level decision makers to consistently learn from their mistakes. They *could*. They're certainly smart enough. But they often have an interest in not learning. For example, Army officers concluded that the Thule accident showed that the system *worked*. It's rather like saying that nuclear power is safe because the Three Mile Island reactor core stopped melting thirty minutes short of breaching containment. The problem is that admitting that their systems are dangerous—more than that, that their systems are *unsafe*—poses severe political risks for those responsible for ensuring our safety. Sometimes they *do* acknowledge the dangers. But we can't depend on it.

Another reason to resist the temptation to see these events as demonstrating that systems are safe is that virtual worse cases, and even non-virtual worst cases, go directly to the question, what's the worst that can happen? The director of emergency programs at Indian Point, the beleaguered power station with two reactors about twenty-five miles from New York City, acknowledged the danger of his industry, but also the pressure from society, when he said that "in our business everything is worst case. We always think about what is the worst that can happen, and we design to accomplish protection for the worst case."[11]

Can they really do that?

I don't think so, partly because whatever we can imagine could always be worse. Tenerife was bad, with 583 casualties, but not *everyone* died. Then there's the remarkable case of Japan Air Lines Flight 123. In August 1985 the 747 was climbing through about twenty-four thousand feet when a bulkhead in the rear of the plane failed. Some of the jet's tail, it seems, fell off. The plane gyrated wildly before slamming into first one and then a second peak on Mount Osutaka. In two blinks of an eye 520 people were dead. It was the worst single airplane crash in history. But still it could have been worse: four people survived.

That's like the World Trade Center disaster. The WTC body count is 2,749 people. But the towers had a working capacity of about fifty thousand people. It's estimated that some thirteen to fifteen thousand people escaped before the towers fell.[12] It takes nothing away from those who died to say that the disaster could have been much, much worse. The first plane struck at 8:46 a.m. Had the hijackings happened one hour later—hardly a fanciful counterfactual—many more bond traders, who begin their working day at 9:30 a.m., would have been at their desks. Or had the towers toppled rather than dropping straight down, engineers say they would have expanded the domain of damage well beyond what it was. Similarly, the *Exxon Valdez* could have lost *all* forty million gallons of its cargo, not just the eleven million it did lose.

COGNITIVE RESILIENCE AND VIRTUAL WORST CASES

The great paradox of worst cases is that ultimately they are never as bad as they could have been. Counterfactuals help us deal with that. It's a comforting message, in the sense that the truly horrible things that we've witnessed could have been even *more* horrible. But it's discomforting too, because it means that we'll never truly be prepared for the worst that humans and nature can throw at us.

I said above that the Thule accident exemplifies decision makers' failure to learn from virtual worst cases. I also said it could be otherwise. Y2K—shorthand for concerns that computers, many of which included only the last two digits of the year in their internal clocks, would malfunction when the year changed from (19)99 to (20)00—involved an outrageous set of what ifs that both averted failure and resulted in a situation of learning. In the two or three years leading up to January 1, 2000, all manner of catastrophe was predicted by experts and nonexperts. Some predicted accidental launches of nuclear missiles, failures at financial institutions that would lead to a depression, or a total shutdown of the electrical grid. Serious people even implied to me that they had moved most of their retirement funds into gold. It was, some said, going to be worse than a Hollywood disaster movie. Of course, there were no real experts in the problems that might be created by Y2K. There were experts in social and organizational failure (including yours truly), experts in computers, experts in networks, experts in fearmongering, experts in spending money. There were a lot of careless commentators making predictions that went far beyond their domains of real expertise. Computer experts didn't hesitate to predict widespread panic, even if they had no clue about research on panic. Social and psychological scientists didn't hesitate to say that nuclear plants were at high risk for failure, although probably none of them were nuclear engineers. In truth, none of us had the overarching expertise with social organization *and* political organizations *and* networks of computer networks that would have been needed to predict what actually happened: almost nothing.

That almost nothing happened prompted a great hue and cry. It was a boondoggle, some said, just a lot of hysteria drummed up by alarmist pessimists dwelling on worst case potential. Amazingly, the evidence for that position was the lack of significant failures of computers, electrical grids, and so on. We were all suckered, according to this view, by extremists who see worst cases around every corner, crying wolf and screaming about the falling sky.

I was one of those who feared the failures. I did not expect or predict the worst, but I knew that there had been next to no preparation in poor countries, some of whom have old industrial facilities without sufficient regulatory oversight. I still can't explain why those places didn't have more trouble in computer-sensitive installations. But I can explain why there weren't more failures in rich places such as the United States, Canada, Great Britain, and Australia: people worked out the worst case scenarios and convinced those with power and money to fix the machines. They used the what ifs as a warning. There was undoubtedly some overstatement in how they built their counterfactuals, and some resources probably were wasted in preparing for Y2K. But none of that means that the Y2K alarm was a false one or that the entire effort was a boondoggle. All you have to do is talk to people in the trenches—information technology specialists in investment banks, network experts in defense organizations, programmers in high-tech industries—to discover that there *were* significant failures. But those people tested their systems well before the Y2K rollover. When the vulnerabilities and potentials for failure became clear, the IT experts had a good case to make to those in positions of power that it was worthwhile to spend large sums of money and person-power on upgrades. In the case of Y2K, what ifs lead to effective worst case preparation.

Increasingly, people are relying on virtual worst cases that *might happen*. Regulators and corporations in dangerous industries spend more time than they used to worrying about how their activities could lead to massive damage. September 11 strengthened that inclination. Let's look at a few examples to see what purpose such considerations might serve.

Most people in the United States think that earthquakes in their country happen on the west coast. A much smaller proportion know about the New Madrid fault, which runs from northeast Arkansas to southern Illinois and could affect people in nine states. Some day the New Madrid fault will break, as it did in the early nineteenth century, wreaking a great deal of damage.

But what if a major earthquake happened under Manhattan? Who thinks of that? Why think of that? There have been several movies about earthquakes in Manhattan. They are all great fun. We can think of those movies, perhaps of all disaster movies that aren't documentaries, as exercises in counterfactual thinking. But they are also literary treatments, and I'll leave their analysis to more literary minds.

There is a little known group of experts called the New York City Area Consortium for Earthquake Loss Mitigation, or NYCEM, which has tried to estimate potential human and property losses from earthquakes under Manhattan. The researchers initially looked to other earthquakes for guidance, but those were not terribly useful because it's hard to find a comparable case that's realistic.[13]

Recent earthquakes under Manhattan have been small. A January 2001 tremor, with its epicenter on the Upper East Side, near 102nd Street, registered 2.4 on the Richter scale. An October 2001 quake centered just south of Columbus Circle, on the southern tip of Central Park, registered 2.6. (For comparative purposes, the collapse of the first World Trade Center tower registered 2.1 on the Richter scale; the second, 2.3.) There have been bigger quakes in New York City, estimated at between 4.9 and 5.5 Richter, but those occurred in 1737, 1783, and 1884. Each of those earthquakes cracked plaster, knocked down chimneys, and scared people. The largest quake to strike the United States, so far, was the 9.2 event in relatively unpopulated Alaska, in 1964. The deadliest was the 1906 event in San Francisco, at 7.7 Richter.

The NYCEM scientists estimated the consequences of magnitude 5, 6, and 7 quakes. Steel buildings would be safest in a big quake and there are relatively more of them in the financial district (where the WTC used to be), midtown (a lot of modern buildings), and the richer residential sections of town. If you're in Los Angeles when a big earthquake comes one of the safest places to be is in a skyscraper. Not so in Manhattan. Most of its buildings were constructed around the turn of the twentieth century; 80 percent are made of unreinforced masonry, others of concrete, which are the kinds of structures most at risk when the ground shakes. Seismic codes only apply to new construction—prior to 1996 earthquakes weren't even considered in building codes. In those upscale residential areas, the big condo buildings would be fine, but the lovely, expensive brownstones would not.

So what happens in a worst case? In a magnitude 7 earthquake more than 50 percent of Manhattan's buildings suffer moderate damage or worse; seventeen hundred buildings collapse completely. The experts estimate a total loss of about fifty billion dollars (in 2001 dollars). I suspect this is an underestimate. The casualty numbers seem even more implausibly low: assuming the earthquake occurs at 2 p.m. on a workday, NYCEM estimates that about 540 Manhattanites would either die instantly or suffer life-threatening injuries, while about 3,000 would require hospitalization.

There are several ways that people die in earthquakes. Big kill numbers don't come only from buildings or things in buildings falling on people. That happens in poor places like Turkey or Iran, but in New York fire would the biggest culprit. It wasn't the direct effects of the earthquake that killed so many in San Francisco in 1906. It was the fires that raged through vulnerable, populated areas. Similarly in Manhattan, water mains would break, debris would prevent firefighters from getting to victims, fire stations and medical facilities would disintegrate (with personnel and their equipment in them). Fires could easily rage out of control. In New York's worst case scenario only about 25 percent of its medical facilities are operative, which means they would be massively overloaded. Most of the schools would be out of operation, which is important because people always use schools for shelter in emergencies. Only 4 percent of police facilities would be usable. Very few fire stations would be functional. Perhaps seventy thousand people would be at risk of suffering a fire. As the New York City Area Consortium for Earthquake Loss Mitigation puts it, "M = 7 events would cause virtually unmanageable situations."

Creating earthquake scenarios for Manhattan seems quaint after the September 11 terrorist attacks. But eventually the significance of 9/11 will be seen more in cultural and political terms than in terms of disaster. If a large earthquake breaks under New York, 9/11 will seem like a mosquito bite. These kinds of counterfactuals can be used for public education, and for organizational learning. They can be used to garner political and economic resources in the name of preparation. Of course, it's unlikely that Manhattan will devote resources to prepare for a such an event. What politician would propose the massive spending that would be required? "It's too unlikely," people would say, "so let's be reasonable." That such admonitions would be right does not gainsay the value of thinking through the alternatives. After all, *reasonable* usually indicates probabilistic, not worst case, thinking.

But what difference, really, does worst case thinking make? As with the Y2K preparations, it could help experts and officials think through how social and technical systems are connected. We live in a highly networked world—people are networked, their organizations are networked, their computers are networked, and all these networks are networked. Learning about how networks of networks might fail is key to thinking through the kinds of disaster preparations that might be necessary. We can use these worst case scenarios to become smarter about how the world works, and what could happen if the world breaks.

BIOTERRORISM AND VIRTUAL WORST CASES

Never before has it been so important to engage in possibilistic thinking, especially regarding terrorist threats. For some time now, since probably the mid-1990s, top officials in Washington, D.C., have been especially worried about biological attacks. As a result of that worry, they've run some tabletop exercises that simulated such attacks. Let's briefly review one of those exercises.

Over a two-day stretch in June 2001 the Johns Hopkins Center for Civilian Biodefense, along with a few similar agencies, ran an exercise they called Dark Winter, which simulated a smallpox attack in the United States. People had run tabletop exercises before, but not like this. There were only twelve participants, but they were no ordinary people. The exercise attracted much interest, in part because the researchers persuaded famous people to participate: former Georgia senator Sam Nunn played the president, former FBI director William Sessions played the FBI director, former CIA director James Woolsey played the CIA director, and so on.[14]

In the simulation, three hundred people were initially infected in three simultaneous smallpox outbreaks, which began in shopping malls in Oklahoma City, Philadelphia, and Atlanta. Most of the researchers' assumptions were extrapolated from available scientific literature, for instance that thirty grams of smallpox virus was enough to cause three thousand infections. Based on data from a 1972 outbreak in Yugoslavia, which has been well studied, they assumed that each person infected would infect eleven others. This was not a worst case assumption, however. All the factors that made SARS travel so quickly would probably elevate the transmission rate significantly. By the simulation's day 6, there were two thousand smallpox cases in fifteen states and vaccine was running out. Political arguments about borders were intensifying, and the country's health system was overloaded. By day 13, there were sixteen thousand cases and a thousand deaths. The simulation ended at that point, with the expectation that over the following twelve days there would be seventeen thousand additional cases and ten thousand total deaths.

There are critics who say that spending scarce resources on smallpox and the like is wasteful. After all, the risk of a smallpox epidemic *is* small, and most people in the business know that. Weaponized smallpox is hard to manufacture and hard to deliver. But the possibility of an outbreak is very frightening. Few doctors have ever seen a case of smallpox, so it would likely be misdiagnosed at first (in the same way that SARS was mistaken for flu). Ironically, Americans are at greater risk because the virus has been eradicated—very few Americans have been recently vaccinated, whereas many in the third world have. Too, the Soviet Union maintained a twenty-ton stockpile of smallpox, which has not been fully accounted for. The virus has a fatality rate of about 30 percent. Here again is a case where the possibilities are more worrisome than the probabilities.

Dark Winter was a productive virtual worst case. The authors drew a number of lessons from it, all unsurprising though important: that America's leaders are pretty clueless about bioattacks and related policy issues, that not having enough vaccine limits policy options, that medical and public health data would be important, that the United States lacks "surge capacity" in its health care system, that federal and state policies might conflict, and that everyday people will be key in the response. "President" Sam Nunn said, "The federal government has to have the cooperation from the American people. There is no federal force out there that can require 300,000,000 people to take steps they don't want to take."

There are three additional things to note about Dark Winter. First, although the biological assumptions were drawn from available scientific literature, assumptions about *social* responses were more questionable. For instance, in one scenario the governor of Texas closed the state's borders to Oklahomans. That's plausible, of course, but why assume it? Dark Winter also didn't consider how the public might be used in responding to the epidemic, although there are instances of such programs in America's past. Too, there's nothing much in the scenario on public outreach to inform people of how they should protect themselves and others. It was assumed that violence between citizens and police who try to quarantine possibly-infected people would become a feature of the social landscape. That may be true, but such conflict would not happen in a vacuum. The available examples show that officials usually *cause* those kinds of confrontations. Second, the participants had to decide who would get vaccine and were given several options to consider. They chose to vaccinate those who had come into contact with vaccine patients, "essential" personnel, and everybody in the Department of Defense. Note that elites and their families get vaccinated before everyone else. Third, Dark Winter was stopped in the middle of the "second generation" of smallpox cases. The participants did, however, want to know the worst case projection: three million cases and one million deaths. It's probably safe to assume that worst case thinking is more a part of their cognitive makeup after going through Dark Winter.

But we don't want to make *too* much of these kinds of exercises. Virtual worst cases are representations. But what do they represent? I doubt they represent capabilities to respond to possible events, and I doubt they represent anything close to what might really happen in a disaster or a terrorist attack. Virtual worst cases aren't usually accompanied by much *ground truthing*. In remote sensing—say, mapping out a forest with a satellite—ground truthing is when someone actually goes to the place for on-site observations. Real ground truthing, for disasters, would involve understanding many more things than would be possible to simulate: the full complex of people's cultures, values, constraints, opportunities, and so on. If you want to understand a smallpox terrorist attack, for instance, it's not enough to simulate official behavior. You also need to understand terrorist behavior: their goals, their aims, their methods, their frustrations. It is the lack of ground truthing that led to quagmire for American forces in Vietnam, and in Iraq.

For some situations, ground truthing may be impossible. Terrorists, because they live in decentralized networks and highly flexible organizations, are extremely adaptable, so predicting and modeling strategic interactions with them may be beyond our abilities. In other cases, the realism that ground truthing provides might make it impossible to run an exercise in the first place. For example, American hospitals have no real "surge capacity," so a huge smallpox outbreak would overwhelm them *immediately*. Realistically, that would mean that most people who got sick would die at home. Such considerations were well beyond Dark Winter's scope.

It may be that virtual worst cases are *least* useful when they best approximate reality, or are thought to approximate reality. Virtual worst cases work best as imagination stretchers: *unreality* may in fact be their greatest virtue. They are especially helpful when there is no experience with a particular kind of hazard. If experts want to plan for a disaster like the *Titanic*, they can turn to a slew of passenger ship disasters. If they want to think through the problems caused by a fire aboard an airliner, there are numerous precedents. But what if they want to think through how an Ebola virus outbreak in Atlanta might play out? What if planners are given the task of drafting a response to a large increase in the world's temperatures? There's no obviously meaningful experience to draw on for such possibilities. In my book *Mission Improbable* I showed how such situations often give rise to "fantasy documents," plans that probably won't be very useful should a big disaster happen, mainly because they're based on wild assumptions. There's always considerable risk of creating fantasy documents when experience is lacking, because experience serves as the best reality check on people's assumptions and promises. But fantasy documents can have an upside. As long as people keep in mind that fantasy documents are *fantasies,* they can serve to provoke innovation and out-of-the-box thinking.

Virtual worst cases can teach less about what might happen than about how we learn. It is the process itself that is the "lesson learned," not the degree to which such exercises reveal our level of preparedness. The greatest utility of practicing disaster response is not actually planning but practicing cognitive resilience and creating informal networks. I'll give a quick example. Some of my colleagues and I conducted interviews with various New Jersey county officials about their response to the anthrax attacks of fall 2001. One of the counties had set up a bioterrorism task force well before September 11. As it happened this particular county had no real cases of anthrax, but officials did get about 120 calls a month for several months from people reporting suspicious situations. In one instance where officials had good reason to think they had a bona fide anthrax exposure, a detective was able to direct the patient to what he considered the most "competent medical authority." I asked the detective if he wouldn't have referred the patient to the hospital anyway. He replied that of course he would, but he wouldn't have "advocated bypassing two other hospitals." He wouldn't have known which hospital to recommend without the exercises that the county's task force had run.

HOW DO YOU TELL A GOOD WHAT IF FROM A BAD ONE?

Perhaps by now, dear reader, you are convinced that ignoring worst case what ifs can be not only unwise but downright dangerous. But you may be frustrated by the "infinite possibilities problem": how do you know when to stop making up scenarios?

Hindsight is always twenty-twenty, and that can be a problem. It isn't hard to look back at any event and reconstruct it such that the outcome changes. This is done all the time with disasters, and especially worst case ones. Because of the drama, the tragedy, and people's sense of personal vulnerability, calamities and catastrophes garner public and media attention. Most of us can't resist looking when we pass car crashes. It's not that we take pleasure in the macabre; instead we are imagining ourselves in a similar situation. Anyway, it's easy to say that an ocean liner should have zigged instead of zagged. It's child's play to reedit the tape so that the *Titanic* doesn't sink. Even a simpleton can imagine how Chernobyl could have been avoided.

The issue here is how to tell the difference between a good and a bad what if. By what standards can we construct reasonable counterfactuals? We want to avoid elevating something trivial to importance. One could argue, for instance, that if one of the 9/11 terrorists had caught the flu on September 10 then the World Trade Center would still be standing in New York. Mohamed Atta, the alleged ringleader, could have been so delirious with fever that he crashed his car on the way to the airport, which in turn might have led to the whole operation, or at least the part that originated in Boston, being called off. While that might be true in the absolute sense—almost *anything* is possible—it's too trivial to warrant serious consideration. To ask, on the other hand, what might have happened differently if Atta and the accomplice traveling with him had missed their flight *is* reasonable, both because it almost happened and because missing connecting flights is common in air travel.

Because hindsight is nearly perfect, we have to be careful when passing judgment on what people could or should have done differently. If counterfactual analysis is done carelessly then the practical implications are significantly diminished. However, if it's possible to tell the difference between reasonable and unreasonable what ifs, then, in principle at least, we can become smarter about the world, more intelligent in imagining worst cases and possibilities for great harm. If we can do *that* then we ought to be able to plan better, to better prepare for some of the worst cases that may come our way.

Let's look at a few of the problems posed by asteroids and comets. This is a set of problems that's only recently come to popular attention. If the following two examples are merely wild speculation then they aren't useful for counterfactual inquiry. If they are *reasonable* what ifs, however, then they can point the way for purposes of disaster preparation.

Consider the question, what if a space rock the size of a soccer field explodes over a large city? This isn't a wild hypothetical, because in June 2002 an asteroid about that size passed within the moon's orbit, about seventy-five thousand miles from earth. We know from the Tunguska event, and from physics and chemistry, the potential explosive yield of an object that size. We know that such an explosion would not be a planet killer. But a huge part of, say, Paris could be incinerated. That's not just guesswork. Because of the experience and science we have to draw on, this is not a silly what if. Whether we *ought* to plan for the obliteration of Paris is another issue entirely. Thinking through the possibility, though, is a rational thing to do.

Another scenario that those who watch near earth objects worry about is whether a space junk explosion could spark a nuclear war? It's a harder question to answer, because it involves anticipating not just the extent of the damage caused by the initial explosion but also people's responses. People are less predictable than explosions. Anyway, there is a legitimate worry that such an event at a time of crisis could lead one of the world's eight or ten nuclear countries to think it was being attacked. The physical issues are easily knowable. In June 2002 an object—astronomers call them bolides—exploded over the Mediterranean with the force of a ten-kiloton bomb. Imagine that India and Pakistan are standing toe to toe, ready to blow each other back to the Stone Age in yet another skirmish over Kashmir. Tensions are high, controls are loose, and both sides have a strong incentive to fire first. Meanwhile, only a few countries have equipment sophisticated enough to distinguish a naturally occurring explosion from a nonnatural one. A bolide explodes and U.S. military intelligence detects it but can't decide whom to warn. Millions of people are incinerated in the ensuing five-minute war.

How can we tell if this is a reasonable counterfactual? One way is to line up arguments for and against its believability. On the positive side:

- People often overreact in times of high tension.
- India and Pakistan have almost blown each other to smithereens before.
- Long-standing hatred between the countries could easily lead to a large war.

- Either country could be so on edge that it would not second-guess an interpretation that a first strike had been launched.
- Nuclear weapons have a built-in logic that requires first-strike use if they are to be effective.

But on the other hand:

- There's never been an all-out nuclear war, so it probably won't happen in the future.
- People don't want a nuclear war and so would second-guess the impulse to launch.
- American officials would probably tell someone that the explosion was from space.

There are mitigating factors, to be sure. And undoubtedly there are other issues that I've missed. What would happen after making our lists is that we'd adduce evidence and examples to support each argument. All the times that United States officials have withheld important information from others would be countered by instances in which the opposite was true. Those who expect rationality from people, even in crisis, would be countered with examples of the myriad ways that officials and countries behave irrationally. And so on.

But again we have the problem of judging whether thinking about whether a bolide could trigger nuclear war is a productive thing to do.

WHAT IF RULES

Are there general principles that might be used to decide? It turns out that there are. These principles cannot, I stress, decide the issue of whether an asteroid-induced nuclear war is possible. They can only decide whether the question itself is mere speculation or a good counterfactual.

One rule to follow when looking backward is the *minimal rewrite-of-history rule*. There's an unavoidably subjective judgment involved here, because reasonable people can disagree on what "minimal" means. Still, imagine arguing that Bill Clinton would have been our greatest president *if only* he had been faithful to his wife *and* he was not hounded by the political far right *and* he had been more savvy about international politics *and* he had found a way to unite Americans on issues of poverty, racism, and health care. It's just too much to ask, too many things would have had to be different for this to qualify as a good counterfactual.

Looking forward, would there be too many things that would have to happen in just the right way for a naturally occurring explosion in the atmosphere to trigger a nuclear war? Probably not. We can find instances in which officials overreacted to or misinterpreted events in dangerous ways. During the Cuban Missile Crisis, an Air Force sentry in Minnesota shot at a fence-climbing intruder and sounded the sabotage alarm. At a Wisconsin airfield the wrong alarm—indicating that a nuclear war had begun—rang. Pilots of nuclear-armed interceptors got their planes ready. Luckily, the planes were stopped before they took off. The intruder in Minnesota turned out to be a bear. There have, as well, been numerous instances in which American defense officials mistakenly thought that nuclear missiles had been launched against the United States. Finally, it is a mere fact that only a few countries have the technological sophistication to distinguish a nuclear explosion from a natural one in space. I think that all of these examples and arguments come down in favor of the idea that this is a plausible counterfactual. It doesn't violate the minimal rewrite rule, and none of the posited conditions are far removed from actual experience.

There's another rule to use. This one, the *possible worlds rule,* says that the action being reimagined had to have been possible for the actor to think about and act upon. It makes no sense, for example, to posit how World War I would have come out had Germany had nuclear weapons, because it was a scientific impossibility for anyone to have had nuclear weapons at the time. But again on this count, I think we'd have to judge as reasonable the counterfactual prediction that a nuclear war *could* be started by a naturally-occurring atmospheric explosion. Certainly, confusion and ambiguity are possible among participants in a crisis situation. We can even expect them. And it is a hallmark of strategic thinking about nuclear weapons that a first strike can be the most rational course of action for a combatant facing the prospect of nuclear war. "Use 'em or lose 'em" is the essence of nuclear strategy.

It is sometimes said that playing with hypothetical scenarios and concentrating on consequences is unproductive. But if we can do those things in a reasonably disciplined way, we can be smarter and more imaginative. Judging good from bad what ifs does not have to be mere speculation. The practical significance of this, it seems to me, is that policy makers and managers could, should they choose to, make good use of experts skilled in building counterfactuals. That kind of imagining doesn't have to stay behind the doors of think tanks and esoteric departments in intelligence organizations.

IMAGINATION BREAKDOWN

We can't ever truly answer the question, what is the worst thing that can happen? But we can at least ask and try to answer the question, what is the worst thing that people *think* can happen? This question is not just an academic one; it has considerable practical importance. For we expect our leaders and organizations to think outside the box, to imagine worst case possibilities and to do whatever is in their power to make people safe. Often enough, though, we instead see imagination breakdown.

Imagination breakdown occurs when people's thoughts and imaginings are insufficient to encompass worst case possibilities. Of course *some* people's imagination breakdowns are more important than other's. It doesn't matter much if a third-grade schoolteacher in Iowa fails to anticipate a 9/11 or a meltdown at the Indian Point nuclear power station, just outside Manhattan. But it matters a great deal if disaster planners in New York City or the federal government have the same failure.

We know from social psychologists that individuals will change what they think about, or even what they *see*, if they are placed in a room with other people who all agree that they see something different. Similarly, social networks shape people's perceptions of risk, possibility, and danger. Just to be the CEO of a big company, rather than a middle manager, can lead to different ways of imagining the future. Such influences can also, of course, shape how people imagine potential disasters. But what kinds of things lead to imagination breakdown?

Simple ignorance sometimes leads to imagination breakdown, as when officials won't tell people when one of their facilities has had a mishap because they fear "public panic." The problem with this is that panic in disasters is quite rare, at least in the United States. The ground will shake, towns will burn, and the hurricane will blow down everything in its path, and still people do not run screaming through the streets in a frenzied attempt to save themselves. Real life is not like reel life. Disaster movies are fun to watch, but they don't reflect reality very well. When elites fail to inform the public of risky situations they use incorrect assumptions about collective behavior in disaster situations; they are ignorant of how people actually behave.

More subtly, a potential future can simply be off someone's radar screen. Before 9/11 the Nuclear Regulatory Commission, which is supposed to regulate nuclear power in the United States, conducted terrorist simulations on nuclear plants that were little more than symbolic. Off-duty guards would pretend to attack a facility, whose on-duty guards would have prior notice of the drill. The pretend attackers couldn't really surprise the guards because that could be awfully dangerous. At the time NRC rules specified that there could be only one inside "attacker" and three outside ones. Even with such minimal requirements nearly half the plants tested between 1991 and 2000 failed. The NRC's simulation was so unrealistic that it could hardly be regarded as a test of anything. But it served the agency's needs to be able to say that *something* was being done about a possible terrorist attack. A more realistic attack apparently couldn't be conceived.

And that's just the problem, isn't it? We need to know how it is that some things aren't even considered possible.

Hubris is often the culprit. When New York City officials, particularly Mayor Rudolph Giuliani, insisted on creating the city's emergency command center at 7 World Trade Center their imaginations neglected some what ifs. The thirteen-million-dollar facility was built, to the mayor's credit, after the 1993 terrorist attack on the World Trade Center. It was a state-of-the-art facility with the ability to monitor traffic throughout the city, coordinate the myriad organizations called to any sort of disaster, and generally fill the information needs that agencies have in times of crisis. It could even surreptitiously tap into the camera feeds of news helicopters, which, in a disaster, can be key sources of information for emergency responders. The command center was also able to notify public health officials of oncoming flu epidemics. And it monitored the 911-emergency database, as a way of detecting possible biological attacks. The emergency operations center had Kevlar in its walls and could withstand two-hundred-mile-per-hour winds. It was designed to handle worst cases.

But the Port Authority of New York and New Jersey, the organization that owned the World Trade Center, decided to put two six-thousand-gallon diesel fuel tanks—which generators would use to provide emergency power should the command center lose electricity—*inside* the building. Putting the fuel inside the building provided a superb source of fire. Had the fuel tanks not been inside the building, perhaps 7 World Trade would not have collapsed after the 9/11 attacks.[15]

How, one might reasonably wonder, did such an option come to be considered acceptable? Would the local fire department allow someone building a house in a suburb, or a brownstone in a city, to do something similar? Not a chance. But the Port Authority was not required to meet New York's fire codes. The Fire Department warned that putting the fuel tanks inside was dangerous. But the Port Authority couldn't imagine that the tanks would precipitate catastrophe. They put eight-inch thick masonry enclosures around them, and said that made them fireproof. Even after the building fell, later in the afternoon of 9/11, Port Authority officials believed that the masonry enclosures couldn't have been breached, an incredible notion to anyone who saw the huge gashes in buildings caused by debris from the falling towers. The Port Authority acted hubristically, as is often the case with powerful organizations with little oversight or competition.

Experience is the root of all wisdom. That's the main reason young car drivers are so dangerous. The same goes for imagining and planning for catastrophe. People plan better when they have relevant past events to look to for lessons. Experience with a problem or set of problems is generally thought to be a good thing: the more experience we have, the smarter we can be. Generally speaking, that's true. Experience makes us smart about a great many things: investing, friendships, car buying, and almost anything where events repeat. People who have learned to get around in New York City are at low risk for getting lost or being mugged. Their experience prepares them for the contingencies of negotiating New York. Without experience in planning for, say, high-rise fires, firefighters would be at much greater risk than they already are. So, it is true to say that experience generally provides a kind of intelligence and competence at dealing with the untoward.

But it's not always true. Experience can also prevent people from imagining well, hemming in imaginations so that possible futures, especially worst case ones, are neglected. Trusting experience too much can lead to imagination breakdown. In 1966 a coal tip in Aberfan, Wales, slid down a hillside and buried a school, killing 144 people, 116 of whom were children. Those responsible for coal safety in Britain had focused exclusively on underground hazards rather than the waste tips on the surface, because that's where they'd encountered problems in the past. They relied on experience and it led them astray.

Steven Weber, a political scientist at the University of California, Berkeley, says that people carry around with them "official futures," ideas and theories about what the future will hold that assume tomorrow will be like today. "Good scenarios challenge this official future," he says, "by focusing precisely on what makes people uncomfortable: discontinuities, events that don't make sense in standard theories/language, and the like." We are continually rewarded for using official futures, because most of the time today is remarkably like yesterday. And for most people, most of the time, yesterday didn't have a worst case in it. This inclination to regard the present as the norm leads us to neglect worst case possibilities, causing imagination breakdowns that rule some futures out of consideration.

The official futures issue, with a dollop of production pressure thrown in, seems to have been at the root of the more interesting failures in the horrendous case of the USS *Indianapolis*. It is a story of worst cases inside of worst cases. On July 26, 1945, the *Indianapolis*, a heavy cruiser, delivered parts of the bomb that would soon incinerate Hiroshima to the South Pacific island of Tinian. It then reported to headquarters in Guam for its next assignment. Headquarters directed the cruiser to Leyte in the eastern Philippines, where it would prepare for the invasion of Japan. The *Indianapolis* was unescorted by any gunships, which was unusual because she had no antisubmarine weaponry on board.

The weather was clear on the night of July 29 so the captain of the *Indianapolis*, Charles McVay, following Navy rules, was sailing in zigzags. The idea was that a zigzagging target would be harder to hit. But as midnight neared the skies clouded over, so McVay ordered a stop to the zigzagging and went below decks. Before doing so, however, he instructed his highly capable officers to resume the evasive maneuver should the weather clear. Apparently, sometime around midnight, the sky cleared for a few moments, and at just the time that the Japanese submarine I-58 surfaced for a look around. Commander Hashimoto— whom the Navy would later call to testify at McVay's court martial, where he said that the zigzagging wouldn't have mattered—fired six torpedoes. Two found their target. The first torpedo blew forty feet off the bow. The second one blew a huge hole amidships, wiping out all communications, along with lights and power in the forward half of the ship. The second explosion also destroyed the ship's radio, radar, and fire control systems. The *Indianapolis*, with 1,196 sailors aboard, sank in less than twelve minutes. Three hundred men went down with the ship, and the rest went into the water. Of those, only 316 survived to be rescued, almost five days later. Most of the rest were eaten by sharks. It was the worst naval disaster in American history. Among the survivors was Captain McVay, who was subsequently scapegoated by the Navy.

Two sets of failures doomed the *Indianapolis*. The first set sent the ship into extreme danger without protection. The second set prevented prompt rescue of the sailors who survived the torpedoes. McVay had requested an armed escort, because his vessel was unarmed, but a vice admiral said none was needed. That decision seems to have been driven by reasons of economy, even though there had been sightings of Japanese submarines between Guam and Leyte. Had the *Indianapolis* been escorted, I-58 would probably not have surfaced, so would never have seen the *Indianapolis* to begin with. Production pressure, then, narrowed the vice admiral's imagination about a worst case at sea. We've seen that sort of imagination-shaper time and time again.

But why weren't the *Indianapolis*'s sailors rescued sooner? Several events and choices came together to foster a collective imagination breakdown. The ship's mission was secret, owing to the preciously deadly cargo that the *Indianapolis* delivered to Tinian, so there weren't as many people expecting her arrival at Leyte as might otherwise have been the case. Personnel aboard the *Indianapolis* sent out at least three SOS messages before she sank. These messages were received at Leyte, but least one of them was dismissed as Japanese trickery. Not fitting into official expectations, it was considered inconceivable that such a message could be legitimate. An officer at Leyte tried to inform his commodore about an SOS that had come in. But the commodore had left word that his card game was not to be disturbed. On his own initiative, the officer ordered two seagoing tugs to the last-reported position of the *Indianapolis*. When the commodore discovered this, he reversed the order. Yet a third message was delivered to a commanding officer, who, apparently drunk, dismissed the order and said, "No reply at this time. If any further messages are received, notify me at once."[16] Since the *Indianapolis* had by then been sunk, no more SOS's were possible. On top of all that, the chief of naval operations had ordered that no combatant ship be officially reported upon arrival at Leyte, an attempt to keep the enemy in the dark about the strength of naval operations.

So there was no mechanism that would lead to the realization that a combatant ship had *not* arrived. As a result, the day after the *Indianapolis* was supposed to arrive, her name was simply erased from a schedule board. The assumption was that she was in port. Amazingly, the U.S. Navy even intercepted a message from Hashimoto claiming that he had sunk a battleship. The message was dismissed, because they just couldn't imagine that it was possible for a ship of that size to disappear.

As perhaps befits a worst case story, it was only luck that the remaining sailors were rescued when they were. A Navy flight patrol happened to pass over the scene of the disaster. The officers in the cockpit did not notice anything amiss. But a flyer had climbed into the rear gunner's blister to fix a problem with an antenna. When he looked down he happened to see a big oil slick, and, on closer inspection, people in it.

THE INTELLIGENCE COMMUNITY'S
FAILURE TO IMAGINE SEPTEMBER 11

It is appropriate to assess here the intelligence community's failure to anticipate the September 11 attacks on the World Trade Center and the Pentagon. That kind of thinking is, after all, exactly what the FBI, the CIA, the National Security Agency, the national security advisor, and the rest of the intelligence community, are supposed to do. But, although a lot of the pieces were there, they didn't connect the dots, as the saying goes.

Now, some argue that the intelligence community did *not* fail. That's certainly the position of the Bush administration. Their argument is that there was too much noise, too much data to digest, and no obvious patterns in the intelligence that would have led experts to imagine the attacks before they took place. President Bush's press secretary, Ari Fleischer, expressed the view well when he said, "So I think, again, people can look back with 20/20 hindsight, people can look back and second-guess . . ."[17] "It's no surprise to anybody that Osama bin Laden wanted to attack the United States," he'd said, dismissing criticism, but the intelligence didn't say "how, what methods, where, when."[18] By these criteria Mohammed Atta, the ringleader of the attackers, would have to call up the president to say he was on his way to New York before they would "know" anything. Republican congressional representative Christopher Shays said, "I think we can already tell you right now who's at fault. We're all at fault. And we know what broke down. It won't even take a board to discover that."[19]

Even Malcolm Gladwell, the erudite, well-informed, and usually critical writer for the *New Yorker*, is sympathetic to the view that it was almost impossible to "connect the dots" before September 11, 2001. Here he quotes an August 2001 exchange between two al Qaeda members:

I've been studying airplanes. If God wills, I hope to be able to bring you a window or a piece of a plane the next time I see you.

What, is there a jihad planned?

In the future, listen to the news and remember these words: "Up above" . . . the surprise attack will come from the other country, one of those attacks you will never forget. It is something terrifying that goes from south to north, east to west. The person who devised this plan is a madman, but a genius. He will leave them frozen [in shock].[20]

Gladwell thinks this exchange reveals the evil attacks only in hindsight, that it doesn't differentiate these terrorists from other terrorists talking about doing dramatic things with an airplane. It was not, in other words, a "forecast." Gladwell's larger point is certainly a good one. Patterns in "data," whether the data are a bunch of numbers or terrorist chatter, must be discerned. Data never speak for themselves. Precisely because they never speak for themselves, discerning patterns requires that you have the cognitive organization in your head *before* you can see the patterns.

What were the signs?

One of the least credible demurrals is that no one in their right mind would have imagined using aircraft as bombs to attack buildings. The Japanese kamikaze attacks weren't exactly secret. In July 1945 Lieutenant Colonel William F. Smith Jr. accidentally flew his B-25 bomber into the side of the Empire State Building. Fourteen people died, and many more were injured. It was a shock to everyone, in 1945. But it was obviously a precedent for 9/11. After all, the World Trade Center engineers considered what might happen to the towers if the largest plane at the time, a Boeing 707 (though without jet fuel onboard), crashed into them.

In 1994 four Islamic extremists hijacked a plane in Algiers. They took the Air France Airbus A300, about the size of a Boeing 767, to Marseilles and demanded that it be loaded with twenty-seven tons of fuel. French commandos stormed the plane and discovered dynamite aboard. Officials later learned that the terrorists were aiming to blow the plane up over Paris or crash it into the Eiffel Tower. Also in 1994 an engineer for Federal Express tried to commandeer a cargo plane. He was thwarted by the crew, but it was clear he intended to commit suicide with the plane. Whether he would crash it into a building or try to kill others was unclear, but the incident clearly connects the dots between suicide and airliners. Finally, again in 1994, a single-engine plane crashed on the grounds of the White House, not far from the president's bedroom. To imagine that airplanes could be used as bombs is not a huge stretch: airplanes have been used that way at least since the kamikazes.

And there had been other signs:

- The World Trade Center bombing of 1993.
- An FBI agent's warning precisely of planes being flown into the Twin Towers.
- Intelligence reports from Egypt that a big attack was in the offing.
- Reportedly, a message from bin Laden telling one of his wives to return home quickly to Saudi Arabia.
- A summer 2001 briefing in which the CIA told government leaders that al Qaeda was planning an attack.

Moreover, nine of the hijackers were selected out for special screening when they arrived at their airports on September 11; two had irregularities in their identification documents; and six were chosen for extra computer screening, with inspectors looking for explosives or unauthorized weapons. The hijackers were notoriously incompetent in other aspects of their lives as well, and should have been detected earlier.

Even though there were many pieces of "data" can we really say that were, beforehand, "signs?" Who really thinks such outrageous thoughts? Well, lots of people, actually, though not the everyday person in the street. When it's germane to their lives, as I've said, Joe and Josephine Doe project and think through worst case scenarios adeptly. The everyday person, however, is unlikely to have imagined the 9/11 terrorist attacks because that kind of scenario is not part of their lives. It's just not relevant to them, even when they are passengers on a plane.

But officers in the intelligence community are different. They are being disingenuous when they imply that the 9/11 attacks were so outrageous that no one in their right mind could have imagined them. They seem to be suggesting that everyone's on a level playing field when it comes to imagining such things. That's not so. It isn't the job of the manager in the hardware store to think about such things. It is, however, part of the everyday lives of the military and of the intelligence communities. It is precisely their responsibility to imagine 9/11. They collect information on terrorists and sometimes even try to infiltrate their organizations. They warn their own people, and elites, when terrorists seem to be planning something. And they run simulations of terrorist attacks. They did all these things, on a regular basis, before September 11, 2001.

In 1996 some researchers at the RAND Corporation, a research think tank that works closely with the American military, ran a simulation based on a more or less formal method developed by RAND personnel. It's called "The Day After . . ." methodology, and it's designed to push people to think through crisis scenarios in which parts of the United States, or its allies, are under attack. The 1996 simulation was called "The Day After . . . in the American Strategic Infrastructure."[21] Participants were to assume they were part of a group that included members of the president's cabinet and high-level advisors. There were three parts to the simulation. The first two parts were set in the year 2002 and described a fast-moving series of domestic and international crises, taking place over a seven-day period. Participants were informed of a series of "facts" and asked to deliberate on the best courses of action and come up with recommendations for the president. The last part was set in what was then the present, 1996, and asked participants to revise a memo that would advise the president on the key issues pertaining to keeping the nation's "critical infrastructure" secure, with special attention given to cyberspace.

It was a terrific, and prescient, simulation. The 1996 instructions told participants that the U.S. administration had been elected in 2000 by the "fourth closest electoral college vote in history!" (The Gore/Bush election was actually the second closest.) The simulation's complex set of crises included the following: China is gearing up to take Taiwan by force, or so it appears, and uses as a pretext evidence that Taiwan is trying to develop a nuclear capability. Russia is barely governable, and its leadership loses control of over twenty kilograms of enriched uranium, which the Russian mafia is trying to sell to Iran. The Middle East, in one of the few moments of optimistic projection, is on the verge of a stable peace. But Latin America is in trouble, and Mexico is in a politically explosive condition. The simulation projects that the Internet has grown immense, with large proportions of commerce done online. The nation's critical infrastructure is very information-technology dependent—and vulnerable.

Then the pretend disasters come, reading like a Tom Clancy novel. The commuter rail in Atlanta fails because of a computer logic bomb. There's an airline disaster caused by malevolent computer code. A government aircraft crashes because a chemical has been added to the fuel that turned it into jelly. Hydroelectric plants are attacked and fail. A couple of years later, in the simulation, the San Francisco commuter system is also shut down by a logic bomb. Miami air traffic control has to shut down for five hours because of a computer worm. A huge natural gas explosion and fire, the result of foul play, happen in North Dakota. The electric grid in Turkey fails, New York Stock Exchange data become corrupted, and a forty-eight-inch gas pipeline is blown up in an act of sabotage. Such incidents, around the world but concentrated in the United States, cascade and intensify. Right-wing groups in America are attacking the infrastructure. China is attacking the infrastructure. At the same time, tensions across the globe are heating up. Financial markets are falling apart. And people are starting to protest, especially on the Mall in Washington, D.C. Widespread panic is threatened.

RAND's simulation is a pretty bad worst case scenario—actually a group of worst case scenarios. The real point, for present purposes, is that the intelligence community is both planning and participating in the simulation. It is a perfectly reasonable way to think. One would think that it's their charge to do so. Note the kind of people involved: they were from organizations like Defense Advanced Research Projects Agency, Office of Management and Budget, National Security Agency, Citibank, and the like. This was no cast of extremists.

"The Day After . . ." exercises present impressive sets of counterfactuals. They are deliberately set up to exercise people's imaginations in circumstances that are worse than might be projected by experts. In the telling, of course, it's hardly believable that the phone system would be disrupted just as nuclear power plants are being hacked just as terrorists are exploding bombs near chemical plants just as a plane crash has taken out computers that control railroad tracks (I'm paraphrasing a little), while the U.S. president has been stricken with smallpox. It's plausible that any of those individual failures or disasters could happen, but all at once? Not really. But then worst cases are never credible. If you're trying to push people to think outside the disaster box, "The Day After . . ." exercises are just the ticket.

Note that RAND's "Day After . . ." exercises follow the rules for good counterfactuals. They pose alternatives that are within the conception and reach of the participants and also follow the minimal rewrite rule. But they do more than that. Why, if the U.S. intelligence community can *formalize* projecting that the power grid is failing, gas pipelines are exploding, planes are falling out of the sky, nuclear materials are being traded on the black market (but thwarted by John Wayne–like incursions), and the lights are going out in major cities, would it be unreasonable to imagine the hijacking of a plane to be used as a bomb? In fact it was foreseen. In March 2004 Richard Clarke, who had served in high-level security positions for many years, published his book *Against All Enemies: Inside America's War on Terror.* Among the revelations in Clarke's book is proof that many in the Bush administration were indeed directly and frequently warned about imminent, specific attacks. Clarke's revelations, backed up with quotes and documents, that the administration was preoccupied with Iraq and so missed obvious opportunities to actually combat terror led to the testimony of National Security Advisor Condoleezza Rice before the commission investigating the 9/11 attacks. Her testimony, in turn, led to the declassification of a Presidential Daily Briefing that Bush received on August 6, 2001. Rice said it was merely a "historical document," but that makes little sense. It was entitled "Bin Laden Determined to Strike in US." We know, too, that it included specific intelligence about using airplanes as missiles. The Federal Aviation Administration received *fifty-two warnings,* between April and September 2001, about the threat from al Qaeda, about hijackings and suicide. The FAA even conducted briefings at nineteen of America's busiest airports in mid-2001.[22]

The intelligence community, and the administration of George W. Bush, may have not connected the dots they needed to connect to do something about 9/11. But that doesn't mean there weren't plenty of dots to connect, and plenty of cognitive maps that would have permitted connecting them. The American intelligence community dropped the ball before September 11. Had they done their job the body count, and the horror, would have been diminished on that worst case day.

REFLECTIONS ON IMAGININGS AND SAFETY

Imagination is contracted, and expanded, by the organizational positions that people occupy and by the cultures to which they belong. It is stretched, or not, by social networks—the people with whom we share emotional, economic, or political ties. These larger contexts of life determine whether imagination leads to great foresight, or cognitive blinkering.

Historians say that events are "contingent," which means that reality could be very different but for this or that happening. "If only" stories demonstrate the point. If only the nail had been available for shoeing the horse, the horse would not have been lost, nor the rider, who, as it happened, would have turned the battle. And that particular battle was crucial for the kingdom, which was itself lost. It was all contingent on something as insignificant as a nail!

Worst cases are contingent. The *Titanic* disaster could have been averted. The waters that *Titanic* traveled in were not unpopulated. The *Californian,* with no passengers, was steaming through the same area, but her captain stopped for the night because there was too much ice in the water. *Titanic* could also have stopped. There could have been enough lifeboats. The crew could have been better trained. The captain of the *Californian* would later be severely criticized for not coming to the aid of *Titanic.* The two ships were apparently close enough together to see each other's lights. If only the *Californian* had recognized the significance of *Titanic*'s flares. If only Captain Smith of the *Titanic* had stopped for the night. If only *Titanic* had enough lifeboats. If only.

There were again many "if onlys" when Exxon ran one of its largest vessels up on a well-known rock in Alaska, in clear weather, with no competing traffic. Alyeska, the company that owns and operates the Alaskan pipeline, at one time had an escort service. A tugboat would escort the huge oil tankers out of the Valdez Narrows, into the safer, wider expanses of Prince William Sound. If only the tugs had been there that night when Captain Hazelwood went belowdecks. If only a trans-Canadian pipeline had been built instead. If only the third mate had followed Hazelwood's instructions carefully. If any of those conditions had held, the *Exxon-Valdez* disaster would never have happened.

Looking at such contingencies, the if onlys, makes us realize that reality could be different. Not all disasters can be avoided, of course, but probably more of them can be than is presently the case. In addition, it's almost always true, if you look closely enough at worst cases, that there is a pattern in the if onlys. The pattern is that it's usually those with the most power in a system who make the critical choices that lead to disaster. In a sense this is unsurprising, because it's only the most powerful in *any* system who are in a position to make *anything* happen. But postdisaster analyses often miss that power.

Talking about what could have been, what might have been, and what might be is fantastical. But that's not a bad thing. For what is fantasy but a working of imagination? And yet, we have to say, there's a difference between flights of fancy and fanciful imaginings. Flights of fancy are trivial, while fanciful imaginings are not. We especially need those who claim to protect us to imagine fancifully. We should want them to imagine better and to prepare for the untoward. We want them to prevent terrorists from being able to enact their own fantasies. We want protection. There are limits to their abilities to provide that. But our leaders and the organizations they try to direct are better positioned than the rest of us to anticipate and prepare for worst cases.

Still, we should never be surprised to find that officials, experts, and organizations fail us in imagining worst cases. Because of bureaucratic politics and self-interest, we can expect them to build "worst case scenarios" in ways that are conservative with respect to action they might be required to take. It's hard enough to conceive the "inconceivable," but add bureaucratic inertia and you have to wonder how organizations *ever* respond to disaster productively. We shouldn't be surprised at that because modern organizations are built to be *reasonable* rather than outrageous. And worst cases are always thought to be outrageous.

Thinking about counterfactuals leads us to a paradox of worst cases, which is where I'll end this chapter: once we answer the question, what's the worst that can happen?, we have given a name to that which was previously inconceivable. That, in turn, brings the scenario into the realm of conceivability, so it's not quite the worst case scenario anymore. What's the worst thing after *that*?

4

POWER, POLITICS, AND PANIC IN WORST CASES

We're used to thinking about politics as concerning only the government. But a lot more than just the government is political. Any situation in which peoples, groups, or nations have interests can be analyzed in political terms. This becomes most obvious when there are *conflicts* of interest, but the absence of conflict is political as well. Relationships between parents and children are political. The granting of stock options to employees is political. When professors insist that their students work on exactly the same kinds of problems that they work on, that's political.

Disasters are political too, in both the traditional and the broader sense. As an example of the former, consider how, in the United States, something gets to be an *official* disaster. For a situation to be an official federal disaster, the president must issue a "declaration of disaster or major emergency." You might think that would be a straightforward decision. Did the community get blown away or not? Did the hurricane kill hundreds or just a few? A city destroyed would definitely qualify as a "major emergency." But presidents get a lot of requests for the official designation that aren't even close to being that bad. Political scientist Rick Sylves tells us that "since the first presidential disaster declaration was issued in 1953, until 2001, presidents have turned down about 1 in every 3 governor requests for declarations of major disaster."[1] FEMA, the Federal Emergency Management Agency, has tried to develop objective criteria to guide the president, but the president isn't bound by them. The process was changed considerably in 1974 with the passage of the Disaster Relief Act, which expanded the definition of disaster to include "emergencies." In truth, there's a lot of subjectivity, and politics, involved in deciding what's an official disaster or emergency.

Disasters can also be *politically useful.* The U.S. government put "Remember the *Lusitania!*" on recruiting posters for World War I. I'm sure no one in the government was happy that nearly twelve hundred people lost their lives when a German U-boat torpedoed the passenger ship. They did, however, find the event useful. Winston Churchill even remarked, three months before the *Lusitania* was sunk, that it was "most important to attract neutral shipping to our shores, in the hope especially of embroiling the U.S.A. with Germany. . . . For our part, we want the traffic—the more the better and if some of it gets into trouble, better still."[2] He was not alone in heralding the sinking for inducing American involvement in the war. Similarly, it is no secret that Pearl Harbor had the happy effect of giving President Roosevelt license to enter World War II.

Even talk about disasters, and risky things more generally, is political. In 2002 Claudia Dreifus, a famous journalist with the *New York Times,* interviewed another famous journalist, David Ropeik, for her column "A Conversation With." Ropeik was the point person for Harvard's Center for Risk Analysis, where scholars conduct research on how people think about risk and danger. He was hired to be the mouthpiece for the center because he has extensive training in speaking to the media and so is quite practiced in the art of translating technical studies into popular parlance. He's very good at his work. Before the *Times* interview, Harvard's risk center had come under fire because it relies heavily on grants from corporations that have an interest in convincing people that their products and processes aren't dangerous. The interesting thing is not that the center takes money from corporations—the integrity of its researchers is above reproach—but what Ropeik said when Dreifus asked him about the issue. It wasn't surprising, he said, that the Natural Resources Defense Council, and other organizations concerned with environmental health, wouldn't be interested in "objective" science. He meant, of course, that *real* science wouldn't support their political positions but rather the positions of chemical companies. It's hard to get more political than that.[3]

The problem of politics in disasters can be hard to think about. It would be nice, if it were true, that calamities always led people to put their interests and passions aside to comfort the afflicted. The priorities when people are suffering ought to be, first, to stop the suffering and, second, to put back in place that which has become disordered. After the disaster in New York City on September 11, 2001, people put aside, for a short time at least, their racial hatreds, most of their ethnic dislikes, and even class conflict to work on the common project of recovery. We see a similar response in most disasters, in the form of altruistic actions on the part of the uninjured to give succor and aid to the less fortunate.

But the truth is that politics, and social conflict, are never far away, even in worst cases, even when there is urgent suffering. Power plays between politicians cannot long recede. In the 9/11 drama we did not often see New York Democratic senators Hillary Clinton and Charles Schumer on the same stage as Republicans Rudolph Giuliani and George Pataki. There were even intense struggles and disagreements between the New York City firefighters and, frankly, everyone else who worked on The Pile. The firefighters treated their own dead with more respect than the dead of others; they gave recovery of their "brothers" pride of place, as if some deaths were more valuable than others. Politics is apparent in other situations as well; when a plane crashes a common response by airline officials and even government regulators is to blame the pilot. All these actions—controlling the stage, differentiating the value of the dead, assigning blame—involve the sacrifice of someone's advantage for the sake of someone else's. Those behaviors are strategic, too, in the sense that they are undertaken to influence other people to do something or to think in a particular way.

In this chapter I look at political machinations in several arenas. We will see that politics is often in play both at the micro, or cognitive, level and at the macro, or institutional, level. "Cognitive" matters have to do with how people think, perceive, and talk about life. "Institutional" questions, as I use the term, have to do with organizations and other large-scale sorts of patterns. These concepts often bleed into each other. I analyze four things in this chapter: risk communication, the problem of panic, the greatest worst case risk that Americans face, and issues of scapegoating and blame. Each has micropolitical and macropolitical aspects. Throughout, I'll draw attention to the conflicts that shape the character of danger and how we talk about danger. Power, it turns out, is exceedingly important in talk about disaster, the production of disaster, responses to disaster, and how people make sense of disasters after they happen.

THE "RISK COMMUNICATION" SHELL GAME

Perhaps you've seen a shell game on a street corner or in a public park. The game's operator shows a ball under a shell or cup and two other shells that are empty, then quickly moves the shells around, letting you think that you can follow the shell with the ball under it. If you guess which shell hides the ball you win.

The shell game isn't a game at all, at least not the simple game presented to the mark. In real games rules and procedures known to all parties help prevent great unfairness. They level the playing field. In a shell game there is no such leveling. The "tosser" uses several tools to prevent the mark from following the ball and is in league with shills who almost guarantee the game's outcome. It's not quite thievery because the mark *agrees* to play. But it's not a fair game. Often, the ball isn't there at all when the shells start to slide; it's already been slipped under a piece of paper.

The professional field of "risk communication" is like that. Only a fairly large, and rich, organization (the tosser) can afford to hire the expert risk communicator (the shill), and that alone guarantees an unlevel playing field. The trappings, and sometimes the substance, of science are an important part of the game of trying to convince someone, perhaps a small town or an urban population, of some particular position. It seems to me very political to claim that "objective" science is on one side or another of some dispute. I don't mean that we can't do objective science. I think we can. The problem is the limited number of attributes that are thought to go along with the label "objective": the use of quantitative data, a focus on individual perception, and acontextual conceptions of who people are. There's nothing wrong with those attributes in and of themselves, but they do not exhaust the list of things we ought to consider important.

I'll explain. If only quantitative data are considered real, then interviews by journalists or social scientists, especially in-depth conversations, are ruled out. But interviews are often the best way to access certain kinds of information: how people acted in the middle of a fire, the things a disaster planner considers important to plan for, how people understand what a disaster has done to them, and so on. Focusing on individual perceptions is interesting. But if we really want to understand how people think about risk and danger we have to know more. We need to know more about the relationships people have, because our connections with others shape how we think and feel. For example, if we're studying people's fears of radiation it makes all the difference in the world whether we ask nuclear utility executives, government regulators, or antinuclear activists. The same kind of point can be made about "acontextual conceptions." If a study asks only about, for instance, race and perception, it assumes that race is the most important reason something is perceived one way rather than another. But the most important causes might really be in the larger context of the perceiving.

Imagine preparing a large community for a smallpox outbreak. Two things will be crucial: vaccinating the unsick and keeping the sick away from the unsick. A smallpox outbreak in Milwaukee in 1894 was accompanied by riots and other conflicts, which reduced vaccination rates and impeded quarantine efforts. The problems are all traceable to a high-handed government reaction and an arrogant approach by scientists. Poor people with the disease were forcibly removed from their homes by health officers wearing military-style uniforms, while rich people were allowed to stay home (we'd call this "shelter in place" now). New immigrants especially feared the uniformed officers, and for that were publicly referred to as the "scum of Milwaukee." There were eleven hundred smallpox cases in Milwaukee, and about 300 deaths, far more than there should have been.

Compare that with a 1947 smallpox outbreak in New York City. From the start city officials were honest with the public. The mayor strong-armed reluctant drug companies to make more vaccine, and they complied. There were daily press conferences to keep everyone up to date, and the cooperation of local organizations such as churches and clubs was elicited by making them central parts of the effort. New York City had only twelve cases of smallpox. Two people died.[4]

If we were to focus on perceptions of individual immigrants in Milwaukee we would totally miss the larger context that led to those perceptions. The immigrants' ethnicity wasn't important, except that Milwaukee officials used it as a proxy for their intelligence. What was most important was that they weren't treated respectfully. That New York officials were able to foster cooperation makes the same point that the important cause of people's perceptions is usually in the contexts of their lives.

Back to the uses of "risk communication."

There is an overblown caricature of "risk" in American society today. This caricature seizes a few sensational instances of people over-reacting—going outside to open residential mail during the anthrax crisis in fall 2001, for example—and draws the conclusion that people are so pervasively irrational that they shouldn't have anything to say about complex, technical issues. It says that people are fooled, usually by the media, into thinking they can have zero risk. They worry about anthrax more than smoking, toxic chemicals more than lack of exercise. These are the people who senselessly fear toxic chemicals, nuclear energy, and high-tech in general. Such people don't understand that flying is safer than driving, or if they *do* understand it, they fail to temper their emotions with that superior knowledge. People's irrationalities, goes the argument, then get translated into overregulation of industry, wasting resources on trivial risks while neglecting more important ones.

This story of how people think about and respond to information about risks is especially popular in industry, but it also has plenty of support from academics and popular writers. One popular book, by the lawyer H. Aaron Cohl, is entitled *Are We Scaring Ourselves to Death? How Pessimism, Paranoia, and a Misguided Media Are Leading Us toward Disaster*. The very title is as sensational as the headlines he mercilessly attacks; the media, he tells us, almost always neglect the facts in favor of a punchy headline. "Aren't we logical at all?" Cohl asks, asserting that people now expect life to be risk free. The media, he writes, created "mass hysteria" in 1989 over Alar, a pesticide that when sprayed on apples makes them mature at about the same time. Mothers were apparently irrationally worried about their children getting cancer. And one reason people fear second-hand cigarette smoke, according to Cohl, is that "the issue allows us to vent anger at the people we love to hate," one reason for which is that "tobacco companies are believed to have lied" about the dangers of smoking. And so on, right to the point where we are scaring ourselves to death.

When this story is told in academic work it is done so in more moderate terms. Most academics, after all, aren't too comfortable with strident statements and controversy. I've already mentioned the Harvard Center for Risk Analysis, and if you do an Internet search for "dread factor" you will quickly discover references to other academics and consultants who champion this idea. You will also find references to consultants who make *ten thousand dollars* a day, plus expenses, teaching "risk communication" skills.

Now, there is a lot of truth in the story. The ways it's used, however—to justify undemocratic decisions and to hide the ways that the American public is being made to bear risks disproportionate to benefits—is the great political issue. In fact Americans, indeed most people in prosperous societies, do live longer and healthier lives than their ancestors. Those in rich, democratic societies are, generally speaking, better off than those in poor, undemocratic ones. According to the U.S. National Center for Health Statistics, the average life expectancy of an American born in 1900 was forty-seven years, for one born in 1970 it was seventy-one years, for one born in 2000 seventy-seven years, and the figure continues to climb.[5] Too, we are healthier on all counts compared to a hundred years ago, except rates of cancer and heart disease are higher. Those, though, are mainly diseases of old age—that we die of them is actually an indicator of how long we live.

It's true that the media feature dramatic things, that a lot of the chemicals we worry about have not been proven to cause cancer, and that people misestimate many risks (e.g., crime; heterosexual, non-IV-drug-related AIDS; even cigarettes). But does it follow that people are irrational, unresponsive to reason or evidence? The answer is that human behavior is a lot more complex than simplistic explanations acknowledge. The circumstances that people find themselves in have enormous influence on what they think and how they act. Trying to understand what people do by relying on the most obvious, readily available ideas slights the complexity of people's thoughts and the multiplicity of influences on their behavior.

Let's look at risk communication in a different way, using a method social scientists call "institutional analysis." Institutional analysis involves focusing on the patterns in a situation rather than the personalities. Who can afford risk communication consultants who make hundreds of dollars per hour? Not communities beleaguered by toxic contamination. Certainly not the people of Libby, Montana, where W. R. Grace and Company used a twenty-one-acre piece of ground as a transport center for vermiculite, which it mined nearby. The problem is that tremolite, a form of asbestos, occurs naturally in vermiculite. No one disputes that at least two hundred Libbians were killed by asbestos exposure. The town is roiled in trouble and conflict. This would be a perfect situation in which to diagnose "dread." The people in Libby face an uncertain future but one with considerable catastrophic potential. They use a stretched worst case ruler. A grandmother says her seven-year-old

granddaughter "is asking me if I'm going to die. Why should children that age be thinking about things like that?"[6] That sort of worry
isn't irrational, isn't dread disproportionate to the actual risk, though
it certainly is dreadful. My point, however, is that these people are not
the ones hiring risk communication experts. Instead, such experts are
mainly hired by the organizations (sometimes corporations, sometimes
government agencies) that create the danger in the first place. There's
an institutional pattern there—the more resources you have the better
able you are to hire consultants to help with your fights.

Consider also the board members who have oversight over the
above-mentioned Harvard Center for Risk Analysis. As of 2003 the
executive council had as members the retired CEOs of Eastman Chemical and International Paper and the presidents of Pfizer and the National Association of Manufactures. The advisory council has members
from DuPont, the Insurance Institute for Highway Safety, RAND, and
Exxon Chemical. And the list of funders, which variously provide "un-
restricted" and "restricted" monies, reads like a roll call of top-tier corporations, some of which have had occasion to hire the consultants who
say people are consumed with dread. There are, however, no council members from the National Resources Defense Council, the Sierra
Club, or the Center for Health, Environment and Justice (of which
Lois Gibbs, the founder of the Love Canal Homeowners Association,
is executive director).

Having corporate councilors and funders does not mean that the researchers or the research done at the Harvard Center for Risk Analysis
are corrupt. Most of the center's work is peer-reviewed, which means it
is evaluated by people who don't have even the appearance of a conflict
of interest. It would be exceedingly hard to "cook the books" on the research projects to get results that please the oil companies, the chemical
companies, the insurance companies, the manufacturers, the law firms,
or the drug companies with whom the center is so closely involved. If I
were putting together a center for risk communication I'd have broader
representation on it, but I'd also like to have the Harvard center's sponsors, who are rich and well-connected. Still, the correspondence between the strong representation of industry on its boards and the strong
cost-benefit orientation of the policies and research that the center ad-
vocates is no accident. Here's how its director of risk communication
put it:

Is that kind of rational cost-benefit thinking going to attract Greenpeace, or the Sierra Club, or National Audubon, or whatever? Less likely than it's going to attract corporations who find comfort in that careful, non-emotional, non-value-based, but "just the facts, please," sort of approach.

In noting the correspondence between the type of work the center does and the interests of its funders we see a pattern. It tells us that risk communication as practiced at one of the most prestigious universities in the world, by some of the best scientists in the world, "communicates" in particular ways that resonate with particular interests.

When the communication director says that corporations find comfort in "non-value-based" research he is saying that environmentalists, community activists, and the like assess risks only in accordance with their values. Corporations and the Harvard Center are, by contrast, interested only in real science. Nonsense. Here are some studies we're not likely to see funded by the center's corporate sponsors, although all could certainly be conducted with the same scientific rigor we find in its work:

- A systematic investigation into how chemical companies use language to allay public concern about their own worst cases.
- A survey of contingent workers in the oil industry about safety procedures on oil derricks.
- A benefit-cost analysis of developing alternative energy sources.

Risk communication is what grows up as people come to expect worst cases from organizations within industry or government. It is, for the most part, a semiorganized effort to convince people who might be at risk that they aren't at risk, that their interests are shared by those who often have as much of an interest in deception as protection. Risk communication, as a practical matter, is mostly public relations: remember DuPont's slogan "Better Things for Better Living . . . Through Chemistry." As an academic matter, risk communication wraps the idea of "rationality" around issues of passion, interest, and safety, dubbing those who don't follow the official program "irrational." I've yet to see the study from prominent consultants or scholars in risk communication that calls corporate executives irrational or emotional. Risk communication is premised on the notion that regular people respond badly to bad news and that their threat "perceptions" need to be manipulated. And that's political.

Most risk communication isn't really communication at all. Real communication goes two ways; there's back and forth between the communicators. But professional risk communication (the *scholarly* study of risk communication isn't like this) is political rhetoric. It may be subtle or it may not be, but the goal of it is to convince members of the public that they're not at risk, often by telling them that they're worried about the wrong things. Just think about it in reverse: when local groups protest or demand accountability from officials and experts, that is never called "risk communication." It's called political protest or NIMBYism. Anything that one-sided is suspicious.

Risk communication doesn't have to work like that. It can be an honest exchange of information between risk creators and potential victims. It can diminish rather than merely manipulate public concern over potential hazards. It can make people safer. Take the strange case of Sybron, Inc. Sybron is a chemical plant in New Jersey that, at one point at least, actually enjoyed the trust of the community in which it is situated. Things weren't always like that, according to Caron Chess and Michael Greenberg, professors at Rutgers University.[7] Some years ago an accident at Sybron caused a hazardous materials release, fires, and serious injury to workers. The company was soon in crisis. But rather than follow the usual risk communication strategy, Sybron began a far-reaching review of its training and personnel practices. It invested time and money in upgrading safety equipment. It established a permanent committee of citizens and plant personnel to review safety procedures, risk communication programs, and future expansion plans. It created early warning systems that included people in the community. Sybron took responsibility for its place in the community.

So apparently the public *can* be a part of decision making in ways that diminish danger and increase confidence. Industry and communities *can* work together. But there has to be a willingness on all sides to be open to honest argument. Most importantly, as the Sybron case demonstrates, the concerns of those not in positions of power must be respected. Giving people a seat at the table is the best way of making that happen. Once that happens, we should probably avoid the term "risk communication" altogether, leaving it to the consultants with their shell games. "Risk deliberation" happens when there's a real leveling of the playing field, a meaningful redistribution of power and influence, and genuine back-and-forth about interests and values.

WHO PANICS?

The shell game of risk communication is based on the idea that people respond poorly to bad news. They can't handle the truth, so they over-react. The conclusion is that they need to be educated and calmed. This image of the public has a ramped-up corollary, which applies to how people respond in disasters. Specifically, the idea is that people are prone to *panic*, which the Oxford English Dictionary defines as an "excessive feeling of alarm or fear . . . leading to extravagant or injudicious efforts to secure safety."[8]

You see it in any disaster movie. Whether the tornado rips through town, or the asteroid slams into city buildings, or a nuclear plant blows itself to smithereens, people run wildly through the streets, screaming their heads off and pushing over people in wheelchairs to save themselves. Thank goodness for that. If a movie portrayed people as they truly behave in disasters it would be dull as mud, or a documentary.

We now have nearly fifty years of research on the matter. It's one of the strongest, most robust, findings in social science: people usually behave quite reasonably when their supper club catches fire or their plane crashes. They scream, they yell, they *feel* terrified out of their minds. Their worst case worlds, after all, are appearing before their eyes. But they hardly ever act in their self-interest to the detriment of others, and their actions are usually reasonable given the circumstances. They may even *think* that they panicked, but more likely than not their behavior was anything but that.

This is not to say panic *never* happens. We have good evidence that it sometimes happens, say, when bars or restaurants catch fire. In February 2003 there were two horrific fires at clubs, one in Rhode Island and one in Chicago. One hundred died at the Station nightclub in Rhode Island, and the E2 nightclub fire in Chicago killed twenty-one people. From survivor reports we know that panic happened in both cases.

But we have to look at the larger context to really understand what happened. It's not enough to just say, "Oh, they panicked," and be done with it. In Chicago, doors that should have been open were reported to be locked; in fact the second-floor club had been ordered closed by a judge because of fire code violations. There may have been as many as fifteen hundred people at the E2, and only one exit. On top of that, when the trouble started, security guards used pepper spray and mace after some female patrons started fighting. In Rhode Island a rock band decided to use fireworks to augment their act. But it was a one-story, wood-frame building and the fireworks were not properly supervised. The place had no sprinklers, nor were any required, and was over capacity. There were four exits, but most people tried to use the same door they'd used to enter; they didn't know about the other three.

Looking at the larger context of these two disasters leads us away from facile explanations like "panic." Instead, we might describe such situations as systems that did not *fail gracefully.* A system that fails gracefully is one in which some of the pieces can stop working without bringing down the entire system. In software engineering, an operating system fails gracefully if any particular program can crash without requiring the computer to be rebooted. The air traffic control system in the United States is designed to fail gracefully; a procedure instituted in 2000 tracks data so that if one component fails its replacement is immediately available.[9] In January 2000 a cable on one of the Empire State Building's elevators broke, sending its occupant on a forty-story drop; but other safety systems kicked in to prevent the elevator from crashing. It failed gracefully.

So while we know that panic is rare, we also know that it does happen. The astute observer will note that when it happens, it happens too late. In the flaming examples I just listed people didn't panic until the flames were licking the backs of their necks. Worst case worlds don't necessarily cause worst case reactions.

Panic's real significance lies in its mythical dimensions. People in positions of power frequently use that myth to deny other people access to information. Kathleen Tierney, director of the Natural Hazards Center, at the University of Colorado, says that federal officials received a credible warning involving nuclear material in the fall of 2001 but failed to inform New York City officials.[10] The panic myth is important because it reflects a widely held perception of how people think and behave. And it's important because the idea of it is singularly applied.

Did you ever notice that the tendency to panic is attributed only to ordinary people? Oh sure, it is said that stock traders are subject to panic, and perhaps they are. But that is a fairly limited case. I've never seen panic attributed to presidents, chief executive officers, university officials, physicians, or, goddess forbid, newspaper executives. Imagine the following scenarios:

- A president decides to invade a third world country on the basis of trumped-up and possibly fabricated evidence of weapons of mass destruction. Later senior members of the president's own party say that the invasion was a panic, an unreasonable response to a phony risk.
- An officer of a major commercial bank hears a rumor that a company to which the bank has loaned money may have questionable accounting practices. After consulting with other bank executives, who've heard the same rumors (because they circulate in the same networks), the officer calls in the loans, driving the debtor company out of business. Later, an investigative journalist discovers that it was the commercial bank's accounting practices, and not the creditor's, that were flaky. The consensus on Wall Street is that the CEO panicked, acting in his own perceived self-interest, without bothering to get the facts.

Those scenarios, and we could easily spin a thousand more like them, are technically imaginable. In practical terms, though, they would never happen. Panic is just not something that is attributed to people in positions of power. We may speak of their mistakes, their greed, their self-interest. But never panic. Panic, as a state of mind or an attribute of behavior, is applied only to ordinary people. That in itself shows that the very idea of panic is politically loaded. Because it is used in a systematic way for only some people, it works to their disadvantage systematically.

That's a real shame because the evidence shows the reverse. In disaster after disaster it is regular, ordinary people who've behaved well and officials who've behaved poorly.

AMERICAN BHOPAL: A WORST CASE WAITING TO HAPPEN

Near earth objects could wipe out the planet. Supervolcanoes could plunge much of the world into a cold, dark era, killing millions and fundamentally reshaping what we think of as civilization. "Broken arrows"—nuclear weapons that are not under full control because they are lost or have broken down—could annihilate a large city. We should worry about all those things. But we needn't look to the heavens, the

depths, or the nuclear abyss to find extreme danger. There are more prosaic threats, just waiting to kill thousands, perhaps many, many more.

In 1984 in Bhopal, India, several thousand people were killed or injured after an accident at a Union Carbide plant released a highly toxic
chemical—methyl icocyanate—that seared their lungs and burned
their eyes. It was one of the worst chemical accidents ever. We'd like to
think that such a thing couldn't happen here. They take bigger chances
in India, where regulations aren't tough and people aren't as educated.
At least that's what we'd like to think. The chemical industry tells us
it can police itself. The American Chemical Council represents the industry, and if you read through their material you'll come away feeling
safe and reassured, thanks to risk communicators.

But it is only a matter of time before we have an American Bhopal.
It's a question of when, not if. When it happens it could easily be much
worse than the Indian Bhopal. The two U.S. industries with the greatest worst case potential are not nuclear power and tobacco, they're not
oil transport and hospitals. They're trains and chemicals. Let me quote
from *Toxic Warfare,* a 2002 RAND report: "Many of the chemicals used
or produced in plants throughout the country have the potential to
match or exceed the 1984 disaster in Bhopal, India. This risk is com-
pounded by the frequent movement of these chemicals, typically by rail,
through densely populated areas such as Baltimore and Washington."[11]
That's putting it mildly.

Since 9/11 there's been a lot of worry, talk, and resources directed
toward terrorists getting their hands on weapons of mass destruction,
which usually means nuclear, biological, or chemical weapons. But we
shouldn't forget that the 9/11 terrorists didn't use these sorts of weapons.
They used native technologies. Our greatest worst case threat, from terrorists or otherwise, involves chemicals not intended as weapons.

It is not crazy to fear the worst case possibilities of chemical plants
and of chemical trains. Yale professor Charles Perrow points out the
following frightening possibilities. If even a single rail car of chlorine
spilled its contents near Los Angeles four million people could be poi-
soned.[12] A refinery near Philadelphia keeps four hundred thousand
pounds of hydrogen fluorine on-site, potentially a threat to another four
million people. Three million in Detroit would be at risk in the event
of a chlorine railcar release. In New Jersey, 180,000 pounds of chlorine
and sulfur dioxide could create a toxic cloud that would put twelve
million people at risk. And a Union Carbide plant near Charleston,

West Virginia, has two hundred thousand pounds of the same deadly chemical that did so much damage in Bhopal, a threat to sixty thousand people.

A *60 Minutes* report on the chemical plant danger, which aired in November 2003, included videos of unlocked, broken, and rusty gates supposedly protecting various plants with storage tanks of deadly chemicals. The reporter walked in and around without being detected. Some of the facilities were adjacent to interstate highways.

It is tempting, and comforting, to think that those scenarios involving the release of toxic chemicals are far-fetched, even fanciful. But that's possible only if you believe that worst case thinking is fanciful. If you believe such thinking is in fact wise, or at least useful as a counterweight to probabilistic thinking, then fear and concern, though certainly not panic, are entirely appropriate.

Before I get further into the matter, let me make two important points. First, I am not opposed to the chemical industry; nor do I suffer a train phobia. Far from it. I think that most of what is done in the chemical industry is necessary to people's well-being. I'm of the opinion, as well, that safety statistics in the chemical industry reflect well on the care taken by chemical corporations and on regulatory oversight. There are regular and serious exceptions to this positive judgment, terrible incidents of callous decision making, community contamination, mistreatment of workers and environmentalists, and corruption of the regulatory process. Those, however, are exceptions, rather than essential attributes of the industry. Second, even under the best of circumstances the chemical industry would be dangerous. Many of the raw and refined materials it deals with are inherently risky. It is unreasonable to expect the chemical industry to be zero-risk. Furthermore, many of the processes essential to the industry are necessarily highly complex. When the technical apparatus in the chemical industry fails, it is prone to fail in ways that lead to catastrophe. Complex technologies and inherently dangerous raw materials together mean that, no matter how much oversight and care there is, there will always be the potential for a worst case disaster.

In the late 1990s the Chemical Safety Board, a federal agency, conducted a study intended to provide a snapshot of America's chemical accidents. It was a pioneering study because before it, incredibly, no one had any idea of the total demographics of chemical accidents in the country. Not having a census of *accidents* involving the chemical industry means that no one had a good notion of the overall level of danger posed by the industry, its worst case potential.

The authors of the CSB report, entitled "The 600K Report: Commercial Chemical Incidents in the United States, 1987–1996," tried to draw on five existing government databases for their effort. They wanted, they said, to make "the workplace as safe as an airplane," and argued that having such data would help policy makers make more "objective" evaluations of what ought to be done to make the industry safer. The problem with present policy, according to the CSB, was that it wasn't clear that all the regulations on the industry were "having any positive impact" on health and safety.

In February 1999 a "special Congressional summary" of the report appeared. It starts out with a counterfactual: "Why does the industrial equivalent of two 737 airplanes 'crash' year after year, killing all passengers (256 people)? And why does no one seem to notice?" Good questions. The summary report acknowledged several deficiencies in its database. Each of the five source databases had been collected for a different purpose. Although that's true of most survey efforts, the problem here was the absence of a common set of rules for collecting the data. The authors noted that there were gaps in coverage and that there was no knowledge on "root causes" of the accidents; there was also difficulty eliminating duplicate reports. With those kinds of caveats, it would be prudent to draw conclusions tentatively, and not to subject the data to extremely technical analysis that would be sensitive to such inconsistencies.

The "600K Report" said, alarmingly, that "commercial chemical incidents . . . causing fatalities, injuries, evacuations or property damage . . . happen more frequently than most Americans would ever imagine. They occur all over the country, in every state, on railways, highways and waterways, and in all kinds of industry, government and commercial facilities." Some highlights cover the ten-year span:

- There were 605,000 chemical incidents (thus the "600K" of the title).
- 42 percent of the incidents happened at a fixed location.
- 43 percent were related to transportation (although, inexplicably, marine oil spills were ignored).
- 29 percent of the incidents resulted in at least one death or injury, evacuation of workers or the public, or property damage.

- Over the ten-year period there were almost twenty-six hundred deaths.
- Approximately ten thousand incidents resulted in at least one death or injury.
- California had the most incidents.

Thus, looking at just the *reported* incidents the picture was pretty bleak. The summary notes that "it is probable that many chemical incidents that occurred over those ten years never made it into any national records." The "600K Report" concluded that "the frequency of serious chemical incidents is significant enough to warrant national concern" and that "there is much to be learned about the nature of the 600,000 incidents in the nation's new but nascent composite federal database."

The "600K Report" was a rare example of comprehensive data gathering about a dangerous industry that might serve broad, rather than narrow, interests. That's true notwithstanding flaws in the data. But the Chemical Safety Board never released the Report. A board member told me that it "was never released as a Report because of technical inaccuracies/incompleteness" and said that "the underlying Government data bases that were used in the 600K drafts were found to be unable to support a sound statistical analysis." So much for that.

What really happened is that the chemical industry went ballistic. It's easy to see why. Forget about statistical analysis. Let's be conservative and cut the number of incidents in half. Call it the "300k Report." The problem still looks huge. Clearly the industry poses some fairly serious dangers for Americans.

It is harder and harder to get bad news about chemical accidents in the United States, appearances to the contrary. As part of the 1990 Clean Air Act, facilities with any significant amount of chemicals have to prepare what the EPA calls "Risk Management Plans"—basically worst case scenarios complete with projections of potential consequences. These projections are given the bureaucratic name "offsite consequence analyses," OCAs for short. The idea was to provide information to workers and communities about the risks they face. From the start, the chemical industry complained that terrorists might get their hands on the information. That is a legitimate worry, certainly. But denying terrorists an opportunity also denies workers and communities an opportunity. In 1999 an amendment to the Clean Air Act stipulated that a member of the public with government-issued identification (e.g., a driver's license) could visit a federal "reading room" to see up to ten OCAs each month. After 9/11 the EPA took the OCAs, and even the executive summaries of the risk management plans, off the Internet. The Right to Know Network (http://www.rtknet.org/) continues to provide access to the executive summaries.

The EPA scenarios should give us pause, for they may not represent the worst of the worst cases. They were, after all, produced by the very industry that creates the danger. And the industry's rubber rulers will be short. We can safely assume that their authors had a strong interest in not thinking outside the box in terms of danger. The U.S. chemical industry may be one of the safest in the world, but that should give us little comfort.

That said, I don't think chemical facilities themselves are what most expose us to potential toxic worst cases. They're often well-guarded and people know where they are—just knowing someone is keeping an eye on you will prompt some degree of self-regulation. Something more prosaic has the dubious honor of being our biggest threat: trains. The March 11, 2004, attack in Madrid, where al Qaeda killed nearly two hundred people with ten simultaneous explosions, gave us a peek at the potential carnage. But compared to the trouble that *could* issue from trains, Madrid was a small peek indeed.

WE COULD HAVE LOST BALTIMORE

On July 18, 2001, a sixty-car train owned by CSX caught fire in a tunnel under Baltimore. It was the kind of thing that people with long worst case rulers push regulators to consider. And just the kind of thing that regulators, with their shorter rulers, say is too extreme to worry about.

The train was carrying hydrochloric acid, among other dangerous chemicals, along with several cars of pulp material. It all made for an excellent fire. A high level CSX official would later say that it was the worst train accident he'd ever seen. It was, he said, "just short" of a real worst case.[13] As it happened, it was bad enough to slow down part of the backbone of the Internet and disrupt local telephone service. The train derailed at about three o'clock in the afternoon, and by nine that night all major highways into the city were closed to incoming traffic. A light grey haze drifted over much of central Baltimore. A baseball game at Camden Yards, where the Orioles play, had to be canceled. Seven thousand people in and around the Yards had to be evacuated. Weeks later, a combustible chemical, suspected of coming from the train, appeared in city sewers. A forty-inch water main above the tunnel broke, flooding some streets, collapsing others, hindering firefighting efforts, and knocking out electricity to twelve hundred people. Officials even sounded the city's civil defense sirens—for the first time since they were installed in 1952—although not until two and a half hours after the trouble began.

Baltimore city officials and the press took the event as a worst case wake-up call and began reexamining disaster contingency plans, emergency response procedures, and ways in which their city was vulnerable to chemical accidents and attacks. They discovered that the city wasn't anywhere near ready for a serious chemical incident. As one expert planner put it, "Nothing in [the plan] relates to the worst-case scenario."[14] Worse than that, so to speak, its 440-page emergency response plan barely mentioned chemical spills of any sort. And a *train-related* chemical accident wasn't even included in Baltimore's contingency plans because emergency planners believed a fire in a tunnel would burn itself out and because you can't do much about poison gas anyway. Since there are major chemical companies operating in and around Baltimore, one might have expected planners to be a bit more thoughtful.

But just imagine if a single rail car, which can carry ninety tons of chlorine, had been in the CSX lineup that day and had ruptured. One and a half million people could have been at risk. Baltimore could have been many Bhopals. A FEMA report says, "The derailment was unusual; the shipment was not. CSX reports that 40 freight trains run through Baltimore on an average day. Some days, all of them carry hazardous materials."[15]

The Baltimore tunnel fire was a worst case wake-up call for a lot of people. It has since become a controversial case in the battle over the federal government's plan to bury high-level nuclear waste under Yucca Mountain, in Nevada. Immediately after the fire people began to pose the following counterfactual: what if the CSX train had been carrying high-level nuclear waste? The Calvert Cliffs nuclear station is on the western shore of the Chesapeake Bay; the Department of Energy says that nuclear waste from that plant would be loaded onto a CSX train about sixty-five miles from Baltimore and then transported through the city.

The train's steel freight cars, according to witnesses, were so hot they were glowing orange. There are credible estimates that the fire burned at 1,600 degrees Fahrenheit for three days. Even the most conservative estimates are that it burned at 1,500 degrees Fahrenheit for twenty-four hours. The U.S. Nuclear Regulatory Commission's rule for transporting nuclear waste is that the containers must withstand 1,475 degrees for thirty minutes.

The state of Nevada took note of the fire, and commissioned a study by some experts in nuclear waste. Their models said that significant amounts of cesium-134 and cesium-137 could be released by such an accident. Through careful technical analysis, the consultants determined that a cask would likely have been breached that day in Baltimore. They estimated that twenty-four square miles around the accident site would be "lightly contaminated" or worse, and that the cleanup costs would run to fourteen billion dollars.[16]

Amazingly, officials in the Nuclear Regulatory Commission think the Baltimore experience was a success story. In a presentation to a committee of the National Academy of Sciences whose charge is to investigate the risks of transporting nuclear fuels and wastes, the director of the NRC's Spent Fuel Project Office claimed the case demonstrated the following (bullet points in original):

- Robust Nature of Cask is Evident
- Exposure of Transportation Cask to the Baltimore tunnel fire would not result in radioactive release
- Health and Safety of the Public Protected[17]

The rubber ruler at the NRC is short indeed.

It's not just Baltimore. Atlanta, San Francisco, or Houston could each be Bhopal. Trains run throughout the United States, and they regularly carry extremely dangerous substances. Chlorine is one such substance, and it is very widely used in American society: not just in swimming pools but in waste treatment centers and many industrial processes. Trains also regularly fall of their tracks and run into other things. According to the Federal Railroad Administration there were three thousand train accidents in the United States in 2001. It's a question of when, not if, a train accident—or a terrorist strike—leads to a worst case chemical event.

In June 2003 thirty-one freight cars, loaded with lumber, broke free in a shipping yard in Montclair, California. The train got up to seventy-five miles per hour as it barreled toward downtown Los Angeles. Workers decided to divert the runaway train to a sidetrack, because otherwise it would have slammed into a propane car. At the town of Commerce the train jumped the tracks, destroying six homes in a scene that from afar looked as though someone had dumped a hundred thousand matchsticks on a neighborhood of dollhouses. Luckily, no one was killed or even seriously injured. Luckily, the train wasn't carrying chlorine or nuclear waste.

In January 2005 thousands of people in Graniteville, South Carolina, weren't so lucky. A Norfolk Southern Railway train was rolling along at forty-five miles per hour when it missed a switch and slammed into a parked locomotive. Fourteen train cars derailed, including three that were carrying chlorine. One of the chlorine cars was punctured, and the gas killed nine people, caused hundreds more to seek medical treatment, and kept thousands from their homes while the wreckage was made safe.

You may recall from chapter 3 the terrifying example of the Burlington Northern freight-train accident. That train was carrying inflammable and toxic materials when it derailed near Duluth, Minnesota. The wreck sent more than twenty thousand gallons of toxic chemicals down the Nemadji River. More important, a tank car carrying highly volatile aromatic hydrocarbons fell upside down in the river and broke open. The car's contents evaporated, creating a vapor cloud twenty miles long and five miles wide. Before the crisis was over seventy-three people in Minnesota and neighboring Wisconsin were in the hospital and the National Guard had been called out. Some thirty to forty thousand people from Superior, Duluth, and surrounding areas were evacuated. Duluth could have been Bhopal.

As these few examples indicate, our trains regularly carry dangerous chemicals close to population centers. It can't be otherwise, because we need these chemicals to live our modern, consumption-oriented lives; we also need the trains to transport both the chemicals and our dangerous waste. A couple of million tank car loads of hazardous materials, nationwide, are shipped every year.[18] So our train system—necessary, dangerous, ubiquitous—presents a steady stream of possibilities for worst cases.

There are two further points to make here. One is that the kind of threat posed by these train-borne worst case possibilities represents an expanded domain of damage that is different from some other kinds of threats. Specifically, they have the potential to harm whole communities of people, not merely a bunch of unrelated individuals. Social scientists have pointed out that harming or killing five related people is importantly different than killing five separate individuals. Similarly twenty thousand people scattered across the country dying from cigarette smoke is different from twenty thousand people from the same town dying. It's not that one person's death is more valuable or more important than another's. But the situations are different. If smallpox were to wipe out twenty thousand people in Manhattan there would be losses in addition to the lives: to the culture, to people's sense of security, to their faith in their key institutions, to their networks of personal affiliations. Contrast that nightmare to the reality of twice that number of people dying every year on American roadways. Thus the worst case possibilities of train accidents like the ones in Baltimore or Duluth represent a different kind of assault, ones that it is entirely appropriate to fear and loathe.

In February 2001 the Environmental Protection Agency produced a report called "Lessons Learned in the Aftermath of September 11, 2001." The report was leaked to Greenpeace and other groups. It notes that:

Two specific incidents where security was a specific concern were identified: (1) railroads did not want to ship chlorine in tankers after attacks, but chlorine is needed to guarantee the safety of water supplies, and (2) EPA received requests [to] reroute chemical tankers and trucks away from the population centers.

The real point here is that some of our very worst cases lay in wait for us in the most prosaic of technologies. We can't live without trains, or at least we can't live the way we like to without them. They are part of our infrastructure and they enable our lifestyles. Given their importance, and their vulnerabilities, you'd think there would be a lot of oversight of the industry. There isn't. It's another case where the industry gets to police itself. It's true that railroads have to report their accidents, and it's true that the National Transportation Safety Board investigates important mishaps. That helps. But it's the production and transport of dangerous substances that need more oversight.

We see here another failure of imagination on the part of those who claim they would protect us from terrorism, and from calamity more generally. In addition to the attention to weapons of mass destruction, WMD, we need to worry a lot more about Instruments with Weapons Potential, IWP. Passenger jets are obviously IWP. So are trains.

SCAPEGOATING AND DEFLECTION

In Don DeLillo's novel *White Noise* a family gathers in front of the TV to eat Chinese food, as is their habit on Friday nights. They gather for the spectacle: "There were floods, earthquakes, mudslides, erupting volcanoes," says Jack Gladney, the book's protagonist. In near silence they watch as "houses slide into the ocean, whole villages crackle and ignite in a mass of advancing lava. Every disaster made us wish for more, for something bigger, grander, more sweeping." There is something about this that is not odd. There is an impulse in the culture that almost celebrates catastrophe. We don't actually wish it on people, but we like to watch. People slow down to gawk at the grizzly car wreck. Few things are more fascinating than footage of a plane crash. We all watched the World Trade Center towers fall and fall and fall. I have the clips on my computer and sometimes I play them; it's still almost as fascinating as the day it happened. DeLillo has a character say that we can "enjoy" California's mass murders, earthquakes, and brush fires because deep down "we feel that California deserves whatever it gets. Californians invented the concept of life-style. This alone warrants their doom."[19]

When things go wrong, especially when they go very badly wrong, we need to find a way to talk about it. We need to make up a story that puts the characters in their places, makes sense of the actions, and let's us walk away feeling safer or more superior. Stories about how disasters unfold can be told in many different ways. We can talk about calamity in terms of bad luck, evil spirits, or even randomness. In the Trobriand Islands, at least in Bronislaw Malinowski's day, natives invoked magic when faced with potential or actual danger. "We find magic," he wrote, "wherever the elements of chance and accident and the emotional play between hope and fear have a wide and extensive range. We do not find magic wherever the pursuit is certain, reliable, and well under the control of rational methods and technological processes."[20]

Of course, there are good reasons why modern people don't invoke magic to make sense of crashing space shuttles and pandemics. Why appeal to mysterious forces when we can actually see the cause of the trouble, which is usually "operator error" or "human error"? It's interesting that magic isn't available as an option with which to tell disaster stories. Western culture values, perhaps overvalues, control, and magic just can't provide actual control over anything. It can provide a *sense* of control, but that's not good enough when you want to figure out how to create construction codes so that tall buildings don't fall down when jetliners smash into them.

Be that as it may, one of the chief narratives in disasters, especially worst case ones, involves responsibility and blame. When things go wrong, somebody has to pay. This is especially true when powerful individuals make mistakes or do wrong things—they try their hardest to make others take the fall for them. Rare is the person of power who, like the mythical ship captain, accepts personal responsibility for organizational failure. In one kind of scapegoating one person or just a few are blamed for the shortcomings of others. These are brute-force power plays and they're important, but we've all seen them so often that they scarcely warrant analysis. Some of us have even been the goat. Another kind of scapegoating deflects attention from systemic problems, putting it on individuals.

Let's look at two cases of scapegoating to see how blame attribution works. On February 9, 2001, the U.S.S. *Greeneville,* a nuclear submarine patrolling near Hawaii, was preparing for an emergency drill in which the vessel surfaces rapidly. Commander Scott Waddle knew another vessel was in the area, so he rose to periscope depth to look around. After raising the periscope, he turned it around twice but didn't see anything. He changed the periscope's magnification and raised the submarine an additional two feet to increase his range of vision. Still the *Greeneville* surfaced under a Japanese fishing vessel, the *Ehime Maru,* sinking her and killing nine of the thirty-five people aboard.

The key failures in the *Greeneville* case were that Waddle didn't see the *Ehime Maru* when he surfaced and that no one else on the *Greeneville* corrected his mistake before it was too late. Apparently a technician aboard the *Greeneville* knew the *Ehime Maru* was nearby but never said anything. In the end, Waddle had to quit the Navy, accepting full responsibility for the disaster, which the Navy let him do without protest. Commander Waddle was of course responsible for both his submarine and his poor judgment. But that alone does not "explain" the disaster. A complicating condition was that there were sixteen civilians aboard the *Greeneville,* part of a Navy program that lets important and famous people have a submarine ride. The program is supposed to bolster support for the Navy. The Navy later confirmed the demonstration was done for the benefit of the civilian passengers. For a moment, the *Greeneville's* mission changed from being an instrument of national defense to being an entertainment park ride.[21]

If not for the added submariners, the accident probably wouldn't have happened. The technician testified that the crew may have been distracted from carrying out their duties because civilians were at the controls. Insofar as the Navy's program was responsible for the accident, blaming only Commander Waddle means the real problem wasn't properly diagnosed, and therefore the treatment—Waddle's retirement—wasn't enough to fix it.

Blaming individuals is usually insufficient to create understanding of why systems fail. But it's an easy and comfortable way to diagnose failures. If we can locate the bad guys, the evildoers, or the miscreant then the fix is easy. Just replace the bad guys with good guys. However, if the problem is the system itself—an organization, a technology, a program—then it is harder to fix. Social and technical systems are usually complex, so it's harder even to map out where the problem is.

On November 12, 2001, American Airlines Flight 587, an Airbus A300 bound for the Dominican Republic, crashed soon after takeoff from Kennedy International Airport. Two-hundred sixty people on the plane, plus five on the ground, were killed. Both of the plane's engines, as well as its tail section, were found some distance from where the fuselage slammed into the Queens neighborhood of Belle Harbor. At first there was a lot of speculation that it was another terrorist attack. It was, after all, only two months after 9/11. But investigators ruled out terrorism pretty quickly. They'd found the tail—which includes the rudder and the tail fin—mostly intact and it showed no signs of sabotage.[22]

But how in the world does a tail break off a jumbo jet? Early on, as one might expect, people looked closely at the tail's construction, for which Airbus uses composites, or carbon fiber–reinforced plastic. Commercial airliners started using composites for some airline parts in the 1970s and 1980s. Composites can be incredibly strong and are also very light, weighing as much as 25 percent less than aluminum. Too, they don't rust and are much less likely to weaken with continual flexing. Finally, composites can be made in larger pieces than aluminum, and with less labor. But there are problems with composites. They don't stretch or bend. And damage done to them isn't as readily apparent. Small cracks in composites can eventually lead to failure of the material. American Airlines, along with other airlines, inspected their Airbuses after the Flight 587 crash and said they found no problems. But "you have to be very careful with inspection of any minor cracking," said an engineer from Syracuse University. "It may snap very quickly."

A Japan Airlines 747, with the flight designation JL047, had taken off before American's Flight 587, and that may have contributed to the disaster. JL047 was cleared for takeoff at eight seconds past 9:11 a.m. but didn't actually leave until one minute later. Meanwhile the tower controller cautioned AA587 that there might be some turbulence and to hold position. Most airports wait two minutes between takeoffs, when the first plane is a 757 or larger aircraft, to lessen the effects of turbulence. The doomed flight started its takeoff roll, according to the NTSB, about 101 seconds after JL047. About a minute after AA587 departed the crew heard a squeak and a rattling sound, which has been interpreted as being caused by wake turbulence. About fifteen seconds later the plane yawed strongly to the right; experts say this would have been caused by the rudder, in the tail-section, moving hard right. Soon after the plane yawed to the right the first officer called for maximum power. During all this the airplane was exuding thumps and cracks and creaks, as we would expect of a plane breaking up in flight. As it descended from about twenty-five hundred feet both engines came off the wings. At 9:16 a.m. Flight 587 crashed into Queens.

The pilot and copilot had some indication that all was not well. In the following transcript, TWR means the Kennedy control tower, RDO indicates a radio transmission from AA587, Hot-1 is the pilot, and Hot-2 is the copilot:

0911:36 TWR American five eighty seven heavy Kennedy tower, caution wake turbulence runway three one left, taxi into position and hold.
0913:27.6 TWR American five eight seven heavy, wind three zero zero at niner, runway three one left, cleared for takeoff.
0913:31.7 RDO-1 Cleared for takeoff, American ah, five eight seven heavy.
0913:35.3 HOT-2 You happy with that distance?

0913:38.5 HOT-1 Aah, he's . . . we'll be all right once we get rollin'. He's supposed to be five miles by the time we're airborne, that's the idea.
0913:45.5 HOT-2 So you're happy. Lights?
0913:47.1 HOT-1 Yeah, lights are on.

The problem, everyone agreed, including Airbus officials, pilots, and other aviation experts, was that too much rudder had been applied. The best way to turn a plane is by using the wing surfaces (the ailerons), precisely to avoid excessive yaw. Of course, it's not at all inappropriate to use the rudder too, but you can use it *too* much. The first officer on Flight 587 used both ailerons and the rudder to control the plane, but clearly the rudder was used more. Some of his colleagues, who had trained or flown with him, told the NTSB that he tended to use the rudder too much; others said he didn't.

On February 8, 2002, the National Transportation Safety Board held a press conference about the ongoing investigation. It released two documents that day; one was a speech by the chair of the NTSB, Marion C. Blakey, and the other was a "safety recommendation." The board said that the big problem was "sequential full opposite rudder inputs," which means wagging the rudder back and forth quickly and with too much force. The pilot on Flight 587 was trying to control the aircraft, which was being buffeted to and fro in the 747's wake. Wagging the rudder too hard can be a problem because it can put too much stress on the aircraft's structure.

The board also said that its concern was "industry wide" and not focused only on the French-made Airbus A300. The French counterpart to the NTSB predictably concurred with the recommendations. The chair of the NTSB said, with no apparent irony, "Let me stress here—because it is very important that we all clearly understand that this recommendation is about pilot education and training—and is not a question of pilot error." She did not clarify how it could be anything other than pilot error if the problem was the pilot was slamming the rudder back and forth, causing the tail to fall off the aircraft. She also said, "To address any concern among the flying public—Let me point out once again, we are not aware of any prior events in which rudder movements have resulted in a separation of a vertical stabilizer or rudder." She also mentioned, briefly, that the NTSB was "studying the composite materials that make-up the vertical stabilizer of the aircraft."

The NTSB ended up making several recommendations to the Federal Aviation Administration. It recommended that pilots be instructed more fully about how rudders work; that training manuals be changed to reflect those understandings; and that new training procedures not be allowed to interfere with extant ones. The NTSB urged the FAA to "ensure that flight crews are not trained to use the rudder in a way that could result in dangerous combinations of sideslip angle and rudder position or other flight parameters." The FAA did order an inspection of tail sections of Airbus A300-600s and A310s, but it was a one-time *visual* inspection. No problems were found, but then they weren't really looking for problems in the first place. In March 2002, the FAA, Airbus, and the French civil aviation authority conducted ultrasonic inspections of six planes' tail attachment lugs, found no big problems, and stopped looking further.

The NTSB did not recommend, however, that there be frequent and close inspections of composite materials. It did not recommend an intensive investigation of the use by Airbus of composites in places that must bear significant forces. And it did not recommend an increase in the amount of time between takeoffs.

The effect of NTSB's statements was to blame the humans and exonerate the machines. Pilots call it "blaming the dead guy." That's a highly political move that works in the interests of some and against the interests of others. An alternative to the "pilot error" explanation for what happened to Flight 587 is that the composite material of which the tail was made was not up to the task of keeping the plane flying under adverse conditions. The French government owns a significant stake in Airbus and so naturally has a huge interest in avoiding such a conclusion. Additionally, recall the NTSB chair's statement that the agency didn't know of any "prior events in which rudder movements have resulted in a separation of a vertical stabilizer or rudder." That may be true in a technical sense. But there's a larger story.

On November 25, 2001, a Singapore Airlines Airbus A340 left Singapore with ninety-six souls aboard. Soon after takeoff the pilot started having trouble with the airspeed indicators. This incident, not mentioned in Blakey's announcement, was noted in an NTSB release of April 12, 2002, which said, "Among other things, there were overspeed warnings and large rudder movements *without pilot input*" (my emphasis). Luckily, the plane returned to Singapore without incident. In its final report on the AA587 crash, the NTSB relegated the A340 incident, and another one involving an A340, to a footnote because "neither event showed any evidence of rudder pedal use." The NTSB ruled these events were irrelevant because the rudder moved on its own! I think the Singapore near-accident strongly implicates the aircraft.

Subsequent work by the FAA and Airbus turned up *seven* A300 and A310 aircraft that had experienced strong "lateral" forces, which could have weakened the vertical stabilizers. On May 12, 1997, an A300 was near West Palm Beach, Florida, on descent into Miami, when it experienced many of the same movements that American Flight 587 would four years later. Over a period of about thirty-four seconds the plane dropped from sixteen thousand to thirteen thousand feet, after which it landed safely. The Safety Board decided that "the probable causes of this incident were the flight crew's failure to maintain adequate airspeed during level off, which led to an inadvertent stall, and their subsequent failure to use proper stall recovery techniques. A factor contributing to the accident was the flight crew's failure to properly use the auto throttle." Yet again the people were blamed while Airbus's technology was found blameless.[23]

There is yet another element of a alternative explanation for the crash of Flight 587 that never appeared in the official reports: production pressures in aviation. Flight 587, as noted, followed the takeoff of a Japan Airlines 747 after 101 seconds of waiting. The reason for the required separation between takeoffs is to let the vortices caused by the leading plane dissipate. When planes take off, the tips of their wings create vortices, basically minitornadoes, that trail the wingtips and create turbulence. What would have happened had Flight 587 waited a whopping three minutes? We don't know, and that ignorance deflects our attention from competing explanations for this terrible crash.

This is a sad example of narrowing the imagination so that some worst cases are ruled out of consideration. If the event of interest were stresses on the tails of airplanes it would be hard not to conclude that composites might be a problem. Once again the neglect of worst cases, relying on a short worst case ruler puts us at greater risk.

*

Disasters, even worst case ones, aren't special. Destruction is no more special than construction. Political struggle is also normal, even when the subject is large-scale devastation. Everyday life is political. So are worst cases. If we care about what produces them, how we should respond to them, how we might prevent some of them, we must understand the distribution of power that permeates societies.

Power, interests, and disagreements are shot through disasters and worst cases, often in subtle ways. We're used to thinking about political conflict as something that occurs mainly in the realm of elections, opinion polls, and making government budgets. Turning a political sensibility toward issues of failure, disaster, and worst cases takes us well outside the usual realms. Seeing catastrophe and calamity with a lens that focuses attention on power and interest illuminates many things. We again see, even more clearly, that disaster is entirely normal.

5

SILVER LININGS: THE GOOD FROM THE WORST

Disaster is normal. Worst cases abound. But common sense denies that, and most policy makers and academic writers approach calamity as if it were special. It is a mistake to regard disasters in general and worst cases in particular as separate from the ebb and flow of normal life. It's a mistake in academia, where "disaster studies" is seen as narrow, driven by an agenda set by funding agencies who also see disaster as abnormal. That's unfortunate, because we can use disaster to study important things about how and why people think and behave as they do. It's a mistake in social policy, too, to regard calamity as peculiar because it pushes policy makers to operate on incorrect assumptions about human nature. Bad policy is usually the result. As for common sense, people could make better, or at least more informed, choices about their lives were they to see disaster as normal.

Once we see disaster and catastrophe, like death, misery, happiness, and boredom, as a normal part of life several things are thrown into sharp relief. We see that destruction happens in disasters in ways that are not random: there are patterns. These patterns tend to mirror the ways humans organize their societies: along lines of wealth and poverty, division of labor, access to health care, membership in organizations, to name a few. We see that catastrophe is never bad for *everybody*—alongside suffering and grief is often someone's advancement. We see that disasters provide occasions for the creation of heroes—ordinary people who, as a result of catastrophe, find themselves taking actions that others regard as extraordinarily unselfish and brave. (You can't be a hero unless other people call you a hero.) In this way worst cases provide something that many people, and not just the anointed hero, need. Additionally, once we come to regard calamities—even worst cases—as normal, we see that they provide opportunities to learn about how things work. We may not need airplane crashes, but attentive minds can learn from them. Earthquakes, hurricanes, and fallen bridges can be opportunities to learn of our faults. And disaster *can* lead to general social betterment, to policies or courses of action that redound to the greater good of society.

So disasters aren't all bad. They often have silver linings.

People sometimes say that tragedy builds character, that losing builds strength, and that all things, even bad things, are for the good. That's nonsense. Such homilies are usually meant to get the downtrodden and the disenfranchised to accept their lot in life. If it were so wonderful and fortifying to lose and suffer the rich and powerful would be eager to give away their money and abdicate their positions. We may learn lessons from tragedy, but character is built from living a life according to a sense of moral standards. Character is formed over time, through many experiences and reflections, rather by a single, jarring event. We may, should, learn after a great hurricane that power lines ought to be buried so that the next storm won't again cause them to fall on houses and cause fires. But that doesn't mean that the hurricane, or the house fires, made people stronger.

Individuals don't need disasters. Neither do societies. People don't need to suffer any more than society needs poverty. Groups don't need disasters any more than countries need wars to stay healthy. The main problem with saying that society needs disaster is that such a statement seems to *explain* why disaster happens. If we translate that notion into examples we immediately see how silly it is: tornadoes happen because lumber companies need to sell wood to builders, the World Trade Center was destroyed because the United States needed to feel cohesive. That logic is backward, confusing causes with consequences.

But there are benefits, at least for some, from suffering, poverty, disasters, wars, and terrorist attacks. Debilitating depression provides an income for psychotherapists. Poverty provides the premise for entire government bureaucracies—not to mention a ready scapegoat for right-wing commentators. War can be just fine for the winners, arms makers, and rebuilders. The consequences that disasters can have are

multiple and complex. Society in general can benefit and so can particular individuals and groups.

The point is that worst cases, and disasters in general, are not just
untoward, random events that we try to prepare for and recover from.
Rather they are patterned phenomena with complex causes and effects.
They are also opportunities for learning, for political gaming, for the
development of new ideas, and even for profit. Worst case events aren't
the worst for everybody involved.

STRUCTURED DESTRUCTION AND INEQUITIES OF THE MOMENT

John McPhee describes how the Army Corps of Engineers tries to tame
rivers, especially the Mississippi, in Louisiana:

Something like half of New Orleans in now below sea level. New Orleans,
surrounded by levees, is emplaced between Lake Pontchartrain and the
Mississippi like a broad shallow bowl. Nowhere is New Orleans higher
than the river's natural bank. Underprivileged people live in the lower
elevations, and always have. The rich—by the river—occupy the highest
ground. In New Orleans, income and elevation can be correlated in a lit-
erally sliding scale.[1]

Being poor is worse than being rich in most places. In New Orleans it
can be fatal. Seventy-five percent of those who died in the World Trade
Center collapse were white, and men were considerably more likely
than women to have died. We might even say that in the WTC disaster
white men experienced institutional discrimination, although I don't
expect anyone would actually say that.

Such cases contradict the common way to think about big disasters, which is that they're random. Monster hurricanes do seem capricious, coming from warm waters (usually), striking blindly and indis-
criminately. In such cases, cause and consequence appear untouched
by humans. Even so-called technological disasters, although obviously
not caused by natural forces, appear to be characterized by randomness. At Three Mile Island and Chernobyl a great number of seemingly unrelated failures came together in unpredictable ways. Had the
TMI meltdown breached containment, the effects of massive atomic

contamination would have been somewhat predictable. But the degree of actual contamination would have depended chiefly on wind direction, and the wind is capricious. At Chernobyl, the wind initially blew away from Kiev but then, about ten days later, switched direction and blew toward it. The effects of disasters, especially worst case disasters, seem always to be arbitrary and capricious.

This perception is comforting in the sense that it relieves anyone of the responsibility to do something about them. This happens in other areas too, for instance, poverty. If poverty is caused by, say, the random distribution of genetic factors, then not only is the present distribution of valuable resources natural but there's little that social policies can do to make things better. But if poverty is caused by lack of access to political and material power, then it follows that policies could be instituted to decrease the problem. We could do something, then, about people not having enough to eat, enough medical care, or decent housing. Randomness is reassuring because it fosters the impression that society is fair. If everyone is equally subject to the vagaries of death and destruction we can throw up our hands and say, *c'est la vie.*

The reality is cruelly different. Georgia's "deadliest" tornado since 1944 killed eighteen people in February 2000. "Capricious Georgia Tornadoes Killed Young and Old," announced the headline in the *New York Times:* "The storm selected its victims from across the spectrum of life, taking both those who were nearing the end and those who had barely begun." The article stressed that the dead were separated by place and generation, evidence of the disaster's unpredictability.[2] The response is almost automatic: What a tragedy—there truly is no protection from fickle fate.

But there's more pattern in disaster than might be apparent. The *Times*'s story could have been told differently. All of the dead had lived in trailers. A mother and her infant daughter were killed when their trailer was blown into a field of kale and collard greens. Lee Hancock and his wife lived in a 1900 farmhouse, which was blown to bits but from which they "emerged without a scratch." Mr. Hancock's father, however, lived in a trailer next door. His body was found in a field some distance away.

Or consider the great heat wave in Chicago in 1995. Over seven hundred people died that summer in the "worst heat wave" ever to happen in the United States, according to sociologist Eric Klinenberg.[3] Heat waves in general are underappreciated as causes of misery and death.

Between 1960 and 1995 heat waves accounted for more U.S. deaths than all other meteorological events combined. This one took place over about a week in the middle of July. Unlike many worst cases, this one could have been prevented. Government officials were warned that trouble was coming but failed to implement their heat emergency plan in time. Fully one-half of the people who died could have been saved if they'd just had air conditioning. They didn't have air conditioning because they were poor. In fact everyone who died was poor. Almost all of them were old; they were also disproportionately African American. Men, to the surprise of many, were at greater risk of dying from the heat than women. That's because men's social networks were more fragile than women's. Social networks made the difference between life and death for people who didn't have water and air conditioning. Those who died, died alone. But the point I'm interested in here is that the disaster didn't strike randomly. It singled out people who were poor, old, isolated, and male.

Poor people often suffer disproportionately in disasters. This should be obvious because poor people get the worst of everything we value most. They lack sufficient health care because they can't afford it or because they don't work for large organizations that provide decent health insurance. They lack good schools because the inhabitants of their neighborhoods don't provide enough of a tax base. Their political interests are insufficiently represented because they don't vote and are politically unorganized. Their plight is forever with them.

In environmental studies, a fairly popular and consistent "finding" is that poor people are more likely to be subjected to environmental contaminants. They are more likely to live close to hazardous waste treatment, storage, and disposal facilities. And chemical facilities are more likely to move into, or close to, neighborhoods or communities that are disproportionately poor and black.[4] "Cancer Alley," an eighty-mile stretch along the Mississippi River between New Orleans and Baton Rouge, Louisiana, is cited as the premier example of "environmental racism" in the United States. Cancer Alley is the site of many petrochemical plants, and some studies have found elevated frequencies of cancers among its mostly black and poor denizens.

A small social movement now pushes the cause of environmental justice. Its basic idea is that poor people, especially nonwhite poor people, are more likely than other people, especially relatively rich white people, to be put at risk of such harm. As the above examples suggest, there is evidence for that. Poor people are more likely to live in trailers than rich people, and trailers are more likely than houses to be blown into vegetable fields when a tornado comes screaming through. Poor people are less likely than rich people to have political and economic connections in, say, the Texas and Louisiana governors' offices and, for that reason alone, are more likely to be subjected to the dangers of having a facility with noxious chemicals close by.

Patterns of suffering that follow divisions of race or class, as in the examples above, are examples of *structured destruction*. They are structured because there is some degree of organization, some recognizable shape, to them. Structured destruction is a generic term that is useful in analyzing the consequences of disasters. Once alerted to the idea, we can more easily see how patterns work before and after calamity.

A story of structured destruction arises, for example, from the broken hull of the *Titanic*. Although the myth evolved that the rich sacrificed themselves to save the poor, the truth is darker and more banal. The table on page 135 shows the *Titanic*'s survival rate by cabin location, which corresponds to social class.[5]

It is true that a higher percentage of women and children survived, compared to men. Three times more women and children than men survived in first class, and similarly lop-sided proportions hold for second class and steerage. But if you compare the survival rates *across* classes, it is clear that the rich made out better than the poor. Fully 62 percent of first class passengers survived, as against 41 percent of those in second class and 25 percent of those in steerage. Women and children *were* saved first, but women and children in first class were more than twice as likely to survive as women and children in third class. Men in first class were similarly more likely to survive than their poorer brethren. The *Titanic* illustrates nicely the idea of structured destruction.

Another pattern in big disasters is that women often suffer disproportionately. Disaster researchers refer to "front-line caregivers," people who take care of others; women tend to do more of that than men, performing more of the emotional work involved in disaster recovery. Two researchers note that women are "particularly subject to environmental risks through urban displacement and migration, environmental degradation, migration, poverty, and other limits to choice." That happened after Hurricane Andrew, one of our worst hurricanes ever, struck in 1992. Women's economic losses were often hidden because

Percentage of passengers surviving *Titanic,* by cabin
location and sex (base *n* in parentheses)

	1ST CLASS	2ND CLASS	STEERAGE
Total	62 (325)	41 (285)	25 (706)
Men	33 (175)	8 (168)	16 (462)
Women and children	97 (150)	89 (117)	42 (244)

unpaid work is hard to price. Non-English-speaking women were es-pecial targets for exploitation by landlords and money-grubbers.

So one common pattern, sometimes more asserted than demon-strated, is that the stratification of suffering in disasters mirrors the stratification in society as a whole, following the major lines of inequal-ity: race, class, and gender.

But structured destruction can take other forms. Race, class, and gender—the Holy Trinity in writings about inequality—concern *vertical* conceptions of inequality that focus our attention on power dif-ferentials. They are vertical in that, for certain statements about the categories to make sense, some people have to be seen as "above" and others as "below" on some scale of value. Two social scientists con-cerned with the matter, for instance, say, "Unsustainable global pat-terns of settlement, resource management, social organization, and political economy increasingly put some population groups more than others at risk from disaster. . . . When the dust clears or the waters recede, poor families around the world suffer the greatest losses and have access to the least public, as well as private, recovery assets, both in developing postcolonial societies and wealthy industrial nations like the United States."[6] For such a proclamation to make sense somebody has to control more resources, especially wealth, than someone else. Somebody has to be on the top, and somebody has to be on the bottom.

But people are organized *horizontally* as well as vertically, in ways that involve no hierarchical, or power, relationship. The notion of struc-tured destruction draws attention to the myriad ways that social, eco-nomic, and political life are organized. Not only poor people suffer in patterned ways.

Consider the crash of one of Air France's Concorde aircraft, in July 2000. It was the "worst" Concorde accident ever. The plane caught fire on takeoff and the pilot soon lost control. The plane smashed into a small wooden hotel, demolishing it. One hundred thirteen people died in that crash, four of whom were on the ground. It cost nearly eleven thousand dollars to cross the Atlantic on Concorde, which has since been grounded for cost. Most likely, everyone on that plane was rich.[7] So there was certainly a pattern of suffering in the Concorde case, in that rich people were at disproportionate risk.

People's lives are organized in many ways. During the day, in modern societies, most people's lives are organized by formal organizations, because most people in modern societies work in such places. If people gather for a professional conference of some sort, for a time their lives will be organized by occupational category. Imagine that the Tort Trial and Insurance Practice Section of the American Bar Association is having a conference in Oklahoma City. TIPS, as they call themselves, has twenty-five thousand members. Now imagine that two or three tornadoes rip through Oklahoma City at the same time. That's not as far-fetched as it might sound. An F5 tornado struck Oklahoma City in 1999. F5 is the highest, the worst, rating on the Fujita scale, which is used to measure the destructiveness of tornadoes, and is defined thus:

Incredible Damage. Strong frame houses leveled off foundations and swept away; automobile-sized missiles fly through the air in excess of 100 meters (109 yds); trees debarked; incredible phenomena will occur.[8]

In May 2003 Oklahoma City had two very large tornadoes in as many days, during the nation's most tornado-stricken week on record. If such a storm ripped through a TIPS conference the carnage could be massive. Under their breath some people might mumble about divine justice. But objectively it would be an instance of horizontal structured destruction, with tort lawyers as victims. Or, staying in Oklahoma City, think of the destruction of the Alfred P. Murrah Federal Building, in 1995, America's worst terrorist attack to that point. That disaster wasn't organized by class, or race, or sex. It disproportionately struck people who worked for the federal government.

The idea of structured destruction broadens attention from fairness and equity to the myriad ways that disaster and catastrophe affect people. It's wrong to say that destruction is always distributed so that poor, nonwhite, female people get the worst deal. How shall we assess the damage at the World Trade Center? I am not aware of any systematic research on the differential effects of the attacks. It's common to see enumerations of the many countries that were represented among the victims, which are used precisely to show, incorrectly, that there were no patterns. But bond traders were differentially exposed to risk of death. The brokerage house of Cantor Fitzgerald lost about two-thirds of its thousand employees that morning. Probably few of those employees were poor. In fact most of them were probably white, male, and financially well-off.

These are *inequities of the moment.* Sometimes occupation matters, sometimes the kind of organization that you work for. Sometimes gender or race or class matters. Sometimes the inequality of the moment is geographically based. The Insurance Institute for Highway Safety collects all kinds of information on the chronic American disaster that is automotoring. In July 2000 it issued a press release on the hundreds of annual roadway deaths caused by people running red lights. Phoenix, Arizona, had the highest death rate per one hundred thousand people in crashes where red lights weren't obeyed for the period studied, the years 1992 through 1998. Compared to other places, at least on that dimension, it was more dangerous to live and drive in Phoenix.[9] It's an example of an inequity of the moment.

People suffer and die in the same ways that they live, which is to say in patterned, nonrandom ways. There are patterns in where people choose to live, where they go to work, with whom they eat lunch, and with whom they spend their leisure time. Because of that patterning, disasters in general and worst cases in particular can always be expected to damage some people disproportionately. Thus in yet another way do we see that disaster is a normal part of life.

WINNING AND LOSING IN DISASTERS

Death, destruction, and suffering are aligned with the institutional arrangements that organize our lives. Calamity and horror are thus intimately and inexorably connected to social forces and social organization. Sometimes—I wouldn't dare to guess the frequency—a group of people will win in calamity *because* another group has lost.

Harry Widener was a rich young man who went down with the *Titanic.* His mother wanted to commemorate him so she gave Harvard

University two million dollars, a considerable sum at the time, to build a library. Today Harvard calls the Widener Library the "flagship" of its library system. The sinking of the *Titanic* was good for Harvard.

Short of the total annihilation of humanity, there will be winners as well as losers in calamities. The oncologist needs people to have cancer. The undertaker has more work when more people die. Huge calamities give disaster relief organizations a reason to exist. There are many ways in which groups use and benefit from disaster. Many professions, after all, depend for their existence on misery and mayhem. The police benefit from crime, and the threat of crime. Psychiatrists need individuals' lives to implode, just as dentists need tooth decay. Imagine what would happen if all mental illness and social problems disappeared tomorrow. The carnage caused by tobacco smoking is good not only for tobacco companies but for nurses, radiologists, and hospitals. State governments all over the United States have profited handsomely from suing tobacco companies. A substantial proportion, perhaps a majority, of social scientists depend on failure and breakdown for problems to figure out and things to say in the classroom.

On September 10, 2001, President George W. Bush was an unpopular president, handed the election by a politically biased Supreme Court. He was widely seen as lacking vision and imagination. But his ratings soared after 9/11. A week after the attacks, a Gallup poll found that 91 percent of the population approved of how he was handling the situation, and that general approval of Congress was 75 per cent. This was the highest approval rating Congress had ever garnered.[10] The same could be said of New York mayor Rudolph Giuliani. At the time of the attacks he was facing a hostile public and press over his high-handed dealings and disastrous personal life. After 9/11 Giuliani was a hero and will now be remembered that way.

Byron Callan, an aerospace industry analyst with Merrill Lynch, said that while the space shuttle *Columbia* accident was likely to have a minimal financial impact on Boeing and Lockheed, it raised questions about the future of the nearly thirty-year-old shuttle program and could prompt NASA and Congress to accelerate plans to replace it. "The paradox of this disaster is that it could provide the spark for a rebirth of the industry," said Loren Thompson, an analyst at the Lexington Institute, a military research institute in Arlington, Virginia. "It is finally focusing attention on a problem that needs to be addressed."[11]

Disasters often involve power plays and conflicts of interests. They can create silver linings for specific groups of people. Economists distinguish between private and social goods. A private good is a product or service that benefits a specific agent (a person, say, or a corporation). An automobile is a private good because the benefit from its manufacture and sale redounds to those who made and sold the car. A public good benefits society more broadly, and it is hard to limit them to a select few. Examples of public goods are education or military protection. There is general benefit to society if people are educated; the same is true if everyone is protected.

Catastrophes produce several kinds of public goods. They provide hero stories, they provide impetus for social change, and they provide a stimulus for stretching the imagination. The last two are more important than the first. These are sociopolitical goods in that social change and expanded imagination can lead to the material and cultural advancement of society. Our culture can become more interesting, our political institutions more resilient, our organizations smarter. But first let's look at heroes.

WHAT HEROES DO

One way that people recover from worst case disasters is by building heroes. We imbue people with special qualities. They are especially wonderful, exceptionally brave, or extraordinarily giving. They are strong and protect others. Children may see such qualities in Superman or Batman, adults in John F. Kennedy or John Wayne. Heroes are icons of hope and goodness. They mitigate agony and despair.

In the World Trade Center story firefighters and police officers were celebrated as great heroes. FDNY baseball caps could be seen everywhere, especially on Mayor Giuliani. The iconographic heroes helped in the national healing, since people could tell themselves that in an event marked by evil and horror there were instances of the true and the good. If there were heroes then there was hope. It barely went noticed— and in saying this I do not mean to take anything away from the efforts of the good people who faced down danger that day—that it was these people's job to go into a burning building to help others. Furthermore, they didn't know the buildings were going to collapse when they went charging in. Even the firefighters who were in the north tower when the south tower collapsed didn't know that their immediate environs were likely to disintegrate. The officers and firefighters who died that day were certainly brave, but it was not over-the-top bravery, as was the case with the passengers of Flight 93, who crashed their aircraft into a Pennsylvania field. Those people knew they were likely to die but that their deaths could prevent some unknown but greater terror.

People like to find silver linings, and heroes are one way to do that. The *Titanic* was barely on the ocean bottom before hero stories started to appear. The stories had a particular theme, too, valorizing the rich men in first class who were said to have gallantly sacrificed themselves, deferring to the "rule of the sea": women and children first. There was even a tale of some of these men using guns to prevent poorer men—especially men with darker skin and foreign accents—from claiming places in the lifeboats over the meek and the helpless. Here's an example from the *San Francisco Examiner,* written less than two days after ship went down:

The picture that invariably presents itself . . . is of men like John Jacob Astor, master of scores of millions; Benjamin Guggenheim of the famous family of bankers; Isidor Straus, a merchant prince; William T. Stead, veteran journalist; Major Archibald W. Butt, soldier; Washington Roebling, noted engineer—of any or all of these men stepping aside, bravely, gallantly remaining to die that the place he otherwise might have filled could perhaps be taken by some sabot-shod, shawl enshrouded, illiterate and penniless peasant woman from Europe.

Much of that was riotously exaggerated and even fabricated. The only evidence journalists had to support such a tale was *Titanic*'s last message: "Sinking by the head. Have cleared boats and filled them with women and children."[12] Alas, the vaunted "rule of the sea" has been quite flexible; sometimes it is followed, sometimes not. There is disagreement about whether it was actually applied on *Titanic.* There's never been much evidence that those rich white men committed all those acts of selfless bravery. In fact, given that their survival rates were greater than those of the less-well-off men, we might surmise the opposite. The larger point here is that the *Titanic,* like the World Trade Center and other worst cases, provided opportunities for telling tales about heroes. It is in the tale telling that heroes are created.

Hero stories have other consequences too. In the *Titanic* case the stories helped justify vast inequities of wealth and power. The Astors and others like them were transformed from somewhat suspect plutocrats and leisure seekers into the very essence of goodness, or even godliness. The tale is also one of racism: no stories appeared of swarthy poor people from southern Italy saving anyone, not even the weak. The tale also reconfirms traditional gender roles, affirming that real men take care of their women and children. "In the midst of harrowing recitals," crowed one editorial, "shines the heroism of American manhood, which protected the weak and helpless." Upon their return home, male survivors of the *Titanic* had to endure rumors that they cross-dressed to save themselves.

Could society live without heroes? Probably. It might even be good to dethrone heroes, for they are but ordinary mortals in extraordinary circumstances—or, sometimes, in made-up circumstances. But cultures, like America's, that vaunt individualism as their highest value can make great use of calamities to create heroes. Worst cases provide that silver lining.

IMAGINATION STRETCH

"Catastrophes are great educators of mankind," said the Harvard sociologist Pitirim Sorokin.[13] They can teach us what we're doing right and point out where we need improvement. Calamity can provide new experiences and opportunities for observation that lead to advances in scientific and technical knowledge.

This is a silver lining, but we shouldn't be too sanguine about it. *How* learning happens matters as much as *what* is learned. After big disasters there often follows an investigation by some august government body—the Presidential Commission on the Space Shuttle Challenger Accident, the President's Commission on the Accident at Three Mile Island, the National Commission on Terrorist Attacks upon the United States, and so on. Sometimes the investigation is mainly symbolic, which usually results in poor learning. The Chicago mayor's office investigated the disastrous 1995 heat wave that I mentioned earlier, but the investigators ended up chiefly blaming the dead people for their own plight. That's not learning well. Hindsight is, of course, always twenty-twenty, and investigations too often are conducted in such a way as to find the obvious "failure" or "mistake" and then stop, as if that were The Cause of the disaster. One problem with this sort of approach is that it leads to scapegoating—once we discover that Captain Hazelwood of the *Exxon Valdez* had been drinking there's no reason to look further.

Scapegoating is the antithesis of hero creation, though both emphasize the qualities of the individual. We blame the drunken sailor and pass tougher laws on sailing while drunk. Then the regulators can say they've done their job of protecting the public. Politicians can thump their chests that they've rooted out the problem. And the public, if we buy into this sort of charade, can go back to feeling all's right with the world, at least until next time. Not only is scapegoating unfair, but it's usually wrong, in the sense that it uses simplistic explanations for complex events. Hazelwood may have been drinking (though a jury acquitted him of driving while under the influence), but the instructions he gave to his officers on how to sail the boat were, by all accounts, exactly the right ones. He should have been on the bridge and he wasn't, but it's not as if he were a besotted idiot who slammed his boat head-on into an iceberg. Ultimately the captain bears responsibility for whatever happens on his ship, but that's a legalism and a convention, not an explanation for how a complex system fails.

Here's another example of learning poorly. Leo Tasca is team leader for Special Projects at the Ontario Ministry of Transport, in Canada. Some years ago Tasca wrote his doctoral dissertation on how the idea of "human error" gets built into marine accident reports of the U.S. National Transportation Safety Board. Tasca found that the social context of building accident reports profoundly affected what was identified as the "cause." "NTSB accident analyses," he said, "place an emphasis on shipboard operators and what they did or did not do to avoid an accident." By so doing NTSB analyses often miss the larger context of an accident.[14]

On May 9, 1980, at 7:33 a.m., the freighter *Summit Venture* rammed into the Sunshine Skyway and knocked out a twelve-hundred-foot length of the bridge across the mouth of Tampa Bay. A Greyhound bus, a pickup truck, and six cars fell 150 feet, killing thirty-five people. Most of the dead were in the bus. It is called one of the worst bridge accidents in American history. Personnel aboard the *Summit* said they had zero visibility because heavy thunderstorms were blowing that morning. The NTSB, and the U.S. Coast Guard, duly decided the cause of the accident was the pilot's failure to understand that he needed to stop his vessel when faced with zero visibility, high winds, and loss of "radar presentation," which means the radar couldn't see the bridge. We can all agree that if you're driving a vessel that's nearly six hundred feet long and you can't see where you're going you should stop. The captain was negligent. But, as Tasca says, the story could be told differently. The story could emphasize the ship owner's reliance on an inexperienced crew. Or it could stress production pressure—cargo at rest is cargo losing money—which is probably the deeper reason that the pilot was willing to take the risk in the first place. There is no guarantee that disasters will teach us the right things. We can learn poorly, in which case the lining is leaden, or we can learn well, in which case the lining is silver.

Another example is the Tacoma Narrows Bridge, which twisted itself apart in 1940. "Galloping Gertie" was a beautiful suspension bridge with an innovative, shallow design that gave it a dramatically low profile from the side. The alternative was to use open trusses, which are necessarily deeper but less aesthetically appealing. The problem was that the bridge's sleek design made it work like an airplane wing in turbulence. The bridge had twisted and bounced in production, but the complete, worst case failure of the bridge in forty-mile-per-hour winds was unforeseen by engineers. Their theoretical models said the bridge would perform well, and the similarly designed Bronx-Whitestone bridge in New York City *had* done reasonably well (although that bridge, too, has had its share of problems). Experience had trapped the engineers, limiting their imaginations and visions in ways that confirmed what they already believed. But this is, after all, a chapter on silver linings. The brightest lining here is that such a collapse is not likely to happen again. After Galloping Gertie fell apart, engineers started studying the phenomenon of aerodynamic instability in bridges, an idea previously unformed in their minds.[15]

What happens when we learn well? The generic thing that happens is that routine patterns of thought are disrupted. When such disruptions happen, the opportunity is created to excite the imagination and expand conceptual horizons. Falling back on "human error," as in the marine accident reports, is an example of missing the opportunity. It doesn't have to be that way. Disasters and worst cases can lead to thinking outside the box, as the saying goes. For instance, business scholars Karl Weick and Kathleen Sutcliffe say that some organizations do a better job than others at anticipating the unexpected. A key reason for this, they say, is precisely because some organizations approach failure and disaster in nonstandard ways. In the corporate world, disasters are usually seen as exclusively bad things. After they happen, some worker, manager, or procedure—or, rarely, an executive—is identified as the culprit and then excised. But Weick and Sutcliffe say there's another option.

Effective [high-reliability organizations] both encourage the reporting of errors and make the most of any failures that are reported. In fact, they tend to view any failure, no matter how small, as a window on the system as a whole. They view any lapse as a signal of possible weakness in other portions of the system.[16]

Such organizations think outside the box. Failure is fine. Disaster is an opportunity. Calamities hold silver linings that can lead to the creation of new ideas.

Disasters drive new ideas. Worst cases can lead to *imagination stretch*. They can provide material incentives and situations that propel innovation. In other words, conflicts of interest are both laid bare and spur the creation of new ideas. Out of the Enron and Worldcom catastrophes, in which corporate executives reaped outrageous fortune at employees' expense, there arose new understandings of how aspects of the financial system—especially the granting of stock options as a form of compensation—could make the system more likely to fail and ultimately undermine its legitimacy.

Let's briefly revisit the Triangle Shirtwaist fire of 1911. Owners, some say, had locked the doors to keep the workers at their sewing machines. It was a "disaster waiting to happen"; the building was a "death trap." It was surely bad for the immigrant girls who jumped to their deaths to avoid being burned alive. But out of that worst case fire came considerable good. The poignant stories of the victims led to a "life safety code." The Triangle Shirtwaist disaster was a bellwether in the history of building safety. New fire codes would be written to prevent a recurrence of the catastrophe. It also led to a rethinking of procedures and equipment in fire departments. The Triangle Shirtwaist incident would have been a fire-response success story—firefighters and their equipment arrived on the scene very quickly—except that the firefighters' ladders couldn't reach high enough to save victims on higher floors, and they had no way to catch the jumpers. And it was also a great opportunity for the International Ladies' Garment Workers Union to organize and push for labor reforms. Worst cases can make new ideas possible. They can also make it so that existing rules are enforced. Even before the fire it was obvious that locking doors can be dangerous, but because of it exits were less likely to be obstructed in the future.

When the Soviet Union launched the first Sputnik on October 4, 1957, it was widely regarded within American scientific and political circles as one of the worst things that could have happened. It was a different kind of disaster than the Triangle Shirtwaist fire. But it was a disaster nonetheless, because it indicated that the Soviets now had the capability to send an atomic warhead any place on the planet. Some scientists even speculated that the Russians might send a satellite to blow up the moon with an H-bomb during an upcoming solar eclipse, to commemorate the Bolshevik Revolution. It was a crushing blow for the United States, which had an image of itself as the leader in technological and military prowess. And yet there were gains from Sputnik, and not only for the Soviets. America's space program got a massive infusion of resources. Beyond that, concern that the math and science curricula in America's schools were not sufficient preparation for rocket science led to reforms in education and an increased concentration on those two areas. Between the late 1950s and the 1970s, school expenditures went up 275 percent. State spending on higher education accounted for 21 percent of total expenditures in 1950, 32 percent by 1960, and nearly 40 percent by 1970. Out of a disastrous event came a program that would change the way we look at our universe.[17]

The airline industry provides a final example of idea generation. Few things are dreaded more than the possibility of two commercial airliners smashing together in flight. But there are silver linings in near misses. Research shows that after reported near misses airline pilots increase their own reporting of near misses. It isn't clear if the increase indicates greater danger or if pilots are just reporting more. The Federal Aviation Administration uses the reports as descriptions of possibilities not previously considered. This is an example of creating conditions that lead to wise learning. Pilots can report dangerous conditions anonymously, with few limitations and without fear that their reports can or will be used against them. In aviation, imagination stretch is facilitated by having many interests represented in gathering information about risk and by muting the threats of punishment and blame.[18]

For all the trouble they can cause we are sometimes saved by the stretched imaginations of engineers, emergency planners, policy makers, disaster response personnel, and even insurance companies. Events and imagined events are used as opportunities for learning. Imagination stretch occurs when the usual categories of thought are expanded or added to so that new possibilities are considered. Worst cases and potential worst cases can be remarkably beneficial in creating ideas, advancing knowledge, and even promoting social betterment.

The Y2K scare led to a lot of computers being fixed. Fixing computers, however, was a relatively minor silver lining of Y2K. There were more important gains. One was that organizations that invested in upgrades substantially increased capital improvements, redounding to greater productivity in the future. Even more important, and more to the point in the present context, is that fear of Y2K led to significant amounts of imagination stretch. Y2K contingency planning led organizations to recognize hidden interdependencies in their systems. Y2K preparations helped organizations to learn about *systems of systems*. Extensive preparation, and organizational learning, account in large part for why we did not see important failures on January 1, 2000. Worst case thinking can facilitate organizational learning by forcing managers to imagine possibilities that might not otherwise have occurred to them.

Safety engineers and airline crash investigators regularly rush to the site of tragedy, so they can figure out how to prevent future ones. Without those crashes, investigators would be far less likely to imagine novel conditions that can endanger lives. Most people who fly have probably heard of a "microburst." A microburst is a small downdraft that can create a burst of 150-mile-per-hour winds on or near the ground. Microbursts, a form of wind shear, are shaped like an upside-down mushroom and can have devastating effects on aircraft that fly through them. Because of how the wind spreads out after it hits the ground a pilot can experience a hard downdraft, a headwind, and then an intense tailwind within a matter of seconds.

That's just what happened to an Eastern Airlines 727 on June 24, 1975. Flight 66 was trying to land at JFK airport when it hit the approach lights in a heavy thunderstorm. The plane was destroyed; of the 124 people aboard, 113 perished. But the worst airline disaster caused by a microburst happened at about 4 p.m. on July 9, 1982, when a Pan Am 727 with 145 aboard took off from New Orleans International Airport. There were some showers along the flight's intended takeoff path and a few gusty winds, but neither of those conditions are threatening to aircraft. Yet the plane, according to the National Transportation Safety Board, got only to perhaps 150 feet in the air before it started to descend. It struck trees about twenty-four hundred feet beyond the end of the runway and continued on for another twenty-two hundred feet, hitting trees and houses before finally crashing in a residential area. All 145 souls on board died, plus eight more on the ground; six houses were destroyed and another five sustained major damage. It was, at the time, the nation's third worst airplane crash.[19]

We are much safer from microbursts now. Today, the Federal Aviation Administration requires pilots to train, on simulators, to fly out of microbursts, and commercial airliners' radar must have wind shear alert systems. Too, large airports now have more advanced, Doppler radar systems that can detect nearby microbursts. For that we can thank the imagination stretch of a University of Chicago meteorologist named Tetsuya "Ted" Fujita, who coined the term "microburst" while researching the Eastern Airlines crash at JFK. Fujita—known as Mr. Tornado for creating a scale to measure tornado damage, the F-scale I mentioned earlier—couldn't have done it alone. For years meteorologists couldn't bring themselves to believe that relatively tiny downdrafts could create 150-mile-per-hour winds when they hit the ground. "People didn't imagine something so small really existed in the atmosphere," said an expert at the Naval Research Laboratory in Monterey, California. Without the disasters, Fujita's imagination wouldn't have stretched to conceive of these strange environmental phenomena.[20]

Worst cases, especially as forward-looking scenarios, can accomplish things. Scholarship on "high-reliability organizations" suggests that positive consequences accrue when organizations prepare for the worst. Doing so in a productive way entails using a broad array of insights, from people in a variety of positions, so that the range of possibilities that are imagined is broad. HROs, researchers say, are particularly good at getting their members to contribute their expertise to the construction of worst case scenarios. As such they are better prepared when disaster comes their way. When broad-based worst case planning happens, more alternatives are considered than otherwise would be. Such fostering of imagination is, apparently, largely responsible for the relatively safe operation of aircraft carriers in the U.S. Navy.

We'll look, as we have before, to the World Trade Center disaster for one final example of imagination stretch. For over a year after the

9/11 attacks engineers worked diligently to figure out just how and why the Twin Towers collapsed. It was clear, early on, that the innovative design of the buildings was involved. Particularly important was the fact that architects had made the outer skin of the buildings structurally important. Most modern skyscrapers are held up by interior columns of steel and concrete. But the World Trade Center towers were so tall, and so expensive to build, that those traditional piers would have taken up too much room—valuable office space that could generate revenue. The solution was to make the outer walls bear a lot of the load. After the disaster, it was obvious that the breaking of so many of the columns on the outer walls made the buildings vulnerable to collapse.

But much remained a mystery. Why, for instance, did anybody on the floors that the planes plowed through survive? What exactly happened to the people in the immediate vicinity of the plane crashes? Why was there so much more fire in the North Tower? For answers to these and other questions we can thank an example of imagination stretch that was itself the result of a civil lawsuit. Larry A. Silverstein had barely become the lease holder for the World Trade Center when 9/11 happened. Afterward, he sued the insurance companies for $7 billion, $3.5 billion for each tower, arguing that it was two separate attacks. The insurance companies said it was a single attack. With so much money at stake a good many experts were hired. The experts unsurprisingly tended to produce results that served the interests of their respective bosses. Still, all agree that the imagination that went into the effort was unprecedented.

After pouring over reams of data, photographs, and three-dimensional computer simulations based on super-slow-motion movies, the experts discovered a number of interesting things. They discovered that as the planes sliced through the buildings the concrete floors above them were obliterated. This compressed the aluminum in the planes' skins, saving countless lives—relatively few people were immediately hurt outside the floors where the planes came in. This compression also helps explain why there were actually some survivors on the floors that were hit directly. The simulations also revealed something about the patterns in which the inner structural columns were destroyed. In fact, the simulations said that the south tower should have collapsed immediately, which suggests less that the simulations are wrong than that things could always be worse. Too, the jet fuel from American Airlines Flight

11, the first plane to strike, sprayed out in a much wider pattern than the fuel from United Airlines Flight 175, which struck the south tower and exploded in the fireball none of us will ever forget. That fireball may be seared into our memories, but it worked in favor of the people in the tower by burning up a majority of the fuel.

Figuring all that out was far more than just a technical feat. It was not merely a matter of having faster computers, more money, or better data. "Taken in the aggregate, it represents a milestone in the forensic engineering of a disaster," said Jeremy Isenberg, a member of the National Academy of Engineering.[21] The engineers had to imagine new ways of manipulating and presenting data, new ways of thinking about disorder and collapse, new ways of experiencing mass death. A silver lining of the World Trade Center towers' collapse was the stretched imaginations of experts, ultimately resulting in the building of safer skyscrapers and a better understanding of the risks posed by existing ones.

INSTRUMENTAL AND SOCIAL BETTERMENT

Out of bad things good things can grow. Disasters are rarely complete disasters. Even worst cases can lead to social betterment. Now, social betterment is an idea that must be used with care. For people often use phrases such as "general public welfare" or "public interest" in ways that in fact mask inequities in distributions of economic and political power. Poverty isn't a problem for everyone; for some it is a solution. Drug addiction isn't a sign of the overall ill health of society; it's only a sign of ill health for some.

That said, worst cases, or disasters more generally, can lead to social betterment. They can do so in two general ways. Worst cases can create opportunities for specific actors—individuals, organizations, groups, or classes—or they can create opportunities for greater safety and security for some social unit (e.g., a country, state, or city). It's a good idea to keep straight when you're looking at a situation where some specific actor is benefiting—let me call that *instrumental betterment*—and when there is some more general benefit. The reason to maintain the distinction is that in the former case, where particular people win, other people lose; there's usually a power game involved. Power is always about winning and losing, and to forget that is to neglect the very reason that the world often works as it does. In the case of general social betterment, power figures less prominently because the conditions that are bettered redound to pretty much everyone, regardless of how much individual, political, or economic power they have.

That particular groups can benefit means that disasters can be infused with politics, as we've seen over and over. Always there are power plays and political interests, and always somebody wins and somebody loses. One of the images from 9/11 that is indelibly imprinted on our imaginations is when the huge antenna on top of the north tower of the World Trade Center began to wobble and start its ride to the ground. That antenna delivered television and radio signals to millions of people in the New York metropolitan area. What possible silver lining could there have been in its destruction? When the north tower fell, taking that antenna with it, people who depended on it for over-the-air broadcasts had to switch to cable or satellite, which benefited companies that provide those services.[22]

The 9/11 disaster had other instrumentally positive consequences. Fall is usually quiet for wedding retailers, but in 2001 bridal shops in New York City, as well as Web sites that specialize in wedding merchandise, reported significant upticks in purchases of gowns and rings and in people setting up bridal registries.[23] And Kathleen Tierney, from the University of Colorado, notes, "Emerging homeland security threats provide major revenue opportunities both for the ailing information technology industry and for defense, intelligence, and national security agencies and contractors." The USA Patriot Act, along with amendments to the attorney general's "Guidelines on General Crimes, Racketeering Enterprise, and Terrorism Enterprise Investigations," make it possible for federal agents to acquire the reading records of library patrons and spy on religious groups. Those developments are a major boon for intelligence agencies. The Economic Security and Recovery Act of 2001 passed the House of Representatives on October 24, 2001, providing temporary tax relief to low-income households and huge tax cuts for the largest corporations, eliminating the minimum corporate tax, and permanently reducing income tax rates for high-income earners.[24]

There were some generally positive consequences from 9/11 too. It generated a heightened sense of community among nearly all Americans. Hundreds of thousands of dollars were spent on overtime for cleanup workers. Airline security was beefed up. The Bush administration was pushed to pump an enormous amount of money into the economy just as a recession was beginning. That money, in classical Keynesian fashion, helped bolster consumer confidence and aggregate demand for goods and services, lessening the recession's severity. The need to rebuild sixteen acres of lower Manhattan will benefit building contractors, construction workers, and eventually tax collectors. Thousands in New York and New Jersey—the children of those who died—will be given free college educations, under edicts from those states' governors. That will add to the growing pressure to hire more professors, always a good thing. At the end of the day we may even find—and I say this in a bare whisper—that an ugly complex of buildings is replaced with an elegant architectural creation. It would be wrong to say that the good outweighs the bad in the World Trade Center disaster, but it would be just as wrong to say that nothing good will come of it.

SOCIAL CLEARING AS SOCIAL BETTERMENT

In June 1988 a few fires, sparked by lightning strikes, started in Yellowstone National Park. The National Park Service's policy at the time, which had been adopted in 1972, was that as long as small fires didn't threaten human life or property they would be left to burn. According to the Park Service, "Of the 368 lightning-caused fires that occurred from 1972 to 1987, 235 were allowed to burn; 208 of these fires burned themselves out before covering one acre." Prior to 1988, the worst fire that Yellowstone had ever seen had consumed only twenty-five thousand acres, and experts used that figure as the upper bound of a worst case scenario. They were badly mistaken.[25]

As typically happens when we highlight probabilities and neglect possibilities, the Park Service was caught off guard. Probabilistic approaches, as I've said, are biased in favor of what has already happened, encouraging us to neglect future possibilities. A Yellowstone park ranger revealed the bias when he said, "If we'd of had normal precipitation or eliminated the unprecedented winds or eliminated the extremely dry fuels, these fires would not have burned like they did."[26]

The weather worked against Yellowstone firefighters that summer. Weather Service forecasters predicted two major windstorms for August, but there were six. In fact, weather forecasters were wrong a lot that month. It was, for Yellowstone, a summer of superlatives. It was an unusually dry summer, the "driest" in the 112 years of park records, and much of the timber was just about the right age to go up in flames. There were also unusually high winds, which helped push fires together. It would become the worst fire Yellowstone National Park had ever experienced. You might call it the perfect fire. The rains didn't come until September 11, and the monster wasn't officially declared dead until the snows of mid-November snuffed its last embers. By that time, the government had spent $120 million fighting the fire. Over 1.4 million acres burned, 800,000 of which were in the park itself—36 percent of Yellowstone had burned!

The great Yellowstone fire is another case in which humans helped cause a natural disaster. Before 1972 the Park Service aggressively fought all fires. By 1976 the policy was that human-caused fires would be suppressed but lightning-caused fires would not unless they specifically threatened people or property. Those policies had the unintended consequence of building up fuel in the forests, although allowing *some* fires to burn surely cleared some fuel away. Human efforts to prevent smaller fires were just putting off the inevitable. And when the inevitable finally came—as inevitable things have a habit of doing—the fire turned into a worst case. Forests, people realized, actually need occasional fires to maintain their natural balance. Fires clear out the mess, help fertilize the soil, and make the forest ecosystem healthier in the long run. Yellowstone doesn't look very nice, even fifteen years later, but attractiveness is a human conceit, irrelevant to ecological health. There's a natural balance in local ecologies, and even the worst case fire of 1988 will in the long run be good for Yellowstone National Park.

Society sometimes benefits from such processes as well. We might called these processes ones of *social clearing*. They wipe away the detritus, the underbrush and litter as it were, of human life. As such they are silver linings, forms of unintentional social betterment that create suffering and destruction in the short run but set the stage for greater productivity and even happiness later.

One afternoon in June 1889 a pot of glue caught fire in the basement of a cabinet factory in downtown Seattle, Washington. A worker tried to smother the fire by putting a board on top of the pot. The board caught fire. Then, not understanding the proper way to extinguish such a fire, another worker threw water on the fire. That spread the burning glue throughout the shop. By the next morning Seattle's entire business district was gone, as were most of the city's wharves and its railroad terminals. In all, twenty-five square miles of property were destroyed. It is called the Great Fire, the worst fire in Seattle's history.[27]

It could also be called the best fire in Seattle's history. It is said that a million rats were destroyed or run off by the inferno. And when the city was rebuilt, new city ordinances required that buildings be of brick and stone, making them considerably more resistant to fire than the wooden buildings that had gone up like matchsticks. Moreover, the city's volunteer fire department was severely criticized for its inadequate response to the disaster, so the city created a paid, professional fire department, which made everyone safer.

But the Great Fire yielded another, even more important benefit. Seattle has a lot of rain every year, and the city had been built on mudflats. When it rained the mud could get waist deep. Too, the business districts were at the end of a notoriously unreliable sewer system. It wasn't a very hospitable environment for commerce. After the fire, the city filled in the mudflats and raised the streets by a story. The fire was just what Seattle needed to permit its growth from a small town to a city of considerable commerce and development. The antiquated and dangerous structure of Seattle was socially cleared, making way for a new era in Seattle's development.

Huge areas of Europe were blown to bits in World War II, and suddenly the opportunity was created to put power lines underground and to re-create city street plans in rational grids. Having power lines underground is aesthetically appealing and also lessens the likelihood of fire in a storm or a future bombing; having city streets laid out in a grid makes it easier to develop land and to transport disaster victims to hospital. (The Florida city of Homestead had the opportunity to bury its power lines after Hurricane Andrew in 1992 but failed to seize the moment.) The U.S. Geological Survey estimates that twenty-eight thousand wood and brick structures were destroyed in the 1906 San Francisco earthquake and fire, creating the opportunity to replace dangerous buildings with safer ones. All of these are examples of social clearing as a type of betterment.[28]

The Black Death is another one. It was the start of a series of epidemics that came and went over a period of three hundred years. Those epidemics, along with wars and famines, led to one of the largest depopulations in history. Some European cities lost up to two-thirds of their denizens. Many of the best and the brightest of the young population were lost. Governments and commerce came to a virtual standstill. Every generation over the next two hundred years was affected by the epidemic in one way or another. Jews and women were persecuted. It touched every corner of society.

It may seem callous to suggest there is a bright side of plagues, but there *were* positive consequences. Sociologist James Jasper points out that before 1347, when the first outbreak happened, Europe was quite overcrowded, by which he means the rural infrastructure could not support the numbers of people trying to live there. Europe's population wouldn't match its 1300 levels for 250 years. When the repopulation did happen it was in the towns and cites, rather than the countryside. Land became more plentiful, Jasper says, and "the amount of money per capita went up, as survivors inherited the savings of victims." Most important was that labor had become more scarce, which gave power to those who had only their labor to sell. That sort of conflict put pressure on the lords and the rich. Rebellions popped up all over Europe, with diverse peoples pushing to enhance their lot in life. Ideas about liberties and rights expanded, and "beating and hanging of commoners was no longer the only response to conflicts."[29]

I've said that worst cases usually play out so that some people win and others lose. As Jasper tells it, some took advantage of the "initial confusion" of Europe's great depopulation to move to the towns and cities, away from the oppressive rural areas. Less productive land was abandoned, because there weren't enough laborers to work it. Peasants became healthier because they were better fed. There were more freedoms and possibilities for self-betterment in the cities and towns. So the lower classes became more prosperous, and as they did family size dropped, which is always a sign of modernization. Standards of living in England, for example, improved dramatically. As Jasper says, "Except at the very top, and sometimes even there, the plague opened up the social structure." As male heirs died so did nobility, which helped disrupt the intergenerational transmission of wealth. Just as worst cases have disproportionate local effects, so do silver linings. In the case of the plague, members of the lower classes gained more freedom and a higher standard of living, though to the upper classes these looked like crises.

The plague also helped usher in modernity. People came to enjoy considerably more mobility, which everywhere contributes to modern markets. Because labor was more expensive there were incentives to innovate technologically. For example, the development of the galleon, a ship that relies more on sails than on oars and labor, increased efficiency and thus was a boon to international trade. Fishermen also learned to salt and store fish onboard, rather than having to land some place where the plague might be rampant to perform those tasks. Some have even attributed the invention of the printing press, in 1453, to the plague—before the press manuscripts had been copied by hand. Landowners had to treat peasants better or they would move to other estates (Jasper says this consequence was limited to *western* Europe). "Medieval hierarchies were badly shaken, as were the philosophies and laws that had supported them. New ideas became possible that would suggest economic, political, and legal alternatives to feudalism," Jasper says. In big depopulations there are winners and losers. Often, though wrenching, social clearings make things better for successive generations.

In *The Age of Triage,* iconoclastic Holocaust scholar Richard Rubenstein shows us that even the wholesale murder of large numbers of people can work as social clearing. Rubenstein is primarily interested in the idea of *surplus populations* and how pressures to decrease them were played out in Cambodia, Vietnam, the Holocaust, the British Enclosure laws, and the Irish Potato Famine.[30] My focus is different. Let's look briefly at the Irish famine, in which, between 1846 and 1848, perhaps 2.5 million people of a population of 9 million died. The problem was not a lack of food. There was plenty of food on store shelves. The problem was that the Irish poor had no money to buy the food. If people could pay they could eat. If they couldn't pay they didn't. They were evicted en masse and, having become highly dependent on a single food—the potato—were incredibly vulnerable to disaster.

England's leaders could have come to the rescue but decided to take a laissez-faire attitude toward the famine. They decided to let it run its "natural" course, as one might a common cold. Such an approach seems barbaric but is in truth an essentially modern way to run society. For only in a modern society are moral choices governed by the cold calculus of currency. The silver lining of the Irish famine was obviously not one for the starving people. But Ireland had become vastly overpopulated, and there is no question that the famine not only helped ease population pressures but, as with the Black Death, increased the bargaining power of those that remained. More importantly, by infusing society with a benefit/cost ethos and by thinning out unproductive labor, the Irish Potato Famine helped usher Ireland into modernity.

Of course, there are more humane ways to reduce populations. Raising living standards and providing public health infrastructure, gainful employment, and education all result in lower birth rates and are themselves examples of social betterment. Too, I don't mean to say that massive die-offs are always socially beneficial. AIDS is currently wiping out a huge part of the productive population in Africa. Drastically destructive measures are surely socially wasteful. Still, betterment does sometimes issue from catastrophe.

The sinking of the *Titanic* led to social betterment. After *Titanic* the first International Convention for Safety of Life at Sea was called in London in 1913. The convention drew up rules requiring that every ship have lifeboat space for each person on a vessel. The *Titanic* didn't have nearly enough lifeboat spaces for the passengers it could carry. The convention also required that lifeboat drills be held during each voyage. Further, all passenger ships were required to maintain a twenty-four-hour radio watch. *Titanic*'s distress signals had not been heard by the *Californian,* which was close by, either because no one was in the communications center to hear the call or because the radio wasn't turned on. Finally, the International Ice Patrol was established to warn ships of icebergs in the North Atlantic shipping lanes. The sinking of the *Titanic* led to safer ocean travel for everyone.

The accident at Three Mile Island is our best worst case in the nuclear industry. TMI even benefited utility owners because it brought renewed assurances from the federal government that their legal liabilities would be limited in the event of a truly catastrophic failure. Opponents of nuclear power could declare victory, because proponents' arguments that such an accident couldn't happen in a million years were disproved. But the TMI accident also contributed to the social good. After TMI the federal government required that all nuclear power plants create plans for evacuating people within a ten-mile radius, in what is called the Emergency Planning Zone. That move arguably made life safer for people who live close to nuclear plants. That the point is arguable created an opportunity for Long Island denizens to kill the Shoreham nuclear power station. It would feel silly to say aloud, "Thank goodness for Three Mile Island," but I can't help having the thought.

Drought struck across several American states in 1931, at a time when the entire nation averaged 13 percent below normal precipitation levels. It was the beginning of the Dust Bowl, which added insult to the injury of the Great Depression. The Dust Bowl hit hardest in portions of western Kansas, southwestern Nebraska, southeastern Colorado, northeastern New Mexico, and the Oklahoma and Texas panhandles. Of course, droughts are hardly unusual on the plains, but this was extreme, as worst cases are. There is no historical precedent for the wind erosion, along with the droughts, in the United States in the 1930s. There were fourteen Dust Bowl droughts in 1932, thirty-eight in 1933, twenty-two in 1934, forty in 1935, sixty-eight in 1936, seventy-two in 1937, sixty-one in 1938, thirty in 1939, and seventeen in each of 1940 and 1941. These storms were called "black blizzards," and the suffering they caused inspired Steinbeck's *Grapes of Wrath*. The misery caused by the blight included not just failed crops and poverty but measles, strep throat, respiratory illnesses, and something called "dust pneumonia," which was a plethora of bronchial diseases.[31]

But there were gains from the Dust Bowl beyond *The Grapes of Wrath*, advances in social betterment for a great many people. The devastation gave people a glimpse—to some it was a major insight—of how humans could cause environmental disaster. Farmers had come to the southern plains without much planning for cultivation, determined to reap big profits quickly. There was no concern for the long-term ecological effects of their actions. The waste and exploitation of natural resources was enormous. Tilting toward famine, the Dust Bowl was a powerful argument for government intervention and state expansion to help regulate and rationalize crop production. After the Dust Bowl soil conservation across the nation increased dramatically, perhaps its most important consequence.

Social scientists have long stressed the unintended consequences of people's actions. Especially in complex systems it's almost impossible to anticipate all of the effects of some big event or action. The silver linings I've been talking about are unintended consequences. More emphasis on conservation after the Dust Bowl was an unintended consequence of farmers' neglect of ecological issues.

Focusing on unintended consequences is important because it highlights how much of life is unplanned, or even chaotic. That's a potent antidote to the urges and expectations of modern society that stress control, predictability, and prediction. Earlier I talked about institutional trust and how we often expect too much of officials and organizations. In America especially, we expect government agencies to be able to cure everything from child abuse to a sagging economy. Surely one reason for that is that experts and government officials often overpromise, suggesting that they do indeed command such abilities. We should always hold officials' feet to the fire when they make outrageous claims for their abilities to know and to control. Still, I think people would be happier, and safer, if they understood that there are limits to such control. Highlighting unintended consequences helps us to see that. Knowing about limits helps create humility, an aspect of wisdom that is in insufficient evidence among leaders and led alike.

Of course, nothing guarantees that silver linings will issue from disasters. Someone, or some group, had to be well positioned, and wise enough, to see how the Dust Bowl created an opportunity for advancing conservation. Aviation and structural engineers have to know how to learn well from airplane crashes and bridge failures. It takes intelligence and imagination to be able to capitalize on worst cases. We can't just count on learning and imagination stretch to happen. People, and the organizations they create, frequently fail to imagine things; they fail to see into the future for all kinds of reasons. Sometimes they're just not smart enough. Sometimes they have an interest in remaining blind. Sometimes their routines prevent them from seeing into the future.

Endings are often times of sadness and despair. Worst cases, after all, bring trauma, whether through great destruction of property and loss of life, or in terms of an assault on people's sensibilities. One can't help but be struck with a sense of hopelessness at the worst case projections of the AIDS epidemic. Even when there isn't great loss of life—think of *Hindenburg, Challenger, Columbia*—only the coldest of souls would not pause in horrified reflection.

Yet there are times when we would do well to look to the kings and queens of worst case thinking, the millennialists, for a tempering attitude if not exactly for guidance. They *look forward to* the end-time. The end of the world as we know it looks *good* to them. Part and parcel of their worst case thinking is hope and even salvation. While there's no salvation in worst cases or disasters, there is value in looking beyond the carnage.

Doom and gloom are everywhere, and that's not entirely a bad thing. For when worst case scenarios are created, and thought about carefully, a coming calamity can be made less likely because people can be better positioned to prevent the onslaught or, if prevention fails, to prepare for recovery. And when something happens that everyone agrees is a worst case—Chernobyl, the World Trade Center, *Titanic*—opportunities are created for those who are not direct victims. Every cloud has a silver lining, at least when the sun adorns it from above. We should welcome any reason to be optimistic about the human condition.

6

LIVING AND DYING IN WORST CASE WORLDS

It is often said that September 11 "changed everything." I don't know about that. But it did make the idea of the worst case more salient, at least for Americans. Fears and notions about dramatic, large-scale disasters loom larger now. We may not actually be objectively more vulnerable to terrorist attacks, but we sure feel that way. More generally, we *are* more vulnerable to worst case disasters, though September 11 didn't cause that. We—and especially our policy makers—need to start thinking a lot more seriously about living and dying in worst case worlds.

Imagining worst cases should incite in us appreciation of how we can cause death and destruction in ways more devastating and potentially irreversible than could, say, the Aztecs or the medievals. Our capacity to damage future generations derives from our fearsome technologies. The toxic legacy of societies that fail to do anything significant about what economists call "negative externalities" (the bad stuff, like air pollution, that nobody wants to happen but that goes along with an activity) is something that can live hundreds of years. With high-level radioactive waste, the time horizon is *thousands* of years.

Nature, too, seems more malevolent than it used to. Mostly that's an illusion, one that lets us deny responsibility for our own actions. Nature has *always* been violent, often in the extreme. Human activity can exacerbate nature's violent tendencies, sometimes to the point of creating a worst case. New Orleans, right at the mouth of the Mississippi, is so far below sea level that a storm surge from a large hurricane could submerge a large proportion of the city under twenty feet or more of water. Such storms don't happen often, but they do happen. In 1969 Hurricane Camille, with two hundred-mile-per-hour winds, nearly wiped out Pass Christian, Mississippi, which is only fifty miles from New Orleans, killing more than 250 people. The worst case projections for New Orleans put the death toll in the tens of thousands. Using quintessential worst case language to evaluate the situation, a local director of emergency management said, "There's no way to minimize the amount of devastation that could take place under such circumstances."[1]

A chord I've repeatedly struck is that disasters are normal. Even unexpected incidents that are usually considered weird or bizarre should be thought of as part of the usual ebb and flow of everyday life. Instead of thinking of worst cases as statistically rare, and therefore outside the realm of responsible planning, we should think of them as arising from the institutional makeup of society. Think of the SARS virus. The significance of SARS isn't its mortality rate, as I've said, although that's frightening enough. The significance of SARS is *the rate at which it spreads*. It can traverse the globe in a very short period of time, wreaking havoc in places far removed from its origins. There were people in the SARS story of 2003 that the media dubbed "supercarriers," people whose contagiousness significantly spread the virus. Health officials call those people "index cases," but I think *supercarrier* conveys more information.

Modern technology and social networks enable SARS to do greater damage than it otherwise could. What's the worst that it could do? Imagine SARS slamming a pediatric AIDS ward, or a large nursing home. The virus is especially dangerous to the young and the very old because their immune systems aren't strong enough to fight it off. The worst case potential is there, and we ignore it at our peril. Humans cause their own destruction.

Earthquakes are sometimes seen as the quintessential random disasters. Attempts to predict earthquakes are usually scoffed at as so much alchemy, the considerable efforts of researchers, especially in Japan, notwithstanding. There just seems to be so much uncertainty about what precipitates earthquakes that predicting them is bound to fail. I once heard Dennis Mileti, then director of the Natural Hazards Center at the University of Colorado, give a speech about earthquake risks. He argued persuasively that predicting the timing of an earthquake might be uncertain, but predicting the place isn't: earthquakes are going to happen where they've happened before. Not only that, but really big earthquakes are entirely normal for the earth to experience. Mileti urged his audience to imagine an 8.4-magnitude quake shaking for four minutes. The devastation could be like what we see in movies. But just because it would be a big disaster doesn't mean we should be surprised when it happens. It's not necessary to predict the exact longitude and latitude of earthquakes, and it is only barely more necessary to predict the probabilities of differently sized earthquakes. Because a big one is going to happen again somewhere close to where it's happened before. Of course "close" in earthquake language may just mean within several hundred miles. But the point is that big disasters are normal.

Viruses, earthquakes, and terrorists don't make us more vulnerable to worst cases. For that we can thank ourselves. Some people insist on living atop earthquake faults; others have no choice. We concentrate ourselves in megacities next to the seashore, vulnerable to tsunamis. We're used to thinking that nearly any place on earth is appropriate to build houses: the sides of mountains, next to the Mississippi, even at the bases of volcanoes. But imagine, instead, if we saw the western coast of the United States as the normal and usual place for tsunamis to strike, earthquakes to shake, and volcanoes to blow. Perhaps then fewer people would say, "Oh, let's go live there." It's partly a matter of perspective, then, but just as plainly a matter of hubris.

Others are sounding the alarm. Richard A. Posner, noted judge and prolific author, recently published *Catastrophe: Risk and Response,* in which he uses cost-benefit analysis to argue that we should all be paying more attention to threats that could wipe out millions of people. Sir Martin Rees, the Royal Astronomer of Great Britain, has written a number of popular books that emphasize worst cases of one kind or another. His *Our Final Hour* sounds a loud alarm about near earth objects, particle accelerators, and nanotechnology, among many other potential hazards. His alarmism is specific: "I think the odds are no better than fifty-fifty that our present civilization on Earth will survive to the end of the present century."[2]

It's not all that clear whether Rees intends this in a metaphorical sense (things are bad, but we can make them better) or in a statistical sense, whatever that would mean. But he surely captures the worst case mood, issuing warnings about things that possibilistic thinking suggests we ought to worry about. I share his alarmist outlook, although putting probability statements on the end-time is too fantastic for my taste. In any case, in this last chapter I want to confront some practical issues that flow from the preceding pages. I don't have all the answers. Perhaps posing some new questions will at least provide fodder for policy makers and activists to fashion new ideas, which may help create new pathways to a safer world. Maybe a spot of worst case thinking can make us not only alarmed but safer.

CRITICAL INFRASTRUCTURES

Even before September 11 government officials were working on problems of what they call "the critical infrastructure." Recall the massive power blackout of August 2003, where within about twenty minutes a huge part of the American midwest and northeast went dark. The electrical grid is *critical* because without it society can't function; and it is *infrastructural* because so many other systems depend on it for proper operation. The usual view is that the critical infrastructure is made up of those systems required to maintain life. President Bill Clinton signed an executive order in July 1996 which created the President's Commission on Critical Infrastructure Protection. The CI, as experts refer to it, includes telecommunications, electrical systems, gas and oil storage and transportation, banking and finance, transportation, water supply systems, emergency services, and continuity of government.[3] All of those systems are vital to our way of life. They are also quite vulnerable. Just consider a few worst cases.

If a small nuclear device were detonated on the day that a new president was being inaugurated, there very likely would not be "continuity of government" at the federal level. Society might not fall apart after such an attack, but it would be severely disrupted. Or imagine if terrorists blew up ten or twenty switch-points in the network of gas pipes— largely unguardable—that traverse the United States, in the dead of an extreme winter, just when OPEC had restricted oil production. Or what if they targeted a liquefied natural gas tanker? There are only four LNG terminals in the United States, which in a sense makes them easier to protect, but also identifies them for terrorists to strike. Worse, LNG tankers load up in Africa, Latin America, and the Middle East, where security might be more dicey. One of the interesting revelations in Richard Clarke's book *Against All Enemies* is that al Qaeda operatives used to find safe passage to the United States on LNG tankers from

Africa.[4] If we had a large outbreak of a highly contagious disease—smallpox is the usual example, but a really virulent strain of flu is more likely and would be more deadly—American hospitals would be *immediately* overwhelmed, because there is no real "surge capacity." It's not that hard to imagine ways to strike our critical infrastructure, and terrorists are surely more creative at it than I am.

My argument throughout this book is that we ought to be thinking about worst cases in more prosaic venues than we usually do. We need to worry about trains tipping over and releasing toxic chemical clouds. We would be wise to think of nursing homes, where an increasing proportion of our population lives, as excellent terrorist targets. Schools, malls, and the like are also places for big, worst case disasters. What happens to our already rattled sense of security, and our civil liberties, if terrorists simultaneously explode big bombs at the five largest universities in the New York metropolitan area?

It is good that our best and brightest are worrying about CI, but the official list of systems that make up the critical infrastructure is too narrow and too short. The list doesn't adequately capture the complexity and interdependency of modern societies. And disasters are often too fast moving, and too extensive, for such a static list of "critical" things to adequately capture reality. The traditional conception of the critical infrastructure neglects softer, more social systems. It's not unusual to regard social aspects of society as superfluous, as if they were extras to be considered after the real business of society is taken care of. But the CI list is an engineer's list.

Let's try to stretch this engineering view of reality. One of our most important concerns should be schools. In America roughly *20 percent* of the population is in K–12 schools for about half of the days in the year. If there's a big chemical accident in, say, the middle of New Jersey, and a cloud of dangerous gas threatens to blanket the area, then the safest place for people would probably be right where they are. It's called "sheltering in place." In that event the first-grade teacher suddenly becomes a key part of the *social infrastructure* of society, no less critical than the chemical plant that has just failed, or been attacked. That's not just because we worry about children. It's also because for almost every kid in school there's at least one adult worrying about that kid. In the chemical-leak scenario it would probably be best if the adults stayed put and didn't put themselves in harm's way. If we want the kid and the parent to shelter in place, at least two key things must happen. One is that the teacher has to know the right things to do (and be equipped to do them), and the other is that the parent has to trust that the teacher will do the right things (I'll leave aside that teachers need to trust that their own children are being cared for.) Otherwise, children and their parents will be at greater risk. Schools can be part of the critical infrastructure, and we need to treat them as such.

Failing to define schools as critical infrastructure entails a faulty view about how society works. Policy solutions to public problems won't work well if they're directed at the wrong problems, which is likely when we have a poor understanding of how institutions change, organizations work, and experts process knowledge. For example, presuming that people will panic, be unproductive and antisocial, and be overly frightened during a bioterrorist attack might lead to a weak and compromised mass vaccination program. Such programs can be done well, poorly, or somewhere in between. It may be difficult, but it is not rocket science. It has been done well in the past.

The 1995 Chicago heat wave showed the same thing. There, hospitals became overwhelmed because they couldn't handle all the bodies that came their way. Refrigeration trucks had to be used to keep bodies from decaying in plain view of the public. Hospitals would be included in anyone's definition of critical infrastructure, but refrigeration trucks? In this case they were indeed critical for maintaining physical and mental public health.

The problem I'm talking about here—how social interdependence calls for a more expansive conception of "infrastructure"—is also well illustrated by the 1918 Spanish flu. In Philadelphia the telephone company nearly had to close down because the absentee rate among workers skyrocketed. Worse, one of the most important groups of service providers nearly came to a complete standstill: morticians. In a grave shortage of morticians, so to speak, two things happen: bodies pile up and, in the words of noted historian Alfred Crosby, "the accumulation of corpses will, more than anything else, sap and even break the morale of a population. When that happens, superstitious horror thrusts common decency aside, all public services collapse, friends and even family members turn away from one another, and the death rate bounds upward."[5]

These are hard issues, because to truly prepare for disaster means rethinking the major categories of thought that dominate political arguments about the matter. *Teachers* as first responders? *Grave diggers* as critical infrastructure? It may seem strange, but worst case thinking is like that. The term "critical infrastructure" is a convenient fiction, useful for organizing our thoughts and resources to some degree. But we should not allow ourselves the comfort of thinking that our categories will hold in a worst case event like the 1918 flu epidemic. All manner of society's institutions become critical when the fabric starts to fray. We need the social infrastructure of daily life to stay healthy just as much as we need electrical hardware and oil production.

DISORGANIZING FOR WORST CASES

Throughout this book I've pointed to lessons about effective leadership, organization, and policy that we can glean from big disasters. There are a few less conventional lessons to mention, and they have to do with *destructing* or *devolving*. They are about *disorganizing* for disaster. We rich countries have made a lot of progress in preparing for and responding to calamity. But we could do more. And I don't think we're at all prepared for the mass-casualty attacks that terrorists would like to mount against us.

We need to demystify the illusions of control that are proffered to us by our leaders and expected by the public. We need to break organizational strangleholds on the idea of disaster response. We need to make the places were we live—communities, places of work, schools, faith-based organizations—more resilient. I'm none too sanguine, however, that policymakers will think out of the box on these matters, although I know some who do. Because of narrowed imaginations, because of professional blinders, because of political interests, because of turf protection, I'm afraid the thing most likely to generate the political and popular attention that these issues deserve is more worst cases.

Worst cases should humble us more than they do. For they throw into sharp relief how limited our control of nature and society actually are. Western culture is marked by an emphasis on, even an obsession with, control. I do not begrudge the money given to family members of 9/11 victims. It would have been wrong for any of them not to take it. What's interesting is that the giving and the taking are not seen as unusual; everyone involved has a sufficiently developed sense of entitlement that it is *expected* they would be paid. The expectation on the part of the recipients is that government will control, or at least appear to control, the damage that has been done to their lives. One of the worst things you can say about anyone in our society is, He's out of control. Worst cases should temper our sense of what it is reasonable to expect of leaders. There's too much complexity in the systems we build, and too much contingency in how history plays out, for leaders to have total control.

Besides, there are forces and interests that leaders can't control, which attenuates their power. Recognizing that is important for understanding the production of worst cases as well as responses to them. One such set of forces concerns the centralization of valuable resources. Bureaucracies tend to consolidate information; a complementary tendency hordes and protects information from outsiders. That's the main reason why after every big disaster investigative reporters discover that the government's right hand didn't know what its left hand was doing. Crucial information about the 9/11 hijackers, for example, was not shared freely between the CIA and the FBI. The ever-present "turf battles" are partly responsible for such disconnects, but there are other reasons too. Whenever there are big problems our culture prescribes creating formal rules to solve them. Formal rules are the life's blood of bureaucracies.

There are problems, though, with responding to all problems through rules and bureaucratic organization, especially when it comes to disasters. One problem is that many of the demands that disasters place on society are not well met by bureaucracies. There is, in other words, a mismatch between problem and solution. We find this mismatch in the areas of causing disasters, preventing them, and responding to them.

Concentrated, high-technology systems are more prone to catastrophic failures than others. Charles Perrow's book *Normal Accidents* shows that many of our most dangerous technologies actually *require* centralized organizations to function properly. Nuclear power plants, for example, simply can't be run by anything other than a highly secretive bureaucracy that's utterly dependent on expert knowledge. That's fine when everything is going well, but when things start to go badly people in highly centralized organizations have a hard time recovering from cascading failures, they have a hard time learning from their mistakes, and society has a hard time looking inside of them to regulate them properly. I realize, of course, that the American nuclear industry hasn't had a major accident in about twenty-five years. America's nuclear plants do, however, have "incidents" regularly. And the safety record of the last twenty-five years is largely a result of the enhanced oversight of the industry after its accident at Three Mile Island in 1979. The point is that bureaucracies are often implicated in worst cases; the way they are organized presents us important dilemmas regarding how to fortify against worst cases.

As power and authority are concentrated in organizations, flexibility is diminished and vulnerability to worst case failures increases. For example, measures proposed to enhance security after 9/11 included such advanced technological detection devices as retina scanners, face-recognition software, and computer chips on driver's licenses. Government officials, egged on by private interests, urged the development of a large national network of connected databases designed to track people. None of those measures would have even slowed down the 9/11 hijackers, let alone actually thwarted the attacks, but that didn't seem to matter. Beyond that, though, are more fundamental problems. The scheme actually creates larger vulnerabilities by concentrating in one place information about people's credit card numbers, social security numbers, buying histories, and so on. It's like making a target as large as possible, then hanging a sign on it that says, shoot me here. Huge, highly concentrated bureaucracies are unlikely to fail gracefully. The post-9/11 security measures taken by the federal government involve centralization and concentration of valuable resources: information, authority, and technology. In fact what's happened is that they have created a vast new bureaucracy, which will be good at some things but very bad at others.[6]

An estimated five hundred thousand people left Manhattan on 9/11 in one of the largest water-borne evacuations in history. How did that happen? Barges, fishing boats, pleasure boats, ferries, all manner of watercraft carried people to safety. It wasn't driven by an official plan. No one was in charge. Ordinary people, though terrified, boarded the vessels in an orderly way. As a rescue system, it was flexible, decentralized, and massively effective.

Don't get me wrong. We can't live a modern lifestyle without big organizations. I certainly wouldn't want to return to a time without them. My warning is that organizational factors can, often enough, be just as lethal as bullets and terrorists. We also can't trust bureaucracies for rescue, although we often have little other choice. The wiser person remembers that when the environment starts to degrade precipitously, when worst cases set upon her, she should look for help to neighbors, friends, or even the stranger sitting next to her on the train. Social networks, rather than formal organizations, are far more likely to save her life. Still and all, a message from the foregoing chapters is that by peering into the abyss of disaster we can glean suggestions on how to organize, and disorganize, for catastrophe.

Remember I said that schoolteachers can become part of the critical infrastructure. There's another point to make about schools. In the official disaster community, made up of the multitude of professionals, consultants, and agencies that in some way depend on disasters for their existence, considerable emphasis is placed on "first responders." In official parlance, first responders are the police, firefighters, ambulance operators, and the like. These are the people often imagined to be rescuers, those we turn to in times of grave danger. They wear uniforms. Of course you should call the fire department if your office building catches fire. If anyone is going to put the fire out, they will. But the plain truth is that by the time these putative first responders get to the scene of a disaster most of those who are going to die are already dead. It's more helpful, more accurate, to dub the police and so on "official responders" rather than first responders. This is not a mere semantic issue. Really effective preparation for disaster requires that we push resources down to the very local level, preparing everyday people rather than just officials and those who wear uniforms. If your office building really does catch fire and you are for some reason incapacitated, it will be your coworker who saves your life.

In fact, in many ways individuals respond to disasters more effectively than formal organizations. Formal organizations are best at handling routine sorts of problems: disciplining a recalcitrant student, fixing broken computer networks, making guns. Disasters, and especially worst case disasters, are too unexpected and overwhelming for organizations to fold into their standard operating procedures. So they often drop the ball. Individuals, and social networks, on the other hand, are much more flexible. Hero stories are always trumpeted by the media after disasters. It almost seems miraculous that Joe or Josephina Doe put aside self-interest to rescue a stranger. He or she may well be a hero, but that sort of behavior isn't unusual in the least.

What does this mean we ought to do? It means we should eschew the centralization of disaster resources in large bureaucracies. Such centralization actually increases vulnerabilities, because centralization is more likely to create systems that don't fail gracefully. It means officials should see the public as an asset in disaster planning and response, rather than as a hindrance. People can generally handle bad news if they believe they are being dealt with honestly and with fealty. It means that local citizens groups should be involved in setting policies. Above all, it means that important choices should be made in a more open and transparent manner. This will necessarily entail inefficiencies and irrationalities, but that is of little consequence in the larger scheme of things.

PREEMPTIVE RESILIENCE

I'm recommending that we foster *preemptive resilience*. An example of preemptive resilience is the case of United Airlines Flight 93. That doomed flight, you'll recall, slammed into a field in Pennsylvania on 9/11. Passengers used cell phones to gain and share solid intelligence; they made a coordinated choice and acted decisively. Indeed, they acted just the opposite of our intelligence organizations, which were paralyzed by turf battles and politics and couldn't make the hard choices that needed to be made. The people could be trusted but the organizations could not be.

Years of research on disasters shows that top-down, command-and-control approaches aren't the way to go. Bottom-up, citizen-based responses are often more effective. After all, disasters happen at the *really local* level, so the more people at that level are prepared for the untoward the more resilient they will be. I don't advocate some libertarian world of self-sufficient communities. Command and control is necessary for tasks such as large-scale prepositioning of supplies, setting standards so that communication devices speak to each other, and redistributing resources to counter extreme inequalities between communities.

Still, it was preemptive resilience when a spontaneous network of regular citizens successfully evacuated half a million people from lower Manhattan on 9/11. Regular people, not bureaucracies, made that happen. Preemptive resilience helped evacuate the infirm from the World Trade Center towers. It would be fostering preemptive resilience if we prepared schoolteachers to be first responders in anticipation of a chemical attack or accident in our neighborhoods.

The issue of preemptive resilience was a great gap in the debate over what President Bush knew and when he knew it in the run-up to 9/11.

Supporters of the Bush administration said nothing could have been done. Critics said they didn't do enough. Nobody seemed to recognize the importance of providing information to *nonbureaucrats* so that they could act intelligently. Yet American citizens can and have played key roles in averting disaster throughout our history, from Paul Revere's Ride to September 11 itself.

What could Bush have done in August 2001 (or earlier)? He could have *told us* what the intelligence community was worried about. In July 2001 the FBI advised Attorney General John Ashcroft not to fly commercially. That was clearly a policy driven by intelligence. Of course, the general public doesn't have the luxury, made available to Ashcroft, of flying in Gulfstream aircraft at the price of nearly two thousand dollars an hour. Only rich people, or people with considerable access to public funds, can do that. The administration could have given better instructions to safety officials and security personnel. A marshal could have been put on every flight.

The president wasn't hog-tied. He could have gone on television and said:

We have clear intelligence that terrorists are operating within our borders. They are probably affiliated with Osama bin Laden, whose radical Islamic group has been involved in several previous attacks against us. He has said he wants to strike inside the United States. Our information is not specific about the place, time, or method of attack. But there is chatter about hijacking airplanes. The FBI has noticed suspicious activity that might be preparation for hijackings and has noticed suspicious activity around federal buildings in New York. The FAA has advised airlines to be on the lookout. I want to warn all Americans to also be on high alert.

Everything in that hypothetical statement would have been consistent with existing intelligence. None of it would have revealed national security secrets. None of it would require any strong analytic power to "connect the dots." And notice how drastically different such a statement would be from the unspecific color-coded alerts that issue from the Department of Homeland Security. If President Bush had made such a statement, Americans wouldn't have become paralyzed, indifferent, or inured by the barrage of ominous intelligence, as intelligence organizations did. Nor would they have "panicked." They might have curtailed their travel a bit, but would that have been unwise?

Such an alert might well have made a difference on 9/11. After all, the nonbureaucratic general public thwarted 25 percent of the planned attacks. If travelers that morning had been suspicious, they might have more quickly spotted the hijackers, who were all flying first class and all looked remarkably similar, and foiled their plans. In the worst case, perhaps they would have commandeered more of the hijacked aircraft and crashed them, like our heroes on Flight 93. If the hijacking of American Airlines 11, the first to strike the World Trade Center, had been foiled the body count of September 11 would have been cut in half.

The power of individuals and their networks shouldn't be underestimated (note the effectiveness of al Qaeda). It should be bolstered and facilitated by organized government agencies. Rather than centralize, we ought to shore up resilience at the levels of society where people actually live, where they actually experience disasters, where they actually die.

CONNECTING THE DOTS:
USING COUNTERFACTUALS WISELY

Surely a relevant policy issue in the present context is the problem of failed imagination. We've seen many examples in this book. But if we want our officials to do better at anticipating disasters it's not enough to simply complain and demand or expect smart imaginings. The problem with blinkered imaginations runs deeper than that.

In everyday life people often use counterfactuals, though usually without realizing it. Counterfactuals are, after all, the cognitive complement to the emotion of fear. It's not just fearful *feelings* that are important if you drive up to your house and it's engulfed in flames. It's also the quick imagining that you have to find a new place to live.

We need to start using *what ifs*, counterfactuals, more extensively and in smarter ways. Earlier, I showed how scholars have laid out some reasonable ways of deciding what's a good counterfactual, and there's no reason we couldn't see more reliance on them in the formation of disaster-related policy. To some, this might sound like a prescription for infinite fantasizing, mere flights of fancy that would keep policy makers from doing their *real* jobs. But using the good-counterfactual rules would mean that policy makers wouldn't get bogged down in an infinite number of imagined realities. There's no point in arguing that a nuclear power plant can explode like an atomic bomb because that's physically impossible. But way too little counterfactual attention is being given the threats from trains, those ever-present but largely invisible potential disasters. Besides, probabilistic analyses could also go on infinitely in a futile attempt to include every potential contingency, but they don't. The same is true for counterfactual thinking.

Serious counterfactual thinking can teach us about things we ought to think we need to know. But knowledge isn't enough to ensure action. There must also be a collection of political interests sufficiently energized to do something with the knowledge. The environmental movement is an example of that, and although there are many accomplished worst case thinkers in the movement, they sometimes *sound* too extreme because they're not sufficiently disciplined in how they go about building counterfactuals.

Experts and organizations have a special responsibility to engage in disciplined counterfactual thinking. This is because the consequences of organizational failures in imagining worst cases can harm a great many people and their communities. A single individual can cause a lot of damage, of course. Someone could, and occasionally does, drive drunk into a family of five, wiping them out. That's certainly a worst case for the family and probably for the drunk driver too. Similarly, many people continue to neglect the worst case possibilities of smoking cigarettes, hang gliding, and other nonessential activities that risk life and limb. But only collections of people, arranged in formal organizations or networks, seem to have the capacity to wipe out *many* families at once, to poison a community, or to make decisions that will affect future generations across a broad swath of society.

That's one reason that power is crucial to making people safer, or putting them in greater danger. And where there is power there is politics. After the *Exxon Valdez* oil spill the Natural Resources Defense Council wrote a report on oil spills in three of America's busiest harbors: San Francisco, New York, and Los Angeles. The report played with some what ifs. It imagined, for example, a repeat of the *Exxon Valdez* spill on the American east coast, demonstrating that the oil would spread from Massachusetts to North Carolina. There are thousands of tanker visits in each of the three ports every year. And every year, in each port, there are hundreds of little oil spills. The system is a catastrophe waiting to happen. The vessel traffic system is basically self-regulating. There is nothing like air traffic control, the boats are huge, and the environment in which they move is, in varying degrees, a hostile one for them.

The case of the SS *Sansinena* illustrates the point. In 1976 the *Sansinena* was moored at a Union Oil Terminal in Los Angeles when it exploded. Six crew members died and twenty-two were injured. There were also several dozen injuries among the general public. The vessel, full of fuel, was ripped in two and sank to the bottom of the harbor. Of course the *Sansinena* accident could have been much worse. The point in the present context, however, is that major oil spills are to be expected, and using counterfactuals shows the danger.

Just think about Valdez Harbor. The Trans-Alaska Pipeline ends there, after bringing its precious cargo from Alaska's North Slope. There are eighteen huge holding tanks next to the harbor, which together can hold 385 million gallons of oil. Earthquakes are not uncommon in Alaska. Far from it. They are as normal as hurricanes in Florida. If tomorrow a huge earthquake hits Valdez and spills 300 million gallons of oil—which would be more than twenty-seven times what spilled from the *Exxon Valdez*—we shouldn't be in the least surprised. If there were more public talk about this potential worst case we could more fully assess the risks of oil transport.

THE PROBLEM OF THE PUBLIC GOOD

The threats from near earth objects, as I've said, are underappreciated. If an NEO the size of a football field slipped through the atmosphere it could turn Miami into a smoking ruin in a matter of seconds. So, naturally there's some talk about how to mitigate the threat. Ideas for mitigation even include the wild Hollywood scenarios in which nuclear weapons are used to nudge an asteroid off its perilous path. Policy makers and experts, including yours truly, hold conferences and give interviews to the press concerning the problems of NEOs. They sometimes talk about the worldwide effort that would be necessary should a large piece of space debris be discovered on a collision course with Earth. For example, NASA, which in 1998 established the Near Earth Object Program at its Jet Propulsion Laboratory in California, says, after noting it would be extremely difficult to deflect an asteroid, that

In the absence of active defense, warning of the time and place of an impact would at least allow us to store food and supplies and to evacuate regions near ground zero where damage would be the greatest.[7]

It would be nice to think that, should such a monstrous threat come to pass, everyone would bind together in a common rescue mission. People use the phrase "world community" as a shorthand to indicate that somehow we're all in this together. Something like that happened after the World Trade Center was destroyed; countries from all over the world offered condolences, ceremonies, and aid. Few countries even expressed disapproval when the U.S. government attacked Afghanistan. It also happened, however briefly, after the big tsunami in December 2004, when people and countries all over the world pitched in for the relief effort. On a smaller scale, disaster researchers have for years found that, most of the time, communities come together after a destructive event, residents offering each other succor and salvation in a common effort to rebuild. "I see a bottomless well of generosity," said a fundraiser for the Red Cross, speculating about another attack on American soil. "One of the characteristics of Americans is the willingness to support one another, no matter what the frequency or gravity of the disaster."[8]

That kind of sentiment may capture the American response to an NEO strike *in America*. Americans would undoubtedly bind together whether Des Moines or Denver were designated as ground zero. But I doubt it would be a universal response. Imagine two scenarios. In the first scenario we can't predict where the rock is going to strike. In the second we can make the prediction. Neither of these scenarios is fanciful. With some regularity astronomers do see large pieces of space material *after* they've passed fairly close to Earth (say, within a third or half the distance between Earth and the moon). Sometimes NEOs come at us from the other side of the sun, where we can't see very well, and rush toward us in the glare. It's like standing in the outfield of a baseball stadium and losing the ball in the lights.

So, assume London is hit by surprise. How would the world respond? There would be expressions of sorrow and sympathy from all quarters, but that would be about it for most of the world. What, after all, could Zimbabwe really do to help England recover? The U.S. government would offer military protection and lots of loans. But the response wouldn't be uniform even within the United States. The religious right would probably say Londoners brought it on themselves; it was divine retribution for sinful behavior. Russia could do little. In fact there would be little that *any* country could do. Eventually London would recover, but the recovery process would be uneven, with some people suffering a great deal longer and more deeply than others. My guess is that present inequities in British society would be reproduced in the recovery.

Now imagine the second scenario, in which scientists have enough data and expertise to predict where the NEO will strike. Imagine that they have determined that the NEO will strike or explode over sub-Saharan Africa, specifically over Lusaka, the capital of Zambia. Ten million people live in Lusaka. If the object were big enough, the force of the blast could easily destroy the city. In fact, it could well destroy the better part of the country. Should Lusaka go up in smoke, the surviving countries would be faced with either helping the country rebuild or providing the refugees a new home. It's hard to imagine scenarios with satisfactory outcomes. Could we really expect one of Zambia's neighbors, say Zimbabwe or Angola, to take all the refugees? It's hardly unimaginable that even the rich, Western countries would write them off. Fifty percent of Lusaka's population is unemployed—the truth is that they are superfluous in the global economy—and so of little value to others. Twenty percent of Zambia's adult population is infected with AIDS; in its cities one of every four adults is infected. Rich countries have already written off Zambia.

I don't mean to sound coldhearted, but if we're really going to think smartly and imagine well about worst cases we have to be honest about political realities. The happy conclusion of disaster researchers—that altruistic communities form after calamity—has limits. Continuing to talk about "the public good," as if there really were one, obscures political realities, letting us comfortably ignore that we're not all in this together.

USING PROBABILISM SMARTLY

Possibilistic thinking can be nutty, so we have to be careful. For example, Martin Rees, whose wonderfully frightening book *Our Final Hour* I mentioned before, talks about experiments in particle accelerators that could ruin the galaxy. It is theoretically possible that experts at Brookhaven National Laboratory, on Long Island, could create a black hole that sucks everything into it. Similarly, *it is possible* that they could create "strangelets," a new form of matter that could turn everything else into that form. Or they could create a sort of vacuum that would consume the universe. I'm glad someone as smart as Rees is thinking about such possibilities, and I think it is fine to use his work as a brief for keeping watch over the physicists on Long Island. But we can put strangelets low on our list of worries.

But worst case possibilities are too often dismissed as wild fantasies, and too often ignored. NORAD apparently learned nothing from the B-52 crash in Thule, which I discussed in chapter 3. SAC Commander General Thomas Power subsequently claimed that Operation Chrome Dome had a "perfect safety record."[9] That was wrong, of course, and dangerously so. You have to be willing to see to learn from possibilistic imaginings. The main justification that people use for ignoring them is that focusing on consequences rather than probabilities is irrational and extreme. The problem is not, most of the time at least, that high-level decision makers simply don't care about the what ifs. No one said, "Well, I don't care if *Challenger* blows up. Let's light the candles and see what happens." They said, in effect, "There's only a low probability that the O-ring will freeze and crack, leading to a catastrophic explosion that will kill all seven astronauts and plunge NASA into a huge crisis. As we've done before, let's light the candles and keep our fingers crossed. The chances are in our favor." What happened in the *Challenger* case was that engineers and managers became so used to making choices on the basis of probabilities, neglecting possibilities, that they lost sight of the big picture. Their imaginations were not driven by the what ifs. Their everyday routines were built so that the best possible face was put on bad news. It was a bad habit.

We might well be smarter, and potentially safer, if the overemphasis on probabilistic thinking were balanced with possibilistic thinking. We need to put probabilism in its place. Experts and policy makers need to stop claiming and acting as if probabilistic thinking is the only rational way to approach problems. Let me repeat that I'm not saying we need to throw it out altogether. But we do need to moderate our reliance on it. For all its advantages—and they are legion—probabilism can also be quite limited in its usefulness as a guide for making choices. If you know that half of all modern marriages end in divorce, what purchase does that provide on *your* chances? Does it mean that half of your marriages will end badly? Or that half of your friends will divorce? Does it mean that you have a fifty-fifty chance of staying married? What if you have a child, or four children? Do the probabilities change then? What if you marry your high school sweetheart or marry much later than most people? It could mean some of those things, all of those things, or none.

For individuals the important facts about marriage are not in aggregate probabilities but in the micro possibilities.

One reason we haven't paid enough attention to how vulnerable we are to worst case events is the lock that probabilistic thinking has as the "rational" way to think about risks. I think we ought to prepare more for possibilities of untoward events that are out of control and overwhelming. It's perfectly sensible to plan for the consequences of global warming (even if we can't agree on what causes it), colossal airplane disasters, nuclear waste releases, volcanic eruptions, and asteroid strikes.

I realize that what I'm saying might be expensive. Probabilism looks most reasonable when it comes to the issue of setting spending priorities. I have no magical formula that would say when we should spend more on the catastrophic potential of nanotechnology as against the African American infant mortality rate, which is about twice that of whites.[10] But policies are sometimes set and actions taken without regard for what would be most economical: preparing for a nuclear plant meltdown or continuing to refine safety in commercial airline travel. We shouldn't ignore cost, but it isn't the holy grail in measuring value.

In some parts of the world there is something called the *precautionary principle*. Growing out of debates over the untoward possibilities of biotechnology and food engineering, the precautionary principle has been developed by environmental activists and policy makers as a principled way, so to speak, to have their concerns reflected in policy. It is quintessentially worst case thinking. The so-called Rio Declaration, issued at a 1992 United Nations Conference on Environment and Development, put it this way:

In order to protect the environment, the precautionary approach shall be widely applied by States according to their capabilities. Where there are threats of serious or irreversible damage, lack of full scientific certainty shall not be used as a reason for postponing cost-effective measures to prevent environmental degradation.[11]

Another way of putting this is that when faced with considerable uncertainty about a possible course of action, the precautionary principle says, first, do no harm. It's a controversial, and somewhat simplistic, idea. It's simplistic because it's not always that easy to figure out what "do no harm" means: Should we widely deploy nuclear power plants to reduce greenhouse gasses, or shun them because of the waste and risk problems?

It may be telling that industrial concerns most vociferously fight the precautionary principle. They say that it's too conservative, that it can't work, that it brakes societal progress. The Heritage Foundation, a think tank "whose mission is to formulate and promote conservative public policies based on the principles of free enterprise," includes on its Web site a paper that claims the precautionary principle is a "threat to technological innovation" and that it was the invocation of the precautionary principle after Three Mile Island—rather than the accident itself—that killed nuclear power in the United States.[12] It's easy to find similar examples.

Conceptually, the precautionary principle shifts the burden of proof regarding new substances, technologies, or courses of action with potentially significant effects to those who are promoting those new things. There are no forces anywhere that can stop companies from pushing high technology, the bioengineering of foods, and so on. Globalization and private interests are just too strong. The precautionary principle is a tool that can sometimes be used to make some of those interests consider worst case possibilities. It can push policy makers to be explicit about the values they're pursuing, to specify the uncertainties in their decision processes, and to imagine alternatives they might otherwise ignore.

Would that McDonnell Douglas experts had used the precautionary principle in maintaining their DC-10s. In May 1979 an American Airlines DC-10 crashed at Chicago's O'Hare Airport, killing 273 people onboard and two people on the ground. Because of a shortcut in a maintenance procedure, the pylon that held the left engine to the plane failed. Having an engine fall off a DC-10 isn't enough to cause the plane to crash, but as it fell the engine ripped some hydraulic cables, ultimately causing problems with the left wing's leading-edge slats that made the plane impossible to fly. There were dramatic photographs of the plane, without the engine, banking hard to the left and then crashing. It was, and as of this writing is, the worst airplane crash ever in the United States. There had been four similar events and McDonnell Douglas, the DC-10's manufacturer, knew about them. The company did some studies and decided that the probability of an engine losing power *and* having damaged slats *while* the plane was taking off was less than one in a billion.[13] It was another instance of relying on a short worst case ruler. Had a more precautionary approach been at work, perhaps those people would still be alive.

In the longer run we may find that the precautionary principle is most useful for urging policy makers to try to think about unexpected interactions and unintended consequences. A great example of where that's needed is in protecting America's nuclear facilities—power plants, weapons facilities, storage sites—whose vulnerabilities have many worried. A common proposal for such protection is to add redundancy to safety systems, especially more levels of security. While that may sound wise and even unexceptionable, Stanford professor Scott Sagan thinks otherwise. In a prize-winning paper, Sagan shows that hastily implemented redundancies can backfire, making a system more rather than less dangerous. Taken-for-granted assumptions "round off low probability events," he says, and *low probability* is too easily transformed into *impossible*. Although he doesn't use the phrase "precautionary principle," Sagan's disciplined use of it—emphasizing conservative actions but not precluding nonconservative ones—leads to surprising conclusions: safety devices can bring systems down, adding more guards can increase opportunities for failure, having extra people can diffuse responsibility, heaping on redundant devices can increase production pressure. As he says elsewhere, "Things that have never happened before happen all the time. . . ."[14]

It is not just managers and policy makers who could benefit from using counterfactuals to imagine possibilities smartly. We all walk around with ideas, expectations, and theories about what the future will hold. Otherwise, it would be hard to get through the day. These are the "official futures" I talked about in chapter 3. But when it comes to systems whose failure can cause a lot of damage, we need to break out of accepted categories, questioning the ideas and routines that usually make life go smoothly. "Good scenarios," to quote Professor Weber again, "challenge this official future by focusing precisely on what makes people uncomfortable: discontinuities, events that don't make sense in standard theories/language, and the like."[15] Possibilistic and probabilistic thinking are complements, not competitors, to each other.

HUBRIS AND HUMILITY

Hubris is an arrogant presumption of mastery, a conceit. But that alone does not make it a bad thing. Hubris pushes us to innovate. It was the height of audacity to think we could engage in commercial transatlantic flight, just as it was risky and overreaching to send people to the moon. Creative projects don't just appear. They are born in people's imaginations. Hubris makes that happen. Imagine being one of the scientists who created the first nuclear weapons. They were working on little more than theoretical knowledge of physics. How exciting it must have been to think, as some of them did, that they might ignite the atmosphere with that first test shot in New Mexico in 1945. Hubris enables people to push the envelope, to build things never before built, to think of things never before thought.

Hubris leads people to push technological boundaries in a quest for new knowledge. Hubris animated the construction of the *Titanic,* the *Challenger,* and New York's World Trade Center. Of course other motives were at work too. Old-fashioned greed helped motivate construction of the World Trade Center, but the very idea of building something a quarter mile in the sky was hubris writ tall. Most of America's spaceflight program was an extension of military might. Military people needed bigger, more accurate missiles to deliver their ever-developing warheads; they also needed to be able to see when the Soviet Union, or others, had lit candles under their own warheads. But at least in parts of the space program, there was also a genuine thirst for knowledge about astronomy, space travel, the possibility of extraterrestrial life, and so on. The burning drive to know new things is a form of hubris.

If hubris can help the audacious imagination, it can also hurt the impudent one. Hubris is the problem with engineering efforts to control the Mississippi River. The Mississippi is one of the mightiest rivers in the world. Only the Nile, the Amazon, and the Yangtze are longer. Twelve million people live close to its banks, which of course gives the river the potential to cause considerable harm. For the Mississippi, like all rivers, occasionally floods. You would think that people would not put themselves in harm's way like that, but they do, and partly because the United States government provides aid and insurance against the inevitable. At bottom, though, hubris is the culprit.

The Mississippi has been touched by a heavy human hand. One of the U.S. Army Corps of Engineers' missions is flood control and water management. The Corps has taken the job seriously. It has modified the Mississippi's floodplain, tried to shift the direction of the river, and made it generally tame enough to do business on and to live around.

Alas, human activity around the river has led to erosion of the watershed, so the effects of the inevitable floods are intensified. About 80 percent of its wetlands have been drained since the 1940s.[16] Doing that has made it possible for more people to live close to the river, but it also puts them in harm's way. Wetlands are natural reservoirs for floodwaters, absorbing water when there's heavy rain and then releasing it slowly. Levees and other human artifices, all designed to control the river so that more people can use it, concentrate the amount of water that's held in the channel. But if a levee breaks, the resulting flood is larger than would otherwise have been the case. It's hubris again, creating opportunity and risk at the same time.

In 1993 the Mississippi pushed back against its human controllers. The flood that year is called the worst flood in American history, in terms both of the amount of land that was underwater and of the monetary damage that resulted. In Des Moines, Iowa, 150 miles upstream from the Mississippi on the Des Moines River, nearly a quarter of a million people were without safe drinking water for a while. Transportation on the Mississippi itself was disrupted for months. More than seventy thousand people were displaced, fifty thousand homes were damaged or destroyed, and fifty-two people lost their lives. The monetary damages were estimated to be between fifteen and twenty billion dollars. The Mississippi River flood of 1993 might have happened in any case, but it would not have done so much damage if not for human actions. Hubris pushed people to live close to the river, expanding its domain of damage. Hubris led the Army Corps of Engineers to think the Mississippi could be controlled. Hubris leads us not to learn from the '93 flood. Little has changed, so people, property, and activity along the river are perfectly set up for the next worst flood.

What can we learn from paying attention to the dark side of hubris? Culturally, we need a greater appreciation of limits and humility. This is not a call for timidity. But hubris is likely to get us into trouble when we go way beyond the bounds of established expertise: projecting forward in time thousands of years (like the Department of Energy with its nuclear waste), assuming that mighty natural forces will bend to human will (the Army Corps of Engineers and the Mississippi), thinking we can consistently ignore failures with catastrophic potential (NASA and its shuttles), or promising to collect lots of oil on open seas after a tanker accident (the oil industry and its black gold).

We can't expect to change how important actors think about the risks they create by arguing with them about their values. Values hardly ever change that way. Instead, they change when configurations of interest change. That's where our biggest problems lie in trying to do something about the problem of hubris. It is often in experts' and managers' interests to overpromise that their organizations and technologies are safe. It's not that they're lying. Most of the time they believe the stories they tell themselves. But they often can't admit their limits forthrightly because doing so might interfere with getting on with the task at hand. Near Tooele, Utah, for instance, the U.S. Army is burning up America's chemical weapons. The Army assures people that any risk at the Tooele facility is under control, that the facility poses no risk to workers or the public. The technologies used there, says Utah's Department of Environmental Quality, "ensure that no agent is released through the stack."[17] The truth is, though, that there have been several accidental releases, including ones involving sarin and mustard nerve gases. But were the Army to dwell on safety problems it would detract from the important work of destroying America's chemical arsenal.

WHAT MIGHT PROMPT NEEDED POLICY CHANGES?

It is possible that great leaders could lead us into more creative thinking and organization for worst cases. That sometimes happens. It is also possible for people to form social movements that push for the same outcomes. It *is* possible for safety to improve without calamity, and it will be interesting to see if that happens. I'm afraid, however, that the push will most likely come from new disasters. When big disasters happen, that which was previously too expensive, too unlikely, off the radar, or just plain out of the revenue stream suddenly becomes too expensive to ignore.

When one of the two reactors at Three Mile Island had a meltdown in 1979, it was a warning shot. Walter Cronkite, icon of the evening news, remarked that it was "the worst nuclear accident of the atomic age," and he was right.[18] It was also nuclear power's best worst case. It brought to people's attention the real risks of nuclear power, not just the hypothetical scenarios that nuclear proponents used to argue the low probability of serious trouble. Similarly, 9/11 highlighted in brilliant yellow, or blood red, our vulnerabilities, the depth of hatred for Americans abroad, and the ineptitude of the U.S. government in protecting its people. In the same way, I don't think much will happen to prepare for the impact of a near earth object until one hits us. I can not bring myself to say we need an NEO to obliterate a few thousand people. But it's hard to see how the risk is going to get beyond the "giggle factor" without, at the very least, a close call.

Worst cases will always be with us, or just around the corner. That's not all bad.

＊

The poet Thomas Hardy wrote, "If way to the Better there be, it exacts a full look at the Worst."[19] Hardy meant that if enlightenment is to be ours we must put aside illusion and magic, and look coldly in the face of the unknown. This is the heart of the rationalist creed, which demands that tradition and unexamined belief be set aside for a more skeptical mood. We should do more. As we mute superstition and prejudice, we must not lose a sense of amazement. We ought to be more tolerant of the uncertainty that we inevitably find when looking full on at the Worst. We can be wiser, and more interesting, as we come to grips with living and dying in a worst case world.

NOTES

1. "Dead Tree Falls on Moving Car in Indiana," Associated Press, January 2, 2002. "Penn. Woman Killed by Stray Bullet," Associated Press, November 28, 2001. "Woman Dies in Bizarre Key Accident," Associated Press, April 8, 1999.

2. Iver Peterson, "Toms River Still Asking a Question: 'Why Us?'" *New York Times,* December 24, 2001.

3. "Experts Find First Clue to Austrian Tunnel Fire," *Guardian,* November 15, 2000, http://www.guardian.co.uk/international/story/0,3604,397624,00.html (includes the quote from the train company official); "Political Official Says It's a Hard Day for Salzburg: Austrian Tunnel Inferno Kills 170," BBC News, November 11, 2000, http://news.bbc.co.uk/1/hi/world/europe/1017971.stm.

4. Linda T. Kohn, Janet M. Corrigan, and Molla S. Donaldson, *To Err Is Human* (Washington, D.C.: National Academy Press, 2000).

5. WTC demographics, http://wtc.nist.gov/media/P7OccupantBehaviorEgress .pdf.

6. Quotations and facts regarding the Triangle Shirtwaist fire come from Cornell University's Web site: http://www.ilr.cornell.edu/trianglefire/default.html.

7. "Shipwreck off China's East Coast Reportedly Kills 290 People," CNN.com, November 25, 1999.

8. The quote from the poor Dominican guy in Queens: Trade Center Survivor Dies in Crash, Associated Press, Ian James, November 13, 2001.

9. http://walrus.wr.usgs.gov/tsunami/PNGhome.html.

10. Sebastian Junger, *The Perfect Storm* (New York: Norton, 2000). The quotes are from, respectively, pages 150, 152, and 263.

11. Charles Perrow came up with the idea of the rubber worst case ruler and has let me use the idea as if it were my own. He's always been generous with his ideas like that. That's one of the reasons I dedicated my previous book, *Mission Improbable,* to him.

12. Aviation accident statistics come from http://www.ntsb.gov/aviation/Table6. htm, auto accident figures from http://www-nrd.nhtsa.dot.gov/pdf/nrd-30/NCSA/ TSFAnn/TSF2000.pdf.

13. Quoted in Evelyn Nieves, "San Jose Emergency Plans Set Example," *New York Times,* October 29, 2001.

14. Carroll, quoted in Jim Dwyer and Janny Scott, "Horror Arrives in a Safe Haven," *New York Times,* November 13, 2001.

15. "Yucca Mountain Preliminary Site Suitability Evaluation," Department of Energy, 2001, p. 220, emphasis added. http://www.ocrwm.doe.gov/documents/sse_a/ index.htm.

16. The environmental impact statement on Yucca Mountain (http://www. ocrwm.doe.gov/documents/feis_2/vol_3_3/indexv33.htm) contains bureaucratic language at its most infuriating. But it is a very important document.

CHAPTER TWO

1. David W. Chen, "New Gun Owner's First Try Hits Sunbather, Police Say," *New York Times,* August 13, 1998.

2. John McPhee, *The Control of Nature* (New York: Farrar, Straus, Giroux, 1989), 248–55.

3. Richard Preston, *The Hot Zone* (New York: Random House, 1994), 11–12.

4. Kai Erikson argues that toxic hazards threaten us in new ways in his *A New Species of Trouble* (New York: Norton, 1995). Charles Perrow claims that some systems are inherently unstable, and given to catastrophic failure, in *Normal Accidents: Living with High-Risk Technologies* (Princeton, N.J.: Princeton University Press, 1999).

5. Information on longevity in Rwanda comes from the World Health Organization (http://www3.who.int/whosis/hale/hale.cfm?path=whosis,hale&language= english) and the CIA (http://www.cia.gov/cia/publications/factbook/).

6. Mary Douglas and Aaron Wildavsky, *Risk and Culture* (Berkeley: University of California Press, 1983), 10–11. William Clark, "Witches, Floods, and Wonder Drugs: Historical Perspectives on Risk Management," in *Societal Risk Assessment: How Safe Is Safe Enough?,* ed. Richard Schwing and Walter Albers (New York: Plenum Press, 1980).

7. My friend Barry Glassner argues that people "worry about the wrong things" in his *Culture of Fear* (New York: Basic Books, 1999).

8. Bob Berger, *Beating Murphy's Law* (New York: Dell, 1994), 9. Berger has gems regarding smoking as death wish (160) and the safety of nuclear power (174); his claim that worry is a "disorder" is on page 215. Larry Laudan serves up the quotes on Oklahoma and Maine (41), the dangers of Saturday (150), Alaska (15), "curtailing everything risky" (2), probability (5), preparing for the wrong risks (8), and asbestos (16) in *The Book of Risks: Fascinating Facts about the Chances We Take Everyday* (New York: John Wiley and Sons, 1994). His assurances that "everything is getting better" and "many high profile risks don't matter much" are on pages 6 and 9, respectively, of *Danger Ahead: The Risks You Really Face on Life's Highway* (New York: John Wiley and Sons, 1997).

9. Stephen M. Stigler, *The History of Statistics: The Measurement of Uncertainty before 1900* (Cambridge: Harvard University Press, 1986), 65. The quote about Quetelet in the next paragraph comes from pages 171–72 of the same volume.

10. Bill Keller, "Nuclear Nightmares," *New York Times Magazine,* May 26, 2002, Web edition.

11. James Risen, "US Failed to Act on Warnings in '98 of a Plane Attack," *New York Times,* September 19, 2002.

12. Dittemore, quoted in Miles O'Brien, "Fifteen Years after Challenger, NASA Inoculates against 'Go Fever,'" cnn.com, January 18, 2001, http://www.cnn.com/2001/TECH/space/01/18/downlinks.40/index.html.

13. Quoted in Howard W. French, "Nuclear Peril Is Over but Japanese Anger Isn't," *New York Times,* October 2, 1999, http://www.nytimes.com/library/world/asia/100299japan-nuke.html.

14. The story of the Atomic Energy Commission studies is in Daniel F. Ford, "A Reporter at Large: The Cult of the Atom," pts. 1 and 2, *New Yorker,* October 25, 1982, 107–59, and November 1, 1982, 45–98. Quotation is from pt. 2, p. 58.

15. Gina Kolata, *Flu: The Story of the Great Influenza Pandemic of 1918 and the Search for the Virus That Caused It* (New York: Farrar, Straus, Giroux, 2000), 56.

16. Alvin Weinberg, "Science and Trans-Science," *Minerva* 10, no. 2 (April 1972): 209–22.

17. http://www.ocrwm.doe.gov/ymp/about/howmuch.shtml.

18. The Department of Energy, on keeping waste safe for thousands of years: http://www.ymp.gov/about/why.htm. On the risk of volcanic activity: A. W. Woods, S. Sparks, O. Bokhove, A.-M. Lejeune, C. Connor, and B. E. Hill, "Modeling Magma-Drift Interaction at the Proposed High-Level Radioactive Waste Repository at Yucca Mountain, Nevada, USA," *Geophysical Research Letters* 29, no. 13 (2002).

19. Lee Clarke, *Mission Improbable: Using Fantasy Documents to Tame Disaster* (Chicago: University of Chicago Press, 1999).

CHAPTER THREE

1. http://www.whitehousehistory.org/02_learning/subs_k/frame_b_k01.html #nixon.

2. Nevil Shute, *On the Beach* (New York: Ballantine, 1974), 79.

3. Steven N. Ward and Erik Asphaug, "Asteroid Impact Tsunami of 2880 March 16," *Geophysical Journal International* 153 (2003):F6–F10. Also http://neo.jpl.nasa.gov/1950da/.

4. "Preserving Our Institutions: The First Report of the Continuity of Government Commission," American Enterprise Institute and Brookings Institution, May 2003, http://www.aei.org/docLib/20030605_FirstReport.pdf.

5. See, for example, the title essay, by volume editors Philip E. Tetlock and Aaron Belkin, in *Counterfactual Thought Experiments in World Politics* (Princeton: Princeton University Press, 1996), 1–38; Geoffrey Hawthorn, *Plausible Worlds* (Cambridge: Cambridge University Press, 1991); and the fun articles in Niall Ferguson's edited volume *Virtual History* (New York: Basic Books, 1999).

6. http://www.sea-viewdiving.com/shipwreckinfo.htm.

7. "Safety Fears Linger, Decade after Kings Cross Fire," bbcnews.com, November 15, 1997. http://news.bbc.co.uk/hi/english/uk/newsid_31000/31723.stm.

8. Quoted in John Meyers, "Rail Veteran Says Crew Not at Fault," *Duluth News-Tribune,* July 2, 1992, 10a.

9. Some of the material about the Thule incident is drawn from my article "Drs. Pangloss and Strangelove Meet Organizational Theory," Sociological Forum 8, no. 4 (1993): 675–89.

10. Scott Sagan, *The Limits of Safety: Organizations, Accidents, and Nuclear Weapons* (Princeton, N.J.: Princeton University Press, 1993).

11. Quoted in Elizabeth Kolbert, "Indian Point Blank," *New Yorker,* July 17, 2003, 36–41.

12. *USA Today* has done great work dissecting patterns of death, and survival, in the World Trade Center collapse. The facts in this paragraph are from Dennis Cauchon, "For Many on Sept. 11, Survival Was No Accident," *USA Today,* December 20, 2001, http://www.usatoday.com/news/attack/2001/12/19/usatcov-wtcsurvival.htm#more. See also the National Institute of Standards and Technology studies at http://wtc.nist.gov/media/P7OccupantBehaviorEgress.pdf.

13. "Earthquakes along the Eastern Seaboard, and in New York City, Scenario Earthquakes for Urban Areas along the Atlantic Seaboard of the United States," NYCEM, 2002, http://www.nycem.org/techdocs/EconCons/Scenarios.asp. Information in the following paragraphs is also drawn from the NYCEM Web site.

14. My description of Dark Winter is drawn from Tara O'Toole, Michael Mair, and Thomas V. Inglesby, "Shining Light on 'Dark Winter,'" *Clinical Infectious Diseases,* April 1, 2002. Sam Nunn quote is on page 982.

15. The Federal Emergency Management Agency says there was only one OEM tank; see chapter 5 in its World Trade Center study, http://www.fema.gov/library/wtcstudy.shtm. The National Institute of Standards and Technology says there were two; see http://wtc.nist.gov/PublicBriefing_06182004.pdf, p. 29.

16. Quoted in Richard F. Newcomb and Peter Maas, *Abandon Ship! The Saga of the U.S.S.* Indianapolis, *the Navy's Greatest Sea Disaster* (New York: HarperCollins, 2000),286.

17. Ari Fleischer, press briefing, June 4, 2002, http://www.whitehouse.gov/news/releases/2002/06/20020604-19.html.

18. Fleischer, quoted in "Families Of 9/11 Dead Upset That Clues May Have Been Missed," cnn.com, May 17, 2002, http://www.cnn.com/2002/US/05/16/bush.family.reax/.

19. Shays, quoted in "Torricelli Calls for Board of Inquiry," cnn.com, September 29, 2001.

20. Malcolm Gladwell, Connecting the Dots, *New Yorker,* March 10, 2003. Gladwell's logic is sound but insufficiently tempered by evidence. What he neglects is the willful turning away from contradictory evidence on the parts of the Bush and Blair administrations. It wasn't a case of confusion, or the fog of prewar. It was a case of not paying attention, turning a blind eye to signs and evidence, largely because they were so gung ho to get Saddam Hussein.

21. "The Day After . . . in the American Strategic Infrastructure" (Santa Monica, Calif.: RAND, MR-963-OSD, 1998). This document has not been cleared by the Pentagon to be released in full. I got permission from RAND to include these few paragraphs. I thank Roger Mollander for his gracious help with these scenarios.

22. Leslie Miller, "Report: FAA Had 52 Pre-9/11 Warnings," Associated Press, February 11, 2005; Eric Lichtblau, "9/11 Report Cites Many Warnings about Hijackings," *New York Times,* February 10, 2005.

CHAPTER FOUR

1. Richard T. Sylves, *Declaring Disaster: The Politics and Policies of Presidential Disaster Declarations* (Albany: State University of New York Press, forthcoming).

2. Churchill, quoted in John Updike, "Remember the Lusitania," *New Yorker,* July 1, 2002, 88–91.

3. Claudia Dreifus, "A Conversation With/David Ropeik: The Fear Factor Meets Its Match," *New York Times,* December 3, 2002.

4. The definitive source comparing the Milwaukee and New York City smallpox outbreaks is Judith W. Leavitt, "Public Resistance of Cooperation? A Tale of Smallpox in Two Cities," *Biosecurity and Bioterrorism: Biodefense Strategy, Practice, and Science* 1, no. 3 (2003): 185–92.

5. http://www.cdc.gov/nchs/data/hus/hus04trend.pdf#027.

6. Michael Janofsky, "Montana Town Grapples with Asbestos Ills," *New York Times,* May 10, 2000.

7. Caron Chess, Michal Tamuz, Alex Saville, and Michael Greenberg, "Reducing Uncertainty and Increasing Credibility: The Case of Sybron Chemicals, Inc.," *Industrial Crisis Quarterly* 6, no. 1 (1992): 55–70. Some of the story comes from my article with William Freudenburg, "Rhetoric, Reform, and Risk," *Society* 30, no. 5 (1993): 78–81. I am told that Sybron has since been bought by a larger corporation, and that these programs have been dismantled.

8. Some of the material on panic comes from my article in *Contexts,* "Panic: Myth or Reality," 1, no. 3 (2002): 21–26, and from an op-ed I wrote for the *New York Daily News:* "Systems Fail, Not People," February 20, 2003. Some of the ideas about "elite panic" I developed with my colleague Caron Chess.

9. See Diane Vaughan, *Dead Reckoning: Air Traffic Control in the Early 21st Century,* forthcoming.

10. Kathleen Tierney, "Disaster Beliefs and Institutional Interests: Recycling Disaster Myths in the Aftermath of 9-11." *Research in Social Problems and Public Policy* 11 (2004):37.

11. Theodore Karisik, *Toxic Warfare* (Santa Monica, Calif.: RAND, 2002).

12. The facts in this paragraph, put together by Barrow, come from James V. Grimaldi and Guy Gugliotta, "Chemical Plants Feared as Targets," *Washington Post,* December 16, 2001.

13. Quoted in Hilary C. Styron, "CSX Tunnel Fire, Baltimore, Md." (Washington, D.C.: FEMA, 2001).

14. Heather Dewar, Marcia Myers, and Kimberly A. C. Wilson, "Accident Plan Leaves City Unprepared," *Baltimore Sun,* July 26, 2001, http://www.baltimoresun.com/news/local/bal-te.md.plan26jul26.story

15. "One Year Later: What Have We Learned from the Baltimore Train Tunnel Disaster?," Progressive Newswire, July 18, 2002.

16. Robert J. Halstead and Fred Dilger, "Implications of the Baltimore Rail Tunnel Fire for Full-Scale Testing of Shipping Casks," Waste Management 2003 Conference, February 23–27, 2003, Tucson, Ariz.

17. Excerpted from the Brach presentation of "meeting 1," on the National Academy of Sciences Web site: http://dels.nas.edu/radwaste/m1.html.

18. Marcia Myers and Heather Dewar, "Hazardous Materials Pass Daily—and No One Knows," *Baltimore Sun,* July 20, 2001, http://www.baltimoresun.com/news/local/bal-te.md.hazard20jul20.story.

19. Don DeLillo, *White Noise* (New York: Penguin, 1984), 64, 66.

20. Bronislaw Malinowski, *Magic, Science, Religion, and Other Essays* (Garden City, N.Y.: Doubleday, 1954), 139–40.

21. Information on the *Greeneville* case comes from the following sources: NTSB report, http://www.ntsb.gov/events/2001/Greeneville/nolan_m.nts.pdf (Waddle turned periscope twice, p. 21); U.S. Navy Official Court of Inquiry report, http://www.cpf.navy.mil/pages/legal/foia/GREENEVILLE_Combined_COI_Rpt.pdf (Waddle ordered the ship raised, pp. 52, 99; Waddle changed magnification of periscope, p. 52). Subsequent reports on the incident include these from CNN: "Sub Skipper's Lawyer Disputes Navy Report," March 7, 2001, http://www.cnn.com/2001/US/03/07/japan.sub.03/index.html, and "Japanese Want U.S. Sub Captain Court-Martialed," April 20, 2001, http://www.cnn.com/2001/WORLD/asiapcf/east/04/20/japan.submarine.court/index.html.

22. Information on the Flight 587 case comes from the following sources: Matthew L. Wald, "Inquiry Focus: Pilot Training in Emergencies," *New York Times,* November 20, 2001, and "Aircraft Safety and the Case of the Plastic Tail," *New York Times,* November 27, 2001; cockpit voice recording, http://www.planecrashinfo.com/cvr011112.htm; Cockpit Voice Recorder Transcript, American Airlines Flight 587, DCA02MA001, Belle Harbor, NY, November 12, 2001, Docket No. SA-522, Exhibit No. 12A, National Transportation Safety Board, http://www.ntsb.gov/events/2001/aa587/exhibits/241569.pdf; other NTSB documents, http://www.ntsb.gov/events/2001/AA587/iic_stmt.htm and http://www.ntsb.gov/events/2001/aa587/exhibits/ (most blame the pilots, but exhibits on the testing of the tail clearly indicate that water had made its way into the composites and that there was "delamination"); NTSB press conference and speech by Marion Blakey, http://www.ntsb.gov/Speeches/blakey/mcb020208.htm.

23. National Transportation Safety Board, "NTSB Advisory," Washington, D.C., February 25, 2002, http://www.ntsb.gov/Pressrel/2002/020225.htm. The NTSB final report is "In-Flight Separation of Vertical Stabilizer, American Airlines Flight 587, Airbus Industrie A300-605R, N14053, Belle Harbor, New York, November 21, 2001," http://www.ntsb.gov/publictn/2004/AAR0404.pdf.

CHAPTER FIVE

1. John McPhee, *The Control of Nature* (New York: Farrar, Straus, Giroux, 1989), 59

2. Kevin Sack, "Capricious Georgia Tornadoes Killed Young and Old," *New York Times*, February 16, 2000.

3. Eric Klinenberg, *Heat Wave: A Social Autopsy of Disaster in Chicago* (Chicago: University of Chicago Press, 2002).

4. See the examples in Timmons Roberts and Melissa M. Toffolon-Weiss, *Chronicles from the Environmental Justice Frontline* (Cambridge: Cambridge University Press, 2001).

5. As in many disasters, *Titanic*'s body count is ambiguous. *Titanic* tickets were sold at many locations up until departure, so the most reliable tally was on the ship. I've seen 1,523 as the correct body count; the Smithsonian says it's 1,522 (http://www.si .edu/resource/faq/nmah/titanic.htm). A British Inquiry said 1,490 died. The data in the table shown in the text come from Walter Lord's *The Night Lives On* (New York: William Morrow, 1986), page 92, which are in turn from the British Inquiry, commonly referred to as Lord Mersey's Report.

6. Elaine Enarson and Betty Hearn Morrow, "Why Gender? Why Women? An Introduction to Women and Disaster," in *The Gendered Terrain of Disaster: Through Women's Eyes*, ed. Enarson and Morrow (Westport, Conn.: Praeger, 1998), 1–8.

7. Alan Riding, "First Crash of a Concorde Kills 113 Just after Takeoff from Paris Airport," *New York Times*, July 26, 2000, Web edition.

8. http://www.spc.noaa.gov/faq/tornado/f-scale.html.

9. http://www.hwysafety.org/news%5Freleases/2000/pr071300.htm.

10. The data on 9/11 redounding to the benefit of President Bush and Congress are in a paper by Brent K. Marshall, J. Steven Picou, and Duane A. Gill, "Terrorism as Disaster: Selected Commonalities and Long-Term Recovery for 9/11 Survivors," *Research in Social Problems and Public Policy* 11 (2003):73–96. Gallup poll data retrieved September 18, 2001, from http://www.gallup.com.

11. Thompson is quoted in Edward Wong with Leslie Wayne, "Loss of the Shuttle Contractors; Boeing and Lockheed, Prime Builders, Face Questions in Shuttle Inquiry," *New York Times*, February 3, 2003, A22, http://www.nytimes.com/2003/02/03/business/03CONT.html?pagewanted=print&position=top.

12. The *Examiner* quote comes from Biel, *Down with the Old Canoe*, 39; the ship's last message is quoted on page 24. The editorial singing the praises of "American manhood," cited in the following paragraph, is on page 25.

13. Pitirim Sorokin, *Man and Society in Calamity: The Effects of War, Revolution, Famine, Pestilence upon Human Mind, Behavior, Social Organization, and Cultural Life*, (New York: Dutton, 1942), 10.

14. Leo Tasca's great dissertation is "The Social Construction of Human Error,", State University of New York at Stony Brook, 1989, unpublished. The quote is from chapter 1.

15. Henry Petroski, *To Engineer Is Human: The Role of Failure in Successful Design*, (New York: Vintage Books, 1992).

16. Karl E. Weick and Kathleen M. Sutcliffe, *Managing the Unexpected: Assuring High Performance in an Age of Complexity* (San Francisco: Jossey-Bass, 2001), 56.

17. The statistics on how Sputnik was good for schools come from Richard C. Leone, "Why Boomers Don't Spell Bust," *American Prospect* 8, no. 30, January 1997, and Thomas A. Garrett and John C. Leatherman, "An Introduction to State and Local Public Finance," Regional Research Institute, West Virginia University, http://www.rri.wvu.edu/WebBook/Garrett/chapterone.htm#education, table 2.

18. Michal Tamuz, "Defining Away Dangers: A Study in the Influences of Managerial Cognition on Information Systems," in *Organizational Cognition: Computation and Interpretation,* ed. T. K. Lant and Z. Shapira (Mahwah, N.J.: Lawrence Erlbaum Associates, 2000), 157–83.

19. National Transportation Safety Board, "Aircraft Accident Report—Pan American World Airways, Clipper 759, N4737, Boeing 727-235, New Orleans International Airport, Kenner, Louisiana, July 9, 1982," 1983.

20. Quote is from Janet McConnaughey, "Wind Shear Detection Improved since '82 Crash," Associated Press, July 9, 2002.

21. Isenberg, quoted in James Glanz and Eric Lipton, "In Data Trove, a Graphic Look at Towers' Fall," *New York Times,* October 29, 2002.

22. Jayson Blair, "After an Antenna Tumbles, Cable Firms Gain Thousands of New Customers," *New York Times,* March 3, 2002. In the article, Blair claims that cable companies gained "thousands of new subscribers." I don't know if that figure is trustworthy: this is the same Mr. Blair who made up material he used in some articles. I wrote and called the *New York Times* to inquire whether this particular article had been fact-checked. No one responded.

23. Anne D'Innocenzio, "Wedding Shops: Bridal Retailers Report Sales Surge," Associated Press, November 19, 2001.

24. Kathleen Tierney, "Disaster Beliefs and Institutional Interests: Recycling Disaster Myths in the Aftermath of 9-11," *Research in Social Problems and Public Policy* 11 (2004):33–51. How wealthy people and large corporations were disproportionately helped out by the government in the wake of 9/11 is well summarized in Marshall, Picou, and Gill, "Terrorism as Disaster," cited earlier.

25. The National Park Service quote is from "Yellowstone in the Afterglow: Lessons from the Fires," http://www.nps.gov/yell/publications/pdfs/fire/afterglow .htm.

26. The park ranger's quote is from http://www.rockybarker.com/chap9.htm.

27. On the disappearance of Seattle's business district after the big fire, http://www .historylink.org/output.CFM?file_ID=715

28. Some of the facts about the San Francisco earthquake and fire come from http://quake.usgs.gov/info/1906/index.html.

29. James Jasper, "The Effects of Depopulation in the Plague Years," unpublished paper.

30. Richard L. Rubenstein, *The Age of Triage: Fear and Hope in an Overcrowded World* (Boston: Beacon Press, 1983).

31. The list of "regional droughts" comes from http://www.rra.dst.tx.us/c_t/ History1/DUST%20BOWL.cfm. The material on "black blizzards" and health

comes from Brad D. Lookingbill, *Dust Bowl, USA: Depression America and the Ecological Imagination, 1929–1941* (Athens: Ohio University Press, 2001).

CHAPTER SIX

1. Quoted in Jon Nordheimber, "Nothing's Easy for New Orleans Flood Control," *New York Times,* April 30, 2002, http://www.nytimes.com/2002/04/30/science/earth/30ORLE.html?pagewanted=print&position=top.

2. Richard A. Posner, *Catastrophe: Risk and Response* (Oxford: Oxford University Press, 2004). Martin Rees, *Our Final Hour: A Scientist's Warning: How Terror, Error, and Environmental Disaster Threaten Humankind's Future in This Century—On Earth and Beyond* (New York: Basic Books, 2003), 8.

3. John Moteff, Claudia Copeland, and John Fischer, "Critical Infrastructures: What Makes an Infrastructure Critical?" report to Congress, Congressional Research Service, January 29, 2003, http://www.fas.org/irp/crs/RL31556.pdf.

4. Richard A. Clarke, *Against All Enemies: Inside America's War on Terror* (New York: Free Press, 2004).

5. Alfred W. Crosby, *America's Forgotten Pandemic: The Influenza of 1918* (Cambridge: Cambridge University Press, 1989), 76.

6. Charles C. Mann discusses failing gracefully in software engineering in "Homeland Insecurity," *Atlantic Monthly,* September 2002, 81–102.

7. The quote comes from NASA's frequently asked questions page, http://impact.arc.nasa.gov/introduction/faq-neo.html.

8. Quoted in David Crary, "If Terrorists Strike Again, How Will Americans React?" Associated Press, September 11, 2002.

9. Quoted in Scott Sagan, *The Limits of Safety: Organizations, Accidents, and Nuclear Weapons* (Princeton: Princeton University Press, 1993),76–78.

10. http://www.cdc.gov/mmwr/preview/mmwrhtml/mm5127a1.htm.

11. UN Rio Declaration, http://www.biotech-info.net/handbook.pdf.

12. John D. Graham, "The Perils of the Precautionary Principle: Lessons from the American and European Experience," http://www.heritage.org/Research/Regulation/hl818.cfm.

13. Charles Perrow, *Normal Accidents: Living with High-Risk Technologies* (Princeton, N.J.: Princeton University Press, 1999), 139.

14. Sagan, *Limits of Safety,* 12. The earlier quote is from his article "The Problem of Redundancy Problem: Why More Nuclear Security Forces May Produce Less Nuclear Safety," *Risk Analysis* 24, no. 4 (2004):935–46.

15. Steven Weber, *Counterfactuals, Present and Future* (Princeton, N.J.: Princeton University Press, 1996), 279.

16. This and many of the statistics in the following paragraphs come from a University of Akron Web site on the Great Flood of 1993, http://lists.uakron.edu/geology/natscigeo/lectures/streams/miss_flood.htm#modification.

17. http://www.hazardouswaste.utah.gov/CDS/TPICTHP1.HTM.

18. http://www.pbs.org/wgbh/amex/three/.

19. Thomas Hardy, "In Tenebris—II," http://www.theotherpages.org/poems/hardy01.html.

INDEX